THE ULTIMATE

COOKING

WITH

INGREDIENTS

Jean Coates

The Ultimate Cooking With 4 Ingredients

1st Printing   January 2002
2nd Printing   June 2002
3rd Printing   September 2002
4th Printing   October 2002
5th Printing   November 2002
6th Printing   August 2003

ISBN # 1-931294-36-4 Hard Cover
ISBN # 1-931294-37-2 Paper Cover
Library of Congress Number: 2002115116

Illustrations by Nancy Murphy Griffith

Edited, Designed, Published and Manufactured in the
United States of America by
Cookbook Resources, LLC
541 Doubletree Drive
Highland Village, Texas 75077
972-317-0245

Toll Free Orders: 866/229-2665
www.cookbookresources.com

Preserving
The Family Meal

INTRODUCTION

In our fast-paced, rush-here-and-there lives, a home-cooked meal may be considered a luxury. We live out of our cars, placing food orders on cell phones and going to drive-through windows for the night's meal and maybe the family sits down together to eat.

We hope to help families come back to the table and spend quality time while sharing good food to eat. The recipes in "The Ultimate Cooking With 4 Ingredients" are easy to prepare and the ingredients are readily available. Most of them are already in your pantry.

Everyone in the family can cook out of "The Ultimate Cooking With 4 Ingredients". Mouth-watering meals are just minutes away and every minute we spend around the table enriches our lives and helps us grow stronger. Have a good time with this cookbook and don't hesitate to recruit some helpers.

It's a great time for all of us to come back to the table.

Jean C. Coates

Contents

Contents

APPETIZERS
&
BEVERAGES

Chorizo Cheese Dip

1 (12 ounce) package
fresh pork chorizo

1 (2 pound) package mild
Mexican Velveeta

1 (15 ounce) can stewed
tomatoes

Tortillas

• Saute chorizo until cooked; drain. In a double boiler, melt the cheese and tomatoes.

• Combine chorizo and cheese mixture, blending well. Serve with tortilla chips.

Speedy Cheese Dip

2 (10½ ounce) cans
cheddar cheese soup

1 (10½ ounce) can diced
tomatoes and green
chilies

1 (10½ ounce) can cream
of chicken soup

Pinch of cayenne pepper

• Mix all ingredients together in a saucepan (add ½ teaspoon of salt to taste). Serve hot. Serve with chips.

Spicy Beef and Cheese Dip

1 (10 ounce) can
tomatoes and green
chilies

½ teaspoon garlic powder

1 (2 pound) box Velveeta
cheese, cubed

1 pound lean ground beef,
browned and drained

• In a large saucepan, place tomatoes and green chilies, garlic and cheese cut in chunks.

• Heat on low until cheese melts. Add the ground beef, mixing well.

• Serve with tortilla chips.

Egg and Cheese Dip

5 hardcooked eggs,
mashed

1 cup mayonnaise

4 ounces shredded
monterey jack cheese

½ teaspoon prepared
mustard

• In bowl, combine all ingredients and mix
well. Add salt to taste. Refrigerate. Serve
with wheat crackers.

Velvet Dip

1 (2 pound) box Mexican
Velveeta cheese, cubed

2 cups mayonnaise

1 (4 ounce) jar chopped
pimentos

1 (7 ounce) can chopped
green chilies

• Place cheese in saucepan and melt over
low heat.

• Add other ingredients and mix well.
Serve with chips.

Veggie Dip

1 (16 ounces) sour cream

1 (10 ounce) package
frozen, chopped
spinach, thawed, well
drained

1 package dry vegetable
soup mix

1 bunch fresh green
onions, chopped with
tops

• Combine all ingredients (make sure
spinach is well drained).

• Chill for several hours before serving
(adding ¾ cup chopped pecans would be
good in this dip).

Creamy Onion Dip

2 (8 ounce) packages
  cream cheese, softened

3 tablespoons lemon
  juice

1 package dry onion soup
  mix

1 (8 ounce) carton sour
  cream

- Beat cream cheese until smooth. Blend in lemon juice and onion soup mix.
- Gradually fold in sour cream until well blended.
- Chill. Serve with chips, crackers or fresh vegetables.

Cold Curry Dip

1½ cups mayonnaise

2 teaspoons curry powder

1 tablespoon grated onion

½ teaspoon dry mustard

- Combine mayonnaise, curry powder, onion and mustard.
- Chill at least 1 hour before serving. Several dashes of Tabasco may be added.

  Serve with chilled vegetables such as celery sticks, sliced zucchini or carrot sticks.

Fiesta Onion Dip

1 package dry onion soup
  mix

1 (15 ounce) can Mexican
  stewed tomatoes

2 teaspoons chili powder

1 cup grated cheddar
  cheese

- In small saucepan heat soup mix, tomatoes and chili powder. Bring to a boil.
- Turn heat down and simmer for 20 minutes, stirring occasionally.
- To serve, pour into a serving bowl and sprinkle with the cheese. Stir before serving. Serve with chips.

Broccoli Cheese Dip

1 (10½ ounce) can broccoli cheese soup

1 (10 ounce) package frozen, chopped broccoli, thawed

½ cup sour cream, ½ teaspoon seasoned salt

2 teaspoons dijon style mustard

• In a saucepan combine soup, broccoli, sour cream, salt and mustard, mixing well. Heat and serve hot.

Hot Broccoli Dip

1 (2 pound) box Mexican Velveeta cheese

1 (10 ounce) can golden mushroom soup

1 (10 ounce) box frozen chopped broccoli, thawed

Chips

• In saucepan, melt cheese with the soup and stir in broccoli. Heat thoroughly. Serve with chips. Serve hot.

Broccoli Dip

1 (10 ounce) package frozen, chopped broccoli, thawed

1 (10½ ounce) can cream of chicken soup

3 cups grated cheddar cheese

1 (7 ounce) can chopped green chilies

• In saucepan, cook broccoli about 5 minutes in a little margarine and about ½ teaspoon salt.

• Add soup, cheese and green chilies.

• Heat until cheese melts. (If chilies are not hot enough in the dip, add several dashes of Tabasco). Serve with tostados.

Artichoke-Blue Cheese Dip

1 stick butter

1 (14 ounce) can artichoke hearts, drained, chopped

1 (4 ounce) package blue cheese

2 teaspoons lemon juice

• In skillet, melt butter and mix in artichoke hearts.

• Add blue cheese and lemon juice. Serve hot.

Artichoke-Bacon Dip

1 (14 ounce) jar marinated artichoke hearts, drained, chopped

1 cup mayonnaise

2 teaspoons worchestershire sauce

5 slices bacon, cooked crisp, crumbled

• In large bowl, combine all ingredients.

• Pour into a buttered 8-inch baking dish.

• Bake at 350° for 12 minutes.

• Serve hot with crackers.

Sassy Onion Dip

1 (8 ounce) package cream cheese, softened

1 (8 ounce) carton sour cream

½ cup chili sauce

1 package dry onion soup mix

• Beat cream cheese until fluffy.

• Add remaining ingredients and mix well.

• Cover and chill.

• Serve with strips of raw zucchini, celery, carrots, etc.

Cottage Dip

1 (16 ounce) carton small curd cottage cheese

1 envelope dry onion soup mix

½ cup mayonnaise

½ teaspoon garlic powder

- Blend all ingredients.
- Chill and serve with chips, crackers or veggies.

Hot-to-Trot Dip

1 pound ground beef

1 (2 pound) box Velveeta cheese, cubed

1½ cups salsa

Several drops of Tabasco

- Brown ground beef and drain well.
- In saucepan, heat cheese and salsa until cheese is melted. Add Tabasco.
- Combine meat and cheese mixture. Serve hot with tortilla chips.

Five-Minute Dip

1 (8 ounce) package cream cheese, softened

1 cup mayonnaise

1 package dry ranch-style salad dressing mix

½ onion, finely minced

- Combine cream cheese and mayonnaise and beat until creamy.
- Stir in salad dressing mix and onion.
- Chill and serve with fresh vegetables.

Horsey Shrimp Dip

1 (6 ounce) can tiny
  shrimp, chopped and
  drained

3 tablespoons cream-style
  horseradish

⅓ cup mayonnaise

½ teaspoon cajun
  seasoning

- Combine shrimp, horseradish, mayonnaise and seasoning.
- Refrigerate. Serve with crackers.

Spinach-Artichoke Dip

2 (10 ounce) boxes frozen
  spinach, thawed,
  drained

1 (14 ounce) jar
  marinated artichoke
  hearts, drained, finely
  chopped

1 cup mayonnaise

2 cups shredded
  mozzarella cheese

- Drain spinach with several layers of paper towels.
- Combine, spinach, artichoke hearts, mayonnaise and cheese and mix well.
- Cover and refrigerate. Serve with chips.

Sombrero Dip

1 (15 ounce) can chili, no
  beans

½ teaspoon chili powder

¾ cup green chili sauce

1 (2½ ounce) can sliced
  black olives, drained

- Combine chili and chili powder in saucepan. Warm over low heat.
- Stir in sauce and olives. Serve with chips.

Avocado Ole!

3 large ripe avocados, mashed

1 tablespoon fresh lemon juice

1 package dry onion soup mix

1 (8 ounce) carton sour cream

• Mix avocados with lemon juice and blend in soup mix and sour cream. You may want to add a little salt. Serve with chips or crackers.

Talking Tomato Dip

1 (10 ounce) can tomatoes and green chilies, drained

1 (8 ounce) carton sour cream

1½ teaspoons seasoned salt

2 teaspoons horseradish

• Combine all ingredients. Chill. Serve with chips.

Watercress "To Do" Dip

3 ripe avocados

1¼ cups snipped watercress

¾ cup mayonnaise

¼ teaspoon ground cumin seeds

• Peel and mash softened avocados and place in medium bowl.

• Add the watercress, mayonnaise and cumin seeds and mix well.

• Add salt to taste.

• Cover and refrigerate. Serve with chips.

Picante Cream

1 (8 ounce) carton sour cream

½ teaspoon prepared mustard

½ cup hot picante sauce

½ teaspoon celery salt

• Combine all ingredients.
• Chill. Serve with chips.

Whiz Bang Dip

1½ pounds ground beef

¼ cup chopped onion

1 (2 pound) box Mexican Velveeta cheese, cubed

¾ cup mayonnaise-type salad dressing

• In skillet brown meat and onion and drain.
• Combine all ingredients and mix well.
• On low heat, cook until cheese is melted, stirring constantly. Serve with chips.

Pep-Pep-Pepperoni Dip

2 (8 ounce) packages cream cheese, softened

1 (3.5 ounce) package pepperoni slices

1 (12 ounce) bottle chili sauce

1 bunch fresh green onions with tops, chopped

• In mixing bowl, beat cream cheese until creamy.
• Cut pepperoni slices into smaller chunks.
• Add pepperoni, chili sauce and green onions to the cream cheese and mix well.
• Refrigerate. Serve with chips.

Dried Beef and Chips

1 (8 ounce) package
  cream cheese, softened
1 (8 ounce) carton sour
  cream
1 (3 ounce) package dried
  beef, cubed
½ cup finely chopped
  pecans

- In mixing bowl, combine cream cheese and sour cream and beat until creamy.
- Fold in dried beef chunks and pecans.
- Refrigerate. Serve with chips.

Whip-It-Up Dip

1 (2½ ounce) jar dried
  beef, coarsely chopped
1 (8 ounce) package
  shredded cheddar
  cheese
⅔ cup mayonnaise
⅔ teaspoon garlic powder

- Combine all ingredients and mix well. (The easiest way to chop dried beef is with scissors). Serve with crackers.

  If you would rather serve it hot, you may spread the mixture on crackers and bake at 350° for about 8 minutes.

Confetti Dip

1 (15 ounce) can whole
  kernel corn, drained
1 (15 ounce) can black
  beans, drained
⅓ cup Italian salad
  dressing
1 (16 ounce) jar salsa

- Combine all ingredients together.
- Refrigerate several hours before serving. Serve with chips.

Fun Mustard Dip

1 cup white vinegar

1 (2 ounce) can dry mustard

3 eggs, well beaten

1 cup sugar

• Combine vinegar and mustard and mix well. Refrigerate 24 hours.

• Add eggs and sugar and mix well. Cook on low until thickened.

• Pour into jars and refrigerate. Serve with cocktail sausages or any food served with mustard.

Ham-Bone Dip

2 (8 ounce) packages cream cheese, softened

2 (6 ounce) cans deviled ham

1 heaping tablespoon horseradish

¼ cup minced onion

• In mixer, beat cream cheese until creamy.

• Add all other ingredients. Chill and serve with crackers.

Pepper-Pot Bean Dip

1 (15 ounce) can refried beans

1 (pound) box hot Mexican Velveeta cheese, cubed

1 stick margarine

1 teaspoon garlic powder

• In a large double boiler, combine all ingredients.

• Heat on low, stirring often, until cheese and margarine melt.

• Serve hot in a chafing dish. Serve with tortilla chips.

Crunchy Asparagus Dip

1 (14 ounce) can
asparagus spears,
drained, chopped

½ cup mayonnaise

¼ teaspoon Tabasco

½ cup chopped pecans

- Combine all ingredients in a medium bowl.
- Refrigerate.
- Serve with wheat thins.

Party Shrimp Dip

1 (8 ounce) package
cream cheese, softened

½ cup mayonnaise

1 (6 ounce) can tiny,
cooked shrimp, drained

¾ teaspoon creole
seasoning

- Blend cream cheese and mayonnaise in mixer. Stir in shrimp and seasoning.
- Mix well and chill. Serve with chips.

Quickie Shrimp Dunk

1 (8 ounce) package
cream cheese, softened

1 (8 ounce) bottle cocktail
sauce

1 teaspoon Italian
seasoning

1 (6 ounce) can tiny,
deveined shrimp,
drained

- Place cream cheese in mixing bowl and beat until it is smooth.
- Add remaining ingredients and chill. Serve with crackers.

Chunky Shrimp Dip

2 (6 ounce) cans shrimp, drained

2 cups mayonnaise

6 green onions, finely chopped

¾ cup chunky salsa

• Crumble shrimp and stir in mayonnaise, onion and salsa.

• Chill for 1 to 2 hours. Serve with crackers.

Tasty Tuna Dip

1 (6 ounce) can tuna in spring water, drained and flaked

1 envelope Italian salad dressing mix

1 (8 ounce) carton sour cream

¼ cup chopped black olives, drained

• Combine all ingredients, stirring until blended.

• Chill 8 hours. Serve with melba rounds.

Cheesy-Crab Dip

1 (6 ounce) roll processed garlic cheese, diced

1 (10½ ounce) can cream of mushroom soup

1 (6 ounce) can crab-meat, drained

2 tablespoons sherry

• In medium-size pan heat all ingredients until cheese has melted.

• Keep warm in a chafing dish and serve with assorted crackers.

Gitty-Up Crab Dip

1 (8 ounce) package
cream cheese,
softened

3 tablespoons salsa

2 tablespoons prepared
horseradish

1 (6 ounce) can
crabmeat, drained and
flaked

- In mixing bowl, beat cream cheese until creamy.
- Add the salsa and horseradish and mix well.
- Stir in the crabmeat. Refrigerate. Serve with assorted crackers.

Hot, Rich Crab Dip

1 (10 ounce) can cheddar
cheese soup

1 (16 ounce) box Mexican
Velveeta cheese, cubed

2 (6 ounce) cans
crabmeat, flaked

1 (16 ounce) jar salsa

- In a microwaveable bowl, combine the cheese soup and Velveeta cheese.
- Microwave at 1-minute intervals until cheese melts.
- Add the crabmeat and salsa, mixing well. Serve hot with chips.

Crab Crackers

1 (6 ounce) can crabmeat,
drained and flaked

1 (8 ounce) package
cream cheese, softened

2 (10½ ounce) cans cream
of celery soup

1 (4 ounce) can chopped
black olives

- In a saucepan combine all ingredients until cheese melts. Serve hot with crackers.

You might also want to add several drops of Tabasco.

Unbelievable Crab Dip

1 (6 ounce) can white
  crabmeat, drained and
  flaked

1 (8 ounce) package
  cream cheese

1 stick butter

Chips or crackers

• In a saucepan combine crabmeat, cream cheese and butter.

• Heat and mix thoroughly. When mixed, transfer to chafing dish and serve with chips or crackers.

Easy Tuna Dip

1 (6 ounce) can tuna,
  drained

1 package dry Italian
  salad dressing mix

1 (8 ounce) carton sour
  cream

2 green onions with tops,
  chopped

• Combine all ingredients, mixing well. Let set several hours before serving.

California Clam Dip

1 envelope dry onion
  soup mix

2 (8 ounce) cartons sour
  cream

1 (7 ounce) can minced
  clams, drained

2 tablespoons chili sauce

• Combine onion soup mix and sour cream and mix well. Add clams and chili sauce. Chill.

Velvet Clam Dip

12 ounces cream cheese

½ stick margarine

2 (6 ounce) cans minced clams, drained

½ teaspoon worcestershire sauce

- Melt cream cheese and margarine in double boiler.
- Add drained minced clams and worcestershire sauce. Serve hot.

Cottage-Ham Dip

1 (16 ounce) carton small curd cottage cheese, drained

2 (6 ounce) cans deviled ham

1 package dry onion soup mix

½ cup sour cream

- Blend cottage cheese in blender or with mixer.
- Add ham, soup mix and sour cream, mixing well. Serve with crackers.

Speedy Chili Con Queso

1 (16 ounce) box Velveeta cheese, cubed

½ cup milk

1 (12 ounce) jar salsa

Tortilla Chips

- In saucepan, melt the cheese and milk in top of double boiler.
- Add about half the salsa. Serve with tortilla chips.

  Taste and add more salsa as needed for desired heat!

Beef Roll

2 (8 ounce) packages
   cream cheese,
   softened

½ medium onion, grated

2 tablespoons lemon
   juice

1 (2½ ounce) jar dried
   beef

• Whip the cream cheese until fluffy.
  Season with grated onion, lemon juice
  and a couple dashes of Tabasco.

• Place dried beef on a long roll of wax
  paper. Spread cream cheese thinly over
  the beef.

• Roll tightly and refrigerate. Cut into
  thin slices when ready to serve.

Sausage Balls

1 pound hot pork
   sausage, uncooked

1 (16 oounce) package
   grated cheddar cheese

3 cups biscuit mix

⅓ cup milk

• Combine all ingredients and form into
  small balls. If dough is a little too
  sticky, add a teaspoon more biscuit mix.

• Bake at 375° for 13 to 15 minutes.

Hot Cheese Balls

1 (5 ounce) jar cheese
   spread

½ stick margarine,
   softened

½ cup flour

⅛ teaspoon salt

• Mash cheese spread and the margarine,
  mixing well. Add flour and salt. Mix
  well.

• Roll into small balls. Chill one hour.

• Place on ungreased cookie sheet.

• Bake at 425 ° for 10 minutes. Balls will
  flatten as they cook. Serve hot.

Chili-Cheese Balls

1 (8 ounce) package grated sharp cheddar cheese, softened

1 stick margarine, softened

1 cup flour

1 (4 ounce) can chopped green chilies

- Stir cheese and margarine together.
- Add flour, green chilies and ½ teaspoon salt.
- Form dough into 2-inch balls and place on cookie sheet. Bake at 375° for 14 to 15 minutes.

Blue Cheese Ball

3 fresh green onions

1 (8 ounce) and 1 (3 ounce) packages cream cheese, softened

1 (4 ounce) package blue cheese, softened

⅓ cup chopped pecans

- Finely chop white portion of onions and combine with cream cheese and blue cheese, blending well. Shape into a ball.
- Finely chop green portion of onions and combine with pecans and roll cheese ball in the mixture to completely cover.
- Chill at least 3 hours. Serve with crackers.

Ranch Cheese Ball

1 package dry ranch-style salad dressing mix

2 (8 ounce) packages cream cheese, softened

¼ cup finely chopped pecans

1 (3 ounce) jar real bacon bits

- With mixer, stir together the dressing mix and cream cheese.
- Roll into a ball. Roll cheese ball in the pecans and bacon bits.
- Refrigerate several hours before serving.

Olive-Cheese Empanadas

1 cup pimento-stuffed green olives or black olives, chopped, divided

1 cup finely shredded cheddar cheese

4 tablespoons mayonnaise

1 (15 ounce) package of 2 refrigerated pie crusts

- Preheat oven to 450°. Combine the olives, cheese and mayonnaise.

- Using a 3-inch biscuit cutter, cut each pie crust into 12 rounds. Place 1 teaspoon of olive mixture in the center of a pastry round.

- Fold side of the pastry to the other side and press the edges together to seal in the olive mixture.

- Crimp the edge with your thumb and forefinger or use the tines of a fork to seal the edges. If the pastry begins to dry it will not seal properly. Dip your finger in water and lightly brush the edges and then seal.

- Place on a baking sheet and bake for about 10 minutes or until golden brown.

Spinach-Cheese Ball

1 (10 ounce) package frozen chopped spinach, thawed

2 (8 ounce) packages cream cheese, softened

1 (1.2 ounce) package dry vegetable soup mix

1 (8 ounce) can water chestnuts, chopped

- Drain spinach on paper towels. Squeeze or mash spinach into towels several times to make sure all water is gone from the spinach.

- In mixing bowl, beat the cream cheese until smooth. Fold in the spinach, soup mix and water chestnuts.

- Form into a ball and serve with crackers.

Beefy Cheese Balls

2 (8 ounce) packages
cream cheese, softened

2 (2½ ounce) jars dried
beef

1 bunch fresh green
onions with tops,
chopped

1 teaspoon cayenne
pepper

- Beat cream cheese with mixer until smooth and creamy.
- Chop dried beef in food processor or blender.
- Combine the beef, cream cheese, onions and cayenne pepper.
- Form into a ball and chill overnight.

Serve with crackers.

Tuna Melt Appetizer

1 (10 ounce) package
frozen spinach, drained

2 (6 ounce) cans white
tuna in water, drained,
flaked

¾ cup mayonnaise

1½ cups shredded
mozzarella cheese,
divided

- Drain spinach well with several paper towels.
- In a large bowl, combine spinach, tuna, mayonnaise and 1 cup cheese and mix well.
- Spoon into a buttered, pie plate and bake at 350° for 15 minutes. Remove from oven and sprinkle remaining cheese over top. Bake another 5 minutes. Serve with crackers.

Onion-Ham Dip

1 (5 ounce) jar pimento
cheese spread

1 (4 ounce) can deviled
ham

1 cup mayonnaise

1 bunch fresh green
onions, chopped

- In a medium bowl, combine, cheese spread, ham and mayonnaise and mix until well blended.
- Fold in chopped green onions.

Serve with crackers.

Chicken-Cheese Spread

2 (8 ounce) packages
cream cheese, softened

2 tablespoons white wine
worchestershire

2 cups finely shredded,
cooked chicken breasts

¼ cup chopped almonds,
toasted

- In mixer bowl, combine cream cheese and worchestershire and beat until creamy.

- Fold in shredded chicken and almonds. Spread on English muffin halves and toast but be careful not to brown.

English Muffin Pizza

English muffin, halved

Canned or bottled pizza
sauce

Sliced salami or
pepperoni

Grated mozzarella cheese
or cheddar

- Split muffin in half. Spread muffin with canned pizza sauce.

- Add salami or pepperoni.

- Top with grated cheese and place under broiler until cheese melts and begins to bubble.

  If you want to go all out, you can add any combination of the following ingredients: cooked chopped onion, cooked chopped green pepper, sliced jalapeno peppers, and chopped green or black olives.

Sausage Rounds

1 (8 ounce) package crescent dinner rolls

1 pound sausage, uncooked

½ teaspoon garlic powder

½ cup grated cheddar cheese

- Open package of rolls and smooth out dough with a rolling pin, sealing the seams.
- Sprinkle dough with garlic powder and cheese.
- Break up sausage with hands and spread a thin layer of sausage over rolls. Roll into a log. Wrap in wax paper and freeze several hours.
- Slice into ¼- inch rounds.
- Place on cookie sheet and bake at 350° for 20 minutes or until lightly browned.

Jack Quesadillas

¼ cup ricotta cheese

6 (6 inch) corn tortillas

⅔ cup shredded monterey jack cheese

1 (4 ounce) can diced green chilies, drained

- Spread about 1 tablespoon ricotta over tortilla. Place 1 heaping tablespoon of cheese and add 1 tablespoon of chilies. Place a second tortilla on top.
- Repeat to make 2 more quesadillas.
- In a heated skillet add 1 quesadilla and cook 3 minutes on each side. Remove from heat and cut into 4 wedges. Repeat with remaining quesadillas.

Serve warm with salsa.

Pigs in a Blanket

1 (10 count) package
  wieners

3 (10 count) cans biscuits

Dijon mustard

- Cut each wiener into thirds.
- Take each biscuit and flatten slightly and spread with mustard.
- Wrap each wiener piece in a biscuit; pinch to seal.
- Bake at 400° for 10 to 12 minutes.

Toasted Pepperoni

1 box melba toasts

¾ cup chili sauce

5 ounces pepperoni
  rounds

1 cup shredded
  mozzarella cheese

- Spread toast with chili sauce and top with pepperoni slices.
- Sprinkle with cheese and bake on cookie sheet at 375° for 3 to 5 minutes.

Cocktail Sausages

⅔ cup prepared mustard

1 cup plum jelly

½ teaspoon garlic powder

4 (4 ounce) cans Vienna
  sausages, halved

- Mix mustard, jelly and garlic powder. Heat.
- Add sausages; heat thoroughly and serve hot.

Editor's Choice

Green Eyes

4 dill pickles

4 slices boiled ham

Light cream cheese, softened

Black pepper

- Dry off pickles.
- Lightly coat one side of the ham slices with cream cheese and sprinkle on a little pepper.
- Roll the pickle up in the ham slice coated with cream cheese.
- Chill. Slice into circles to serve.

Cheddar Cheese Ring

2 (16 ounce) packages shredded cheddar cheese

1 small onion, finely chopped

1 cup mayonnaise

1½ cups finely chopped pecans plus 2 tablespoons for garnish

- Combine cheese, onion, mayonnaise and pecans. Press into an 8-inch ring mold.
- Cover with plastic wrap and refrigerate until set. Unmold when firm.
- Sprinkle top of cheese ring with additional chopped pecans.
- Slice to serve on wheat crackers.

Bacon-Oyster Bites

1 (5 ounce) can smoked oysters, drained, chopped

⅔ cup herb-seasoned stuffing mix

¼ cup water

8 slices bacon, halved and partially cooked

- Combine oysters, stuffing mix and water. Add another teaspoon water if mixture seems too dry.
- Form into balls, using about 1 tablespoon mixture for each. Wrap a half slice of bacon around each and secure with a toothpick.
- Place on a rack in a shallow baking pan. Cook at 350° for 25 to 30 minutes.

Cheese in the Round

1 cup grated cheddar
cheese

1 stick margarine,
softened

1¼ cups flour

½ teaspoon cayenne
pepper

- Combine all ingredients and form rolls
  1- inch in diameter. Chill.
- When ready to bake, slice into ¼-inch
  thick rounds and bake at 375° for 5 to 8
  minutes.

Garlic Shrimp

1 clove garlic, minced

⅔ cup chili sauce

½ pound thin bacon
strips

1 pound medium shrimp,
cooked

- Add garlic to chili sauce and set aside
  for several hours.
- Broil the bacon on one side only. Cut in
  half.
- Dip shrimp in the chili sauce and then
  wrap with half a bacon strip on the
  uncooked side out; fasten with tooth-
  picks. Refrigerate.
- Just before serving, broil shrimp until
  bacon is crisp.

Special Pimento Cheese

5 cups shredded sharp
cheddar cheese

2 (4 ounce) jars diced
pimentos, drained

1 cup salsa

3 tablespoons
mayonnaise

- Combine grated cheese, pimentos and
  salsa in large bowl.
- Stir in mayonnaise, blending well.
  Store in refrigerator.

Homemade Pimento Cheese

2 cups grated cheddar cheese

½ cup salad dressing (not mayonnaise)

2 tablespoons pimento, chopped

¼ teaspoon white vinegar

• Combine and mix together all the ingredients. Chill several hours, if possible, before serving.

Bacon Nibblers

1 (1 pound) package sliced bacon, at room temperature

1½ cups brown sugar

1½ teaspoons dry mustard

¼ teaspoon black pepper

• Cut each slice of bacon in half. Combine the brown sugar, dry mustard and black pepper in a shallow bowl.

• Dip each half slice of bacon in brown sugar mixture, pressing down so the bacon is well coated. Place each slice on a baking sheet with sides.

• Bake at 325° for 25 minutes, turning once, until bacon is browned. Immediately remove with tongs to several layers of paper towels. Bacon will harden and can be broken in pieces.

Holy Guacamole

4 avocados, peeled

½ cup salsa

¼ cup sour cream

1 teaspoon salt

• Split avocados and remove seeds. Mash avocados with a fork.

• Add salsa, sour cream and salt.

Serve with tortilla chips.

Great Balls of Fire

1 pound lean hot sausage

3 green onions, chopped

1 can chopped tomatoes and green chilies

1 (2 pound) box Velveeta cheese, cubed

• Brown sausage in a large skillet. Drain off fat. Add tomatoes and green chilies; mix.

• Add cheese to sausage mixture; cook on low heat until cheese melts. Serve hot in chafing dish with large chips.

Shrimp Squares Deluxe

1 (6 ounce) can shrimp, drained, chopped

1 cup mayonnaise

1 cup shredded cheddar cheese

10-12 slices white bread, trimmed and cut in squares

• Combine the shrimp, mayonnaise and cheese.

• Spread shrimp mixture on the bread squares and broil until bubbly.

Shrimp-Stuffed Eggs

8 hardcooked eggs

¼ cup mayonnaise

1 (6 ounce) can tiny shrimp, drained

2 tablespoons sweet pickle relish, drained

• Cut eggs in half lengthwise; set aside the egg whites. In small bowl, mash egg yolks with mayonnaise.

• Add shrimp and pickle relish and mix well. Refill egg whites. Refrigerate.

Chili-Cheese Bites

6 slices white sandwich bread

1 cup shredded cheddar cheese

1 stick margarine, softened

¾ teaspoon chili powder

- Trim crusts from bread and cut each slice into 4 squares.
- Combine cheese, margarine and chili powder and mix well.
- Place heaping teaspoonful of mixture on each bread square; place on baking sheet. Bake at 375° for 10 minutes or until puffy and lightly browned.

Whiz Biz

1 (8 ounce) jar processed cheese spread

2 tablespoons dry white wine (or cooking wine)

1 teaspoon prepared mustard

1 teaspoon worcestershire sauce

- Mix all ingredients together. Chill. Serve with crackers.

Water Chestnut Dip

1 (8 ounce) can sliced water chestnuts, chopped

1 cup chopped pecans

1 (16 ounce) carton sour cream

1 (1.8 ounce) envelope leek soup mix

- In a large bowl combine water chestnuts, pecans and the sour cream and mix well.
- Fold in the leek soup mix and mix well. Refrigerate.

Serve with wheat crackers.

Cucumber Squares

1 (8 ounces) package cream cheese, softened

½ teaspoon dill weed

3 medium cucumbers, peeled, grated

1 envelope dry ranch salad dressing mix

• In mixing bowl, combine cream cheese and dill weed and beat until creamy.

• Fold in grated cucumbers and ranch dressing.

• Spread on pumpernickel or rye bread slices.

Artichoke Bites

1½ cups mayonnaise

¾ cup freshly grated parmesan cheese

1 (4 ounce) can chopped green chilies

1 (14 ounce) jar artichoke hearts, chopped

• Mix mayonnaise, parmesan cheese, green chilies and artichoke hearts. (Remove any spikes or tough leaves from artichokes.)

• Put 1 teaspoon of the mixture on bite-size toast rounds. Broil until lightly brown.

Bacon-Wrapped Water Chestnuts

1 (8 ounce) can whole water chestnuts, drained

¼ cup soy sauce

¼ teaspoon cayenne pepper

About ½ pound bacon, cut in thirds

• Marinate water chestnuts for 1 hour in soy sauce.

• Wrap ⅓-slice bacon around the water chestnuts and fasten with a tooth pick.

• Bake at 375° for 20 minutes or until bacon is done. Drain and serve hot.

No-See-Um Chicken Livers

2 white onions, sliced
10-12 chicken livers
4 strips bacon
⅓ cup sherry

- Place onion slices in shallow pan. Top each onion slice with a chicken liver and ⅓-strip bacon. Pour sherry over all.
- Bake uncovered at 350° for about 45 minutes or until bacon is crisp. Baste occasionally with pan drippings.

Border Queso

2 canned jalapeno peppers, reserve 1 tablespoon liquid

1 (16 ounce) box Velveeta cheese

1 (4 ounce) jar pimentos, drained and chopped

3 fresh green onions, chopped

- Seed jalapeno peppers and chop.
- Combine peppers, cheese, pimentos and onion in saucepan.
- Heat on stove, stirring constantly, until cheese melts. Stir in reserved liquid. Serve with tortilla chips.

Toasted Crab

¾ cup shredded cheddar cheese

1 stick margarine, softened

1 (6 ounce) can crabmeat, drained and flaked

6 English muffins, halved

- In a bowl, combine cheese, softened margarine and crabmeat and mix well.
- Spread mixture on each muffin half. Cut each muffin into quarters and place on baking sheet.
- Broil for 5 minutes. Serve hot.

Bubbly Franks

1 package wieners

½ cup chili sauce

½ cup packed brown sugar

½ cup bourbon

- Cut wieners into bite-size pieces.
- Combine chili sauce, sugar and bourbon in a saucepan.
- Add wieners to sauce and simmer 30 minutes. Serve in chafing dish.

Cheese Straws

1 (5 ounce) package pie crust mix

¾ cup shredded cheddar cheese

Cayenne pepper

¼ teaspoon garlic powder

- Prepare pie crust according to package directions. Roll out into a rectangular shape.
- Sprinkle cheese over dough and press the cheese into the dough.
- Sprinkle cayenne pepper over the cheese.
- Fold dough over once to cover cheese. Roll to make a ¼-inch thickness.
- Cut·dough into ½-inch by 3-inch strips and place on a lightly greased baking sheet.
- Bake at 350° for 12 to 15 minutes.

Cheddar Toppers

1 cup chopped black
   olives
1 cup shredded cheddar
   cheese
½ cup mayonnaise
½ cup finely minced
   green olives

• Combine all ingredients and mix well.

• To serve, spread mixture on English
   muffins. Bake at 350° for 30 minutes.
   After baking, quarter the muffins and
   serve as hors d'oeuvres.

Tortilla Rollers

1 (8 ounce) package
   cream cheese, softened
1 (4 ounce) can chopped
   black olives, drained
1 (4 ounce) can chopped
   green chilies, drained
1 (12 ounce) jar salsa

• With a mixer, beat cream cheese until
   smooth. Add black olives, green chilies
   and ¼ cup salsa, mixing well.

*To serve, spread on flour tortillas and roll
up. Refrigerate several hours. Slice in
half inch slices. Insert toothpick in each
slice and dip in salsa.*

Cheese It

1 (5 ounce) jar processed
   cheese spread,
   softened
½ stick butter, softened
½ cup flour
¼ teaspoon salt

• In mixer whip the cheese and butter,
   mixing flour and salt. Make a roll 1½-
   inches in diameter; place in freezer for
   15 to 20 minutes.

• When chilled slice ½-inch thick to make
   small circles.

• Place on ungreased baking sheet and
   bake at 425° for 12 to 15 minutes.

Onion Crisps

2 sticks margarine,
  softened

2 cups shredded cheddar
  cheese

1 package dry onion soup
  mix

2 cups flour

- Combine all ingredients. Dough will be very thick.
- Divide into two batches and form into two rolls. Refrigerate for about 3 hours.
- Slice in ¼-thick slices.
- Bake at 350° for 12 to 15 minutes.

Sausage Pinwheels

2½ cups biscuit mix

⅔ cup milk

1 (pound) package hot
  sausage at room
  temperature

1 green or red bell pepper,
  minced

- In medium bowl. Combine biscuit mix and milk and mix well.
- Divide sough into 3 parts. Roll each piece of dough into a thin rectangle.
- Crumble ⅓ sausage and minced bell pepper on each piece of dough and pat down.
- Roll up like a jelly roll. Cover with foil and chill overnight. Slice into thin slices and bake at 375° for 15-20 minutes.

Sausage Bites

1 (1 pound) package hot
  sausage

1 pound colby or cheddar
  cheese, grated

3¾ cups biscuit mix

½ teaspoon garlic powder

- Combine sausage, cheese, garlic powder and biscuit mix. Kneed thoroughly.
- Roll into 1-inch balls.
- Bake on a cookie sheet at 350° for 15 to 18 minutes until lightly browned.

Hot Cocktail Squares

1 (4 ounce) can chopped green chilies

1 (3 ounce) jar bacon bits

1 (16 ounce) package shredded cheddar cheese

7 eggs

- In a greased 7 x 11-inch baking dish, layer green chilies, bacon bits and cheese.
- Beat eggs with a fork until well beaten. Season with a little salt and several drops Tabasco. Pour over cheese.
- Bake covered at 350° for 25 minutes. Uncover and bake another 10 minutes. Serve warm.

Bits of Frank

1 (8 count) package frankfurters

1 (8 ounce) package of corn muffin mix

½ teaspoon chili powder

⅔ cup milk

- Cut franks into 1-inch pieces.
- Combine corn muffin mix, chili powder and milk. Add the pieces of frankfurters to the corn muffin mix, stirring well to coat each piece.
- Drop one at a time into deep hot fat. Fry for 2 minutes or until brown, then drain. Serve warm with chili sauce for dunking.

Mexican Fudge

1 (16 ounce) package shredded American cheese

4 eggs, beaten

⅔ cup jalapeno green sauce

1 teaspoon worcestershire

- In a sprayed 7 x 11 -inch baking dish, spread half of the cheese in the dish.
- Combine eggs with green sauce and worcestershire and pour over cheese in the dish. Add the remaining cheese.
- Bake at 350° for 30 minutes.
- Cut into squares to serve. May be served hot or room temperature.

Crispy Chestnuts

1 (8 ounce) can whole
water chestnuts

5-6 slices bacon,
quartered

Honey mustard

- Wrap each water chestnut with quartered strip of bacon. Secure with toothpick.
- Broil until bacon is cooked and remove.
- Dip in honey mustard.

Peanut Butter Sticks

1 loaf thin sliced
sandwich bread

1 cup smooth peanut
butter

½ cup peanut oil

1 teaspoon sugar,
optional

- Trim crust from the bread. Cut each slice into four fingers. Place bread and the bread crust in separate pans.
- Bake at 200° for one hour or until crisp, turning often.
- In your food processor make crumbs from the dry bread crust.
- Mix peanut butter and oil. Dip bread fingers into peanut mixture, then roll in breadcrumbs.
- Arrange in layers in an airtight container; let stand overnight. These must be stored in a tightly covered container.

Devil's Spread

1 (4¼ ounce) can deviled
ham

¾ cup mayonnaise

1 tablespoon grated onion

1 (4 ounce) can chopped
green chilies, drained

- Mix all ingredients. Spread on wheat crackers.

Hot Artichoke Spread

1 (14 ounce) can artichoke hearts, drained, finely chopped

1 cup mayonnaise

1 cup grated parmesan cheese

1 package Italian salad dressing mix

- Remove the tough outer leaves, and chop artichoke hearts. Combine all ingredients, mixing thoroughly.
- Pour into a 9-inch square baking pan.
- Bake at 350° for 20 minutes.

Serve hot with assorted crackers.

Artichoke Spread

1 (14 ounce) jar marinated artichoke hearts

1 cup grated parmesan cheese

1 cup mayonnaise

1 teaspoon dried parsley

- Drain artichoke hearts, remove the tough outer leaves and chop. Combine artichokes, cheese, mayonnaise and parsley, blending well.
- Spoon into a non-stick sprayed 9-inch baking dish. Bake at 350° for 20 minutes.

Serve with melba toast rounds.

Smoky Gouda Spread

¾ cup chopped walnuts

1 (8 ounce) smoked gouda cheese

1 (8 ounce) package cream cheese, softened

¼ cup sliced green onions

- Spread walnuts in a shallow baking pan. Bake at 325° for 10 minutes or until lightly toasted. Cool and set aside.
- Trim and discard outer red edge of gouda cheese. Grate cheese. With mixer combine the cream cheese and gouda cheese. Mixing well, stir in walnuts and onions.

Serve with apple wedges or crackers.

Jiffy Tuna Spread

1 (7 ounce) can white
  tuna, drained

½ cup chopped ripe olives

1 package dry Italian
  salad dressing mix

1 (8 ounce) carton sour
  cream

• Combine all ingredients, mixing well.
  Sprinkle with a little paprika for color
  and serve with crackers.

Creamy Cucumber Spread

1 cup seeded, chopped
  cucumbers

1 (8 ounce) package
  cream cheese, softened

½ cup mayonnaise

1 teaspoon seasoned salt

• Before chopping cucumber, make sure
  seeds have all been removed.

• With mixer, beat cream cheese until
  creamy; mix in mayonnaise, seasoned
  salt and cucumber.

  Spread on crackers.

Cucumber-Garlic Dip

2 unpeeled cucumbers

2 (8 ounce) packages
  cream cheese, softened

2 tablespoons lemon
  juice

1 envelope savory herb
  and garlic onion soup
  mix

• With a grater, coarsely grate both cucumbers, reserving juice.

• In mixer bowl, combine cream cheese,
  lemon juice and onion soup mix. Beat
  until cream cheese is fairly smooth.

• Thin mixture with reserved cucumber
  juice as needed. Add salt to taste. Cover
  and refrigerate.

  Serve with vegetable sticks.

Olive-Cheese Appetizers

1 cup pimento-stuffed olives, chopped

2 fresh green onions, finely chopped

1 ½ cups shredded monterey jack cheese

½ cup mayonnaise

• In large bowl, combine all ingredients and mix well.

• Spread on English muffins and bake at 375° until bubbly.

• Cut muffins into quarters and serve hot.

Black Olive Spread

1 (8 ounce) package cream cheese, softened

½ cup mayonnaise

1 (4 ounce) can chopped black olives

3 green onions, chopped very fine

• Cream together the cream cheese and mayonnaise until smooth.

• Add olives and onions. Chill.

Spread on slices of party rye.

Pineapple-Island Spread

2 (8 ounce) packages cream cheese, softened

1 (8 ounce) carton sour cream

1 (8 ounce) can crushed pineapple, drained

½ cup finely chopped pecans

• In mixer bowl, combine cream cheese and sour cream and beat until creamy.

• Fold in pineapple, juice and pecans and mix well. Refrigerate,

Spread on banana nut bread, zucchini bread or use as a fruit dip.

Carmel Apple Dip

1 (8 ounce) package
  cream cheese, softened

1 cup packed brown
  sugar

1 teaspoon vanilla

½ cup chopped dry
  roasted peanuts

• Combine cream cheese, brown sugar
  and vanilla with mixer. Beat until
  creamy. Stir in peanuts. Refrigerate.

Serve with crisp apple slices.

Nutty Apple Dip

1 (8 ounce) package
  cream cheese, softened

1 cup packed brown
  sugar

1 teaspoon vanilla

1 cup finely chopped
  pecans

• In a small mixing bowl combine cream
  cheese, sugar and vanilla. Beat until
  smooth.

• Stir in pecans.

Serve with sliced apples for dipping.

Orange Dip for Apples

1 (8 ounce) package
  cream cheese, softened

1 (8 ounce) carton orange
  yogurt

½ cup orange marmalade

¼ cup finely chopped
  pecans

• In mixing bowl beat cream cheese until
  smooth.

• Fold in remaining ingredients. Refrigerate.

Serve with apple slices.

Orange-Sour Cream Dip

1 (6 ounce) can frozen
  orange juice
  concentrate, thawed

1 (3.4 ounce) package
  vanilla instant pudding
  mix

1 cup milk

¼ cup sour cream

- Combine the orange juice concentrate, vanilla pudding mix and milk. Stir with a wire whisk until mixture is blended and smooth. Stir in sour cream.
- Cover and chill at least 2 hours.

Serve with fresh fruit.

Chocolate Fruit Dip

1 (8 ounce) package
  cream cheese, softened

¼ cup chocolate syrup

1 (7 ounce) jar
  marshmallow cream

Fruit

- In a mixing bowl beat cream cheese and chocolate syrup until smooth.
- Fold in marshmallow cream.
- Cover and refrigerate until serving.

Serve with apple wedges, banana chunks or strawberries.

Juicy Fruit Dip

1 (8 ounce) package
  cream cheese, softened

1 (7 ounce) jar
  marshmallow creme

¼ teaspoon ground ginger

- Cream together with the mixer, the cream cheese and marshmallow creme; fold in ginger.
- Chill.

Serve with apple slices, pineapple sticks, honeydew slices, etc.

Peanut Butter Spread

1 (8 ounce) package
cream cheese, softened

1⅔ cups creamy peanut
butter

½ cup powdered sugar

1 tablespoon milk

• In mixer, cream together all ingredients.
*Serve spread with apple wedges or
graham crackers.*

Fruit Dip for Nectarines

1 (8 ounce) package
cream cheese,
softened

2 (7 ounce) jars
marshmallow cream

¼ teaspoon cinnamon

⅛ teaspoon ground
ginger

• With mixer, combine and beat together
all ingredients. Mix well. Refrigerate.
*Serve with unpeeled slices of nectarines
or any other fruit.*

Sweet and Creamy Fruit Dip

1 (8 ounce) carton sour
cream

3 heaping tablespoons
brown sugar

½ teaspoon ground
cinnamon

Dash ground ginger

• Mix sour cream, brown sugar and
cinnamon.

• Serve with fresh fruit.

Amaretto Dip Spread

1 (8 ounce) package
  cream cheese, softened

¼ cup amaretto liqueur

¼ cup chopped slivered
  almonds, toasted

Banana bread

• With mixer blend cream cheese and
  amaretto. Stir in the toasted almonds.
  Serve with crackers or sliced apples.

*This is also a good spread on banana
bread, zucchini bread, etc.*

Deviled Pecans

½ stick butter, melted (no
  margarine)

1 tablespoon
  worcestershire

2 cups pecan halves

¼ teaspoon cayenne
  pepper

• In a mixing bowl combine the butter and
  the worcestershire and mix well.

• Add pecans, pepper and ¼ teaspoon
  salt. Stir and toss pecans until well
  coated.

• Roast on baking sheet at 350° for 15
  minutes, stirring or shaking the pan
  occasionally.

Classy Red Pecans

½ stick margarine

1½ teaspoons chili
  powder

¾ teaspoon garlic salt

3 cups pecan halves

• In large skillet, melt butter. Stir in chili
  powder, garlic salt and pecans.

• Cook on medium heat, stirring pecans
  constantly for 4 or 5 minutes until
  browned and well coated with chili
  powder.

Cinnamon Pecans

1 pound shelled pecan halves

1 egg white, slightly beaten with fork

2 tablespoons cinnamon

¾ cup sugar

• Combine the pecan halves with the egg white and mix well.

• Sprinkle with mixture of the cinnamon and sugar. Stir until all pecans are coated.

• Spread on a baking sheet and bake at 325° for about 20 minutes. Cool. Store in a covered container.

Toasted Pecans

12 cups pecan halves

1 stick margarine

Salt

½ teaspoon garlic powder

• Place pecans in a large baking pan. In 250° oven, toast pecans for 30 minutes to dry.

• Slice margarine and melt in baking pan. Let pecans get completely greasy, stirring twice.

• After pecans and margarine have mixed well, sprinkle with salt and garlic powder and stir often.

• Toast pecans one hour until margarine has been absorbed and pecans are crisp.

Sugar-Coated Peanuts

1½ cups sugar

1 tablespoon maple flavoring

4½ cups Spanish peanuts

1½ teaspoon salt

- In a large saucepan combine the sugar, ¾ cup water, maple flavoring, and peanuts. Stir over medium heat for 20 minutes or until almost all of the liquid is absorbed.

- Spread on a greased 10 x 15-inch baking pan and sprinkle with salt. Bake at 350° for about 25 minutes or until peanuts are well coated, stirring 2 to 3 times.

- Remove to a wax paper-lined baking sheet to cool. Store in airtight container.

Best Tropical Punch

1 (46 ounce) can
   pineapple juice

1 (46 ounce) can apricot
   nectar

3 (6 ounce) cans frozen
   limeade concentrate,
   thawed

3 quarts ginger ale,
   chilled

• Combine the first three juices and
   refrigerate. When ready to serve, add
   ginger ale.

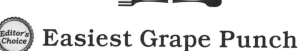

Easiest Grape Punch

½ gallon ginger ale

Red seedless grapes

Sparkling white grape
   juice, chilled

• Make an ice ring of the ginger ale and
   seedless grapes.

• When ready to serve, pour sparkling
   white grape juice in punch bowl with ice
   ring.

   *Sparkling white grape juice is great
   just by itself!*

Great Fruit Punch

1 (46 ounce) can
   pineapple juice

2 (46 ounce) cans apple
   juice

3 quarts ginger ale

Fresh mint to garnish,
   optional

• Combine pineapple juice and apple juice
   and make an ice ring with part of the
   juice.

• Chill remaining juice and ginger ale.

• When ready to serve, combine juices
   and ginger ale and place ice ring in
   punch bowl.

Perfect Party Punch

1 (12 ounce) can frozen limeade concentrate

1 (46 ounce) can pineapple juice, chilled

1 (46 ounce) apricot nectar, chilled

1 quart ginger ale, chilled

- Dilute the limeade concentrate as directed on the can.
- Add the pineapple juice and apricot nectar, stirring well.
- When ready to serve, add the ginger ale.

Ruby Red Punch

1 (46 ounce) can pineapple-grapefruit juice

½ cup sugar

¼ cup cinnamon candies

1 quart ginger ale, chilled

- In a large saucepan, combine pineapple-grapefruit juice, sugar and candies. Bring to a boil, stirring until candies are dissolved.
- Cool until time to serve, stirring occasionally, to completely dissolve candies.
- Add ginger ale just before serving.

Cranberry Punch

2 (28 ounce) bottles ginger ale, chilled

1 (48 ounce) can pineapple juice, chilled

1 quart cranberry juice, chilled

1 quart pineapple sherbet, broken up

- Pour all ingredients in punch bowl. Serve.

Creamy Strawberry Punch

1 (10 ounce) package frozen strawberries, thawed

½ gallon strawberry ice cream, softened

2 (2 liter) bottles ginger ale, chilled

Fresh strawberries to garnish, optional

- Process strawberries through blender.
- Combine strawberries, chunks of ice cream and the ginger ale in punch bowl.
- Stir and serve immediately.

 # Mocha Punch

4 cups brewed coffee

¼ cup sugar

4 cups milk

4 cups chocolate ice cream, softened

- In a container, combine coffee and sugar; stir until sugar is dissolved. Refrigerate for 2 hours.
- Just before serving, pour into a small punch bowl.
- Add milk; mix well. Top with scoops of ice cream and stir well.

Sparkling Pink Punch

3 (6 ounce) cans frozen pink lemonade concentrate, undiluted

1 (750 milliliter) bottle pink sparkling wine

3 (2 liter) bottles lemon-lime carbonated beverage, divided

Lime slices to garnish, optional

- Stir together all ingredients, except 1 bottle carbonated beverage, in an airtight container; cover and freeze 8 hours or until firm.
- Let stand at room temperature 10 minutes; place in a punch bowl.
- Add remaining bottle carbonated beverage, stirring until slushy.

Strawberry Fizz

2 (10 ounce) boxes frozen strawberries, thawed

2 (6 ounce) cans frozen pink lemonade concentrate

2 (2 liter) bottles ginger ale, chilled

Fresh strawberries to garnish, optional

- Process strawberries through blender.
- Pour lemonade into punch bowl and stir in strawberries.
- Add chilled ginger ale and stir well.

  It would be nice to make an ice ring out of another bottle of ginger ale.

Party-Hardy Punch

1 (46 ounce) can pineapple juice

1 (46 ounce) can apple juice

3 quarts ginger ale, chilled

Pineapple chunks to garnish, optional

- Combine pineapple and apple juice in a very large plastic container or any container large enough to hold both juices. You can use two plastic pitchers. Freeze both juices.
- When ready to serve, place pineapple and apple juice in punch bowl and add the chilled ginger ale. Stir to mix.

Cranberry-Lemon Punch

2 quarts cranberry juice

1 (6 ounce) can lemonade concentrate, thawed

⅔ cup maraschino cherry juice

2 liters lemon lime soda, chilled

- Combine all ingredients.

  It would be good to have ice ring made out of cranberry juice, lemon slices and maraschino cherries.

Pina Colada Punch

1 (46 ounce) can
 pineapple juice, chilled

1 (20 ounce) can crushed
 pineapple, undrained

1 (15 ounce) can cream of
 coconut

1 (32 ounce) bottle 7-Up,
 chilled

• Combine all ingredients.

• Serve over ice cubes.

White Wine Punch

2 quarts ginger ale,
 chilled

2 (12 ounce) cans frozen
 limeade concentrate

4 limeade cans white
 wine, chilled

Lime slices

• Make an ice ring with as much ginger
 ale as necessary.

• Combine limeade, white wine and
 remaining ginger ale in punch bowl.

• Serve with ice ring and lime slices.

Sparkling Wine Punch

6 oranges, unpeeled,
 thinly sliced

1 cup sugar

2 (750 milliliter) bottles
 dry white wine

3 (750 milliliter) bottles
 sparkling wine, chilled

• Place orange slices in a large plastic or
 glass container and sprinkle with sugar.

• Add white wine; cover and chill at least
 8 hours.

• Stir in sparkling wine.

Champagne Punch

1 (750 ml) bottle
champagne, chilled

1 (32 ounce) bottle ginger
ale, chilled

1 (6 ounce) can frozen
orange juice
concentrate

Orange slices to garnish,
optional

• Mix all ingredients in punch bowl.
Serve chilled.

Apple Party Punch

3 cups sparkling apple
cider

2 cups apple juice

1 cup pineapple juice

½ cup brandy

• Combine all ingredients and freeze 8
hours.

• Remove punch from freezer 30 minutes
before serving.

• Place in a small punch bowl and break
into chunks. Stir until slushy.

Holiday Egg Nog

1 gallon egg nog

1 pint whipping cream

1 quart brandy

½ gallon ice cream,
softened

• Mix all ingredients.

• Serve in individual cups and sprinkle
with nutmeg and serve immediately.

Amaretto Cooler

1¼ cups amaretto

2 quarts cold orange juice

1 (15 ounce) bottle club soda, chilled

Orange slices to garnish, optional

• Combine all ingredients, stirring well. Serve over ice.

Creamy Orange Drink

1¾ cups milk

½ pint vanilla ice cream

⅓ cup frozen orange juice concentrate

1 teaspoon non-dairy creamer

• In blender, combine all ingredients.
• Blend until smooth.

Banana Split Float

2 ripe bananas, mashed

3 cups milk

1 (10 ounce) package frozen sweetened strawberries, thawed

1½ pints chocolate ice cream, divided

• Place bananas in blender and add milk, strawberries and ½ pint of the chocolate ice cream. Beat just until blended.
• Pour into tall, chilled glasses and top each with a scoop of chocolate ice cream.

Lemon-Banana Shake

1 (6 ounce) can frozen lemonade concentrate, thawed

1 cup diced bananas

1 quart vanilla ice cream

3 cups milk

- In mixing bowl, combine lemonade concentrate and bananas. Beat until it is a heavy consistency.
- For each milk shake, add one scoop vanilla ice cream and ¼ cup of lemon-banana mixture in bottom of glass.
- Fill glass ⅔ full of milk and stir until blended. Top it off with one more scoop of ice cream.

Peanut Power Shake

2 bananas, cut up

½ cup frozen orange juice concentrate, thawed

¼ cup peanut butter

¼ cup milk

- In blender container, combine all ingredients. Cover and blend until smooth.
- Add 1 cup of ice cubes, blending until smooth.

Purple Shakes

1 (6 ounce) can frozen grape juice concentrate

1 cup milk

2½ cups vanilla ice cream

2 tablespoons sugar, optional

- In blender combine all ingredients. Cover and blend at high speed for 30 seconds. Serve immediately.

Kahlua Frosty

1 cup kahlua
1 pint vanilla ice cream
1 cup half-and-half
¼ teaspoon almond extract

• In a blender, combine all ingredients and one heaping cup of ice cubes.
• Blend until smooth. Serve immediately.

Orange Lush

2 (6 ounce) cans frozen orange juice concentrate, thawed
1 pint cranberry juice
½ cup sugar
1 quart club soda

• Combine orange juice, cranberry juice and sugar, mixing thoroughly.
• Just before serving, pour into punch bowl and stir in the chilled club soda.

Fruit Smoothie

1 cup orange juice
1 ripe banana, peeled, thickly sliced
1 ripe peach, cut into chunks
1 cup strawberries

• Put the orange juice into a blender.
• Add the banana, peach, strawberries and 1 cup of ice cubes.
• Blend on high speed until liquefied.

Tropical Fruit Smoothie

2 (8 ounce) cartons
vanilla yogurt

1 cup fresh frozen
blueberries

1 cup fresh frozen peach
slices

1 (8 ounce) can pineapple
chunks, drained

- Process all ingredients in a blender until smooth, stopping to scrape down sides.
- Serve immediately.

Limeade Cooler

1½ pints lime sherbet

1 (6 ounce) can frozen
limeade concentrate

3 cups milk

Lime slices to garnish,
optional

- Beat lime sherbet in mixing bowl; add concentrated limeade and milk.
- Blend all ingredients together.
- Pour into 5 glasses, topping each with an additional scoop of lime sherbet. Serve immediately.

Pineapple-Strawberry Cooler

2 cups milk

1 (20 ounce) can crushed
pineapple, chilled

½ pint vanilla ice cream

1 pint strawberry ice
cream

- In a mixer bowl, combine milk, pineapple and vanilla ice cream.
- Mix just until blended. Pour into tall glasses and top with a scoop of strawberry ice cream.

Strawberry Smoothie

2 bananas, peeled, sliced

1 pint fresh strawberries, quartered

1 (8 ounce) container strawberry yogurt

¼ cup orange juice

• Place all ingredients in blender. Process until smooth.

Orange Slush

2 cups orange juice

½ cup instant, non-fat dry milk

¼ teaspoon almond extract

8 ice cubes

• Add all ingredients in blender and process on high until mixture is combined and thickened. Serve immediately.

Victorian Iced Tea

4 individual tea bags

¼ cup sugar

1 (11 ounce) can frozen cranberry-raspberry juice concentrate, thawed

4 cups cold water

• Place tea bags in a teapot; add 4 cups boiling water. Cover and steep for 5 minutes.

• Remove and discard tea bags. Add sugar mix. Refrigerate tea.

• Just before serving, combine cranberry-raspberry concentrate and cold water in a 2½-quart pitcher; stir in tea. Serve with ice cubes.

Lemonade Tea

2 family-size tea bags

½ cup sugar

1 (12 ounce) can frozen lemonade

1 quart ginger ale, chilled

- Steep tea in 3 quarts water; then mix with sugar and lemonade.
- Add ginger ale just before serving.

Spiced Iced Tea

2 quarts tea

⅔ cup sugar

1 (12 ounce) can frozen lemonade concentrate, thawed

1 quart ginger ale

- Combine tea, sugar and lemonade; chill.
- Just before serving, add the chilled ginger ale.

Frosted Chocolate Milk

2 pints coffee ice cream

½ cup chocolate syrup

¼ cup instant coffee flakes

2 quarts milk, divided

- In a blender, beat ice cream, chocolate syrup, coffee and about half of the milk. Beat until well blended.
- Combine the remaining milk and chill before serving.
- Serve in frosted glasses.

Coffee Milk Shake

1 pint vanilla ice cream, divided

¼ cup milk

½ cup chocolate coated toffee bits

• In blender combine half the ice cream and all the milk. Cover and blend until combined.

• Add remaining ice cream. Cover and blend until desired consistency.

• Add toffee bits and process briefly with on/off pulse to mix.

Chocolate-Yogurt Malt

4 cups frozen vanilla yogurt

1 cup chocolate milk

¼ cup instant chocolate malted milk drink

Mini-chocolate chips, optional

• Process all ingredients in a blender until smooth, stopping to scrape sides.

• Serve immediately.

• Top with mini-chocolate chips.

Spanish Coffee

1 tablespoon sugar

4 cups hot, brewed coffee

¾ cup kahlua

Sweetened whipped cream

• Stir sugar into hot coffee and add kahula.

• Pour into 4 serving cups.

• Top with whipped cream.

Instant Cocoa Mix

1 (8 quart) box dry milk powder

1 (12 ounce) jar non-dairy creamer

1 (16 ounce) can instant chocolate flavored drink mix

1¼ cups powdered sugar

- Combine all ingredients and store in an airtight container.

- To serve, use ¼ cup cocoa mix per cup of hot water.

 # Amaretto

3 cups sugar

1 pint vodka

3 tablespoons almond extract

1 tablespoon vanilla (not the imitation)

- Combine sugar and 2¼ cups water in a large pan. Bring mixture to a boil.

- Reduce heat. Let simmer 5 minutes, stirring occasionally. Remove from stove.

- Add vodka, almond and vanilla extracts. Stir to mix.

- Store in airtight jar.

Hot Cranberry Cider

1½ quarts cranberry juice

1 (12 ounce) can frozen orange juice concentrate, thawed

1½ orange juice cans water

½ teaspoon cinnamon

- Combine cranberry juice, orange juice and water in large saucepan. Bring to a boil to blend flavors.

- Add cinnamon, stirring well. Serve hot.

Peppermint Hot Chocolate

3 cups hot milk, divided

8 small chocolate
  peppermint patties

Pinch salt

1 cup half-and-half

- Combine ½ cup hot milk with chocolate peppermint patties, stirring well.
- Add pinch of salt and remaining hot milk.
- Heat to simmering, but do not boil.
- Add the half-and-half.

Spiced Coffee

1 cup instant coffee

4 teaspoons grated lemon
  peel

4 teaspoons ground
  cinnamon

1 teaspoon ground cloves

- In a small jar, combine all ingredients; cover tightly.
- For each serving, spoon 2 teaspoons of coffee mix into coffee cup and stir in ¾ cup boiling water. Sweeten to taste.

Mexican Coffee

1 ounce kahlua

1 cup hot black coffee

Ground cinnamon

Sweetened whipped
  cream

- Pour kahlua and coffee into a tall mug.
- Sprinkle with cinnamon and stir.
- Top with whipped cream. (You can substitute frozen whipped topping).

Kid's Cherry Sparkler

2 (6 ounce) jars red maraschino cherries, drained

2 (6 ounce) jars green maraschino cherries, drained

½ gallon distilled water

1 (2 liter) bottle cherry 7-Up, chilled

- Place 1 red or green cherry in each compartment of 4 ice cube trays.
- Fill trays with distilled water; freeze for 8 hours. Serve soft drink over ice cubes.

Apricot Punch

1 (12 ounce) can apricot nectar

1 (6 ounce) can frozen orange juice concentrate, thawed, undiluted

2 tablespoons lemon juice

1 (2 liter) bottle ginger ale, chilled

- Combine apricot nectar, orange juice concentrate, lemon juice and 1 cup water. Chill.

- When ready to serve, stir in ginger ale.

Chocolate Mint Fizz

¼ cup white creme de menthe

¼ cup creme de cocao

1 pint vanilla ice cream

1 pint chocolate ice cream

• Place liqueurs into blender container.

• Add ice cream gradually and blend until smooth after each addition.

• Pour into glasses and serve immediately.

BREADS,
BREAKFAST
&
BRUNCH

Creamy Rich Biscuits

2 cups flour

3 teaspoons baking powder

½ teaspoon salt

1 (8 ounce) carton whipping cream

- Combine flour, baking powder and salt.
- In mixer bowl, beat the whipping cream only until it holds a shape.
- Combine the flour mixture and cream; mix with a fork. Put dough on a lightly floured board and knead it for about 1 minute.
- Pat dough to a ¾-inch thickness. Cut out biscuits with a small biscuit cutter.
- Place on baking sheet; bake at 375° for about 12 minutes or until lightly brown.

Quick, Creamy Biscuits

2½ cups biscuit mix

½ pint whipping cream

- Mix biscuit mix and cream. Place on a floured board. Knead several times.
- Pat out to ½-inch thickness. Cut with a biscuit cutter.
- Bake at 375° for 12 to 15 minutes or until lightly brown.

Drunk Biscuits

3¼ cups biscuit mix

¼ teaspoon salt

1 teaspoon sugar

1⅔ cups beer

- Combine all ingredients and spoon into 12 greased muffin cups.
- Bake at 400° for 15 to 20 minutes until golden.

Sour Cream Biscuits

⅓ cup club soda
⅓ cup sour cream
½ tablespoon sugar
2 cups biscuit mix

- In a mixing bowl combine all ingredients stirring with a fork just until the dry ingredients are moistened.
- Turn bowl out onto lightly floured board and knead lightly several times.
- Roll dough into a 1-inch thickness and cut with a biscuit cutter.
- Place dough in a greased 9 x 13-inch baking pan. Bake at 400° for 12 to14 minutes or until golden brown.

Refrigerator Biscuits

1 (8 ounce) package
   cream cheese, softened
1 stick margarine,
   softened
1 cup self-rising flour

- Beat cream cheese and margarine at medium speed with mixer for 2 minutes. Gradually add flour, beating at low speed, just until blended.
- Spoon dough into miniature muffin pans, filling ⅔ full or you can refrigerate dough for up to 3 days.
- Bake at 375° for 15 minutes or until golden brown.

Garlic-Flavored Biscuits

5 cups biscuit mix

1 cup shredded cheddar cheese

1 (14 ounce) can chicken broth with roasted garlic

- Mix all ingredients to form a soft dough. Drop by heaping spoonfuls onto greased baking sheet.

- Bake at 425° for 10 minutes or until slightly brown.

Maple Syrup Biscuits

2¼ cup baking mix

⅔ cup milk

1½ cups maple syrup

- Combine baking mix and milk. Stir just until moistened. On a floured surface roll dough into ½-inch thickness. Cut with a 2-inch biscuit cutter.

- Pour syrup into a 7 x 11- inch baking dish. Place biscuits on top of syrup.

- Bake at 425° for 13 to 15 minutes or until biscuits are golden brown.

  Serve with breakfast.

Speedy Biscuits

6 tablespoons shortening

3 cups self-rising flour

1 cup milk

Butter

- Cut shortening into the flour with a pastry cutter or by hand. Add milk and mix until dough forms a ball. Knead until dough is smooth.

- Place on a flowered surface and flatten slightly. Cut with a floured biscuit cutter and place in a well greased pan, turning to grease both sides of the biscuits.

- Bake at 400 ° for 10 to 12 minutes.

Hot Biscuits

1⅓ cup self-rising flour

1 (8 ounce) carton whipping cream

2 tablespoons sugar

Butter

- Combine all ingredients and stir until blended.
- Drop biscuits by teaspoon onto a greased baking sheet.
- Bake at 400° for about 10 minutes or until lightly brown.
- Serve with plain or flavored butters on page 84 and 85.

Come and Get 'Em Biscuits

2 cups self-rising flour

4 tablespoons mayonnaise

1 cup milk

Butter

- Mix all ingredients and drop by spoonfuls on a baking sheet.
- Bake at 425° until biscuits are golden brown.
- Serve with plain or flavored butters on page 84 and 85.

Date Biscuits

1 cup chopped dates

2 cups biscuit mix

½ cup grated American cheese

¾ cup milk

- Combine dates, biscuit mix and cheese.
- Add milk; stir well to a moderately soft dough. Drop by teaspoonful onto a greased baking sheet.
- Bake in a 400° oven for 12 to 15 minutes. Serve hot.

Cream Cheese Biscuits

1 (3 ounce) package
  cream cheese, softened
1 stick butter, softened
1 cup self-rising flour
¼ teaspoon salt, optional

- In mixer beat cream cheese and butter together. Add flour, mixing well.
- Roll out to ½-inch thickness and cut with a small biscuit cutter.
- Place on a greased baking sheet and bake at 350° for 20 minutes or until lightly browned.

Hot Cheese Biscuits

1 small jar Old English
  cheese spread
½ stick margarine,
  softened
½ cup flour
⅛ teaspoon salt

- Mash cheese spread and the margarine, mixing well. Add flour and salt.
- Mix well. Roll into small balls. Chill one hour.
- Place on ungreased cookie sheet.
- Bake at 400° for 10 minutes. Balls will flatten as they cook. Serve hot.

Sausage-Cheese Biscuits

1 (8 ounce) package
  grated cheddar cheese
1 pound hot bulk pork
  sausage
2 cups biscuit mix
¾ cup milk

- Combine cheese, sausage and biscuit mix.
- Drop on ungreased baking sheet.
- Bake at 400° until lightly brown. Serve hot.

Strawberry Topping for Biscuits

3½ cups sugar

1 (10 ounce) carton frozen strawberries, thawed

1 (6 ounce) can frozen orange juice concentrate, thawed

2 tablespoons lemon juice

- Combine sugar and strawberries in a large saucepan, mixing well. Over high heat bring to a full rolling boil. Boil one minute, stirring constantly.
- Remove from heat and stir in orange juice concentrate and lemon juice. Return to heat and bring to a boil for one minute, stirring constantly.
- Skim off foam off top. You could add red food coloring if you like.
- Pour into jelly glasses and seal with hot paraffin.

This is delicious over hot biscuits.

French Onion Biscuits

2 cups biscuit mix

¼ cup milk

1 (8 ounce) container French onion dip

2 tablespoons finely minced green onion

- Mix all ingredients together until soft dough forms. Drop dough onto a greased baking sheet.
- Bake at 400° for about 10 minutes or until light golden brown.

Old South Sweet Potato Biscuits

1 (16 ounce) can sweet potatoes, drained

1 tablespoon sugar

¼ cup milk

1½ cups biscuit mix

- In a mixing bowl, mash sweet potatoes, add sugar and milk and beat until creamy. Stir in biscuit mix with a fork until most of the lumps are gone.
- Pour mixture onto floured, wax paper and knead 5-6 times. Press down to about ½-inch thick and cut out biscuits using biscuit cutter or small glass. Bake at 450° for 10-12 minutes on ungreased baking sheet.

Toasted French Bread

1 unsliced loaf French
    bread

1 stick butter, softened

¾ cup parmesan cheese

1½ teaspoons Tabasco

- Slice bread in half lengthwise, then quarter.

- Combine butter, parmesan cheese and Tabasco. Spread on top of slices using all the mixture. Place on baking sheet.

- Cook at 325° for about 25 minutes or until heated thoroughly and browned on top.

Parmesan Bread Deluxe

1 loaf unsliced Italian
    bread

½ cup refrigerated creamy
    Caesar dressing and
    dip

⅓ cup grated parmesan
    cheese

3 tablespoons finely
    chopped green onions

- Cut 24 (½-inch thick) slices from bread. Reserve remaining bread for other use.

- In small bowl, combine dressing, cheese and onion. Spread a teaspoon of dressing mixture onto each bread slice.

- Place bread on baking sheet. Broil 4-inches from heat until golden brown. Serve warm.

Bacon-Cheese French Bread

1 (16 ounce) loaf unsliced French bread

5 slices bacon, cooked, crumbled

8 ounces mozzarella cheese, shredded

1 stick margarine, melted

- Slice loaf of bread into 1-inch slices. Place sliced loaf on a large piece of aluminum foil.
- Combine bacon and cheese. Sprinkle bacon and cheese in between slices of bread.
- Drizzle margarine over loaf, letting some drip down in between slices. Wrap loaf tightly in foil. Bake at 350° for 20 minutes or until thoroughly heated. Serve hot.

Ranch French Bread

1 loaf unsliced French bread

1 stick margarine, softened

1 tablespoon ranch-style dressing mix

1 tablspoon mayonnaise, optiional

- Cut loaf in half horizontally. Blend margarine and dressing mix.
- Spread margarine mixture on bread.
- Wrap bread in foil. Bake at 350° for 15 minutes.

Cheese Bread

2 cups shredded sharp cheddar cheese

1 cup mayonnaise

1 package ranch-style dressing mix

10 (1-inch) slices French bread

- Combine cheese, mayonnaise and dressing mix.
- Spread on bread slices and heat in oven until brown.

Green Chili and Cheese Bread

1 loaf Italian bread,
   unsliced

1 stick margarine, melted

1 (4 ounce) can diced
   green chilies, drained

¾ cup grated monterey
   jack cheese

• Slice bread almost all the way through.

• Combine melted margarine, chilies and cheese. Spread between bread slices.

• Cover loaf with foil. Bake at 350° for 25 minutes.

Crunchy Bread Sticks

1 package hot dog buns

2 sticks margarine,
   melted

Garlic powder

Paprika

• Take each half bun and slice in half lengthwise.

• Using a pastry brush, butter all bread-sticks and sprinkle a light amount of garlic powder and a couple of sprinkles of paprika.

• Place on baking sheet and bake at 225° for about 45 minutes.

Creamy Butter Bread

2 sticks salted butter,
   softened

2 cups self-rising flour

1 (8 ounce) carton sour
   cream

• Combine all ingredients, mixing well.

• Drop by teaspoons into miniature muffin cups.

• Bake at 350° for 20 minutes or until lightly browned.

Cheese Sticks

1 loaf thick sliced bread

1 stick margarine, melted

1 cup grated cheddar cheese

1½ teaspoons paprika

- Remove crust from bread and slice into sticks.
- Brush or roll in melted margarine. Place on baking sheet.
- Sprinkle on parmesan and paprika.
- Bake 325° for 20 minutes.

Butter Rolls

2 cups biscuit mix

1 (8 ounce) carton sour cream

1 stick butter, melted

- Combine all ingredients and mix well. Spoon into greased muffin tins and fill only half full.
- Bake at 400° for 12 to 14 minutes or lightly brown.

Poppy Seed-Onion Loaf

2 tablespoons instant minced onions

1 tablespoon poppy seed

1 stick margarine, melted

2 cans refrigerated butter flake biscuits

- Combine the onions and poppy seed with the margarine.
- Separate each biscuit into 2 or 3 rolls. Dip each piece in the margarine mixture, turning to coat.
- Place rolls on edge of a loaf pan arranging rolls into two rows. Pour any remaining margarine mixture over top of loaf.
- Bake at 325° for 35 minutes. Serve warm.

Tea Cakes

1 cup self-rising flour

1 cup whipping cream
(not whipped)

2 tablespoons sugar

⅛ teaspoon ground
cinnamon

- Combine all ingredients and pour into greased mini-muffin cups.
- Bake at 375° for 10 to 15 minutes.

Cheese Drops

2 cups baking mix

⅔ cup milk

⅔ cup grated sharp
cheddar cheese

½ stick margarine, melted

- Spray baking sheet with non-stick spray.
- Mix together the baking mix, milk and cheese. Drop one heaping tablespoon of dough for each biscuit onto baking sheet.
- Bake at 400° for 10 minutes or until slightly browned.
- While warm, brush tops of biscuits with the melted margarine. Serve hot.

Bread Sticks

1½ cups shredded
monterey jack cheese

¼ cup poppy seeds

2 tablespoons dry onion
soup mix

2 (11 ounce) cans bread-
stick dough

- Spread cheese evenly in a 9 x 13-inch baking dish. Sprinkle poppy seeds and soup mix evenly over cheese.
- Separate breadstick dough into sticks. Stretch strips slightly until each strip is about 12 inches long.
- Place strips one at a time into the cheese mixture. Turn to coat all sides.
- Cut into 3 or 4-inch strips. Place on a cookie sheet and bake at 375° for about 12 minutes.

Spicy Cornbread Twists

⅓ stick margarine

⅓ cup cornmeal

¼ teaspoon red pepper

1 (11 ounce) can refrigerated soft breadsticks

- Place margarine in a pie plate and melt in oven. Remove from oven.
- On a piece of waxed paper, mix cornmeal and red pepper.
- Roll breadsticks in margarine and then in cornmeal mixture.
- Twist the breadsticks as label directs and place on a cookie sheet. Bake at 350° for 15 to 18 minutes.

Corn Sticks

2 cups biscuit mix

1 (8 ounce) can cream-style corn

Melted butter

2 tablespoons minced green onion

- Mix biscuit mix, green onions and cream-style corn.
- Place dough on a floured surface and cut into 3 x 1-inch strips. Roll in melted butter.
- Bake at 400° for 15 to 16 minutes.

Sausage Cornbread

1 (10½ ounce) can condensed golden corn soup

2 eggs

1 (8 ounce) package corn muffin mix

⅓ pound pork sausage, crumbled, cooked

- In a medium bowl combine soup, eggs and ¼ cup water or milk.
- Stir in corn muffin mix just until blended. Fold in sausage.
- Pour mixture into a greased 9-inch baking pan.
- Bake at 375° for 25 minutes or until golden brown. Cut into squares.

Mexican Cornbread

½ pound Mexican Velveeta cheese

¼ cup milk

2 (8 ounce) packages corn muffin mix

2 eggs, beaten

- In a saucepan, melt cheese with milk over low heat.
- In a bowl, combine corn muffin mix and eggs. Fold in cheese, mixing just until moistened.
- Pour into a greased 9 x 13-inch baking pan. Bake at 375° for about 25 minutes or until lightly brown.

Mayo Muffins

1¼ cups self-rising flour

3 tablespoons mayonnaise

1 cup whole milk

- Mix all ingredients together and spoon into greased muffin tins.
- Bake at 375° for 20 minutes or until lightly browned.

Filled Muffins

1 box blueberry muffin
mix with blueberries

1 egg

⅓ cup red raspberry jam

¼ cup sliced almonds

• Rinse blueberries and drain.

• In bowl, combine the muffin mix, egg and ½ cup water. Stir until moistened; break up any lumps in the mix.

• Place paper liners in 8 muffin cups. Fill cups half full of the batter.

• Combine the raspberry jam with the blueberries. Spoon mixture on top of batter. Cover with remaining batter. Sprinkle almonds over batter.

• Bake at 375 ° for about 18 minutes or until lightly brown.

Ginger-Raisin Muffins

1 box gingerbread mix
1¼ cups lukewarm water
1 egg
2 (1½ ounce) boxes
   seedless raisins

- Combine gingerbread mix, water and egg, mixing well. Stir in raisins.
- Pour into greased muffin tins filled half full.
- Bake at 350° for 20 minutes or when tested done with a toothpick.

Blueberry-Orange Muffins

1 package blueberry
   muffin mix with
   blueberries
2 egg whites
½ cup orange juice
Orange marmalade

- Wash blueberries with cold water and drain.
- Mix together the muffin mix, egg whites and orange juice; break up any lumps. Fold blueberries gently into batter.
- Pour into muffin tins (with paper liners) about ½ full.
- Bake at 375° for 18 to 20 minutes until toothpick inserted in center comes out clean.
- Top with orange marmalade spooned over top of hot muffins.

Honey-Cinnamon Butter

2 sticks butter
½ cup honey
1 teaspoon ground
   cinnamon
Breakfast breads

- Combine all ingredients in a small mixing bowl; beat until smooth.

   Serve with muffins, toast, French toast or pancakes. Refrigerate any leftovers.

... Orange Butter

⅔ cup butter (not margarine), room temperature

¼ cup frozen orange juice concentrate, thawed

1 pound box powdered sugar

1 teaspoon dried orange peel

- Blend all ingredients together in mixer. Store in refrigerator.

Great on biscuits and hot rolls.

Ambrosia Spread

1 (11 ounce) can mandarin orange sections, drained

1 (8 ounce) container soft cream cheese with pineapple, softened

¼ cup flaked coconut, toasted

¼ cup slivered almonds, chopped and toasted

- Chop orange sections; set aside.
- Combine cheese, coconut and almonds, blending well. Gently fold in orange sections. Refrigerate.
- Spread on date nut bread, banana bread, etc.

This can also be used as a dip for fruits.

Strawberry Butter

1 (10 ounce) package frozen strawberries, undrained

1 cup unsalted butter, softened

1 cup powdered sugar

Breakfast breads

- Place all ingredients in a food processor or mixer and process until well mixed.

Strawberry butter is delicious on biscuits, muffins or breads.

A Better Scramble

1 (10½ ounce) can
    cheddar cheese soup

8 eggs, lightly beaten

2 tablespoons margarine

Snipped chives

- Pour soup into a bowl and stir until smooth.

- Add the eggs and a little bit of pepper, mixing well.

- In a skillet, melt the margarine. Pour in egg mixture and scramble over low heat until set.

- Sprinkle with chives.

Breakfast Wake-Up

12 eggs

2 (7 ounce) cans chopped
    green chilies

2 (16 ounce) packages
    shredded cheddar
    cheese

Salsa, optional

- Drain green chilies, saving juice.

- In a separate bowl, beat eggs with the juice of the green chilies; add a little salt and pepper.

- Spray a 9 x 13-inch pan and spread ½ the cheese on bottom of pan and layer the chilies over this. Top with the remaining cheese.

- Pour eggs over the top and bake uncovered at 350° for 45 minutes.

Cheesy Scrambled Eggs

2 tablespoons margarine

8 eggs

1 (4 ounce) can chopped
    green chilies

½ cup grated cheddar
    cheese

- Melt margarine in a skillet.

- Beat remaining ingredients well, adding a little salt and black pepper; pour into skillet.

- Cook and stir until set.

Creamy Eggs On Toast

½ stick margarine

4 level tablespoons flour

2 cups milk

6 hardboiled eggs, sliced

- Melt margarine in skillet; stir in flour. Add milk.
- Cook over medium heat, stirring constantly until sauce is thickened.
- Gently fold in egg slices.

  Serve over six slices toasted bread.

Baked Eggs

4 eggs

4 tablespoons cream, divided

4 tablespoons cracker crumbs, divided

4 tablespoons shredded cheddar cheese, divided

- Grease 4 muffin cups and place 1 egg in each.
- Add 1 tablespoon each of cream, crumbs and cheese for each egg. Sprinkle with a little salt and pepper.
- Bake at 325° for 12 to 20 minutes until eggs are set.

  As many eggs as required may be prepared at the same time.

 # Mexican Eggs

4 corn tortillas

4 eggs

1 cup green chili salsa

4 ounces grated longhorn cheese

- Dip tortillas in heated oil in skillet and remove quickly. Set tortillas on baking pan to keep warm.
- In skillet, fry eggs in a little butter until the whites are set. Place a fried egg on each tortilla.
- Heat salsa and spoon over each egg. Sprinkle grated cheese on top.
- Place baking pan under broiler just until cheese melts. Serve hot.

Breakfast Tacos

4 eggs

4 flour tortillas

1 cup chopped, cooked ham

1 cup grated cheddar cheese

- Scramble eggs in skillet.
- Lay tortillas flat and spoon eggs over the 4 tortillas.
- Sprinkle with ham and cheese. Roll up to enclose filling.
- Place tacos in a microwave-safe dish. Microwave for about 30 seconds or until cheese is melted. Serve immediately.

Glazed Bacon

1 pound bacon

⅓ cup packed brown sugar

1 teaspoon flour

½ cup finely chopped pecans

- Arrange bacon slices close together, but not overlapping, on a wire rack over a drip pan.
- In a bowl, combine the brown sugar, flour and pecans; sprinkle evenly over the bacon.
- Bake at 350° for about 30 minutes. Drain on paper towels.

Pecan Waffles

2 cups self-rising flour

½ cup oil

½ cup milk

⅔ cup finely chopped pecans

- Preheat waffle iron.
- In a bowl, combine flour, oil and milk. Beat until well mixed.
- Stir in chopped pecans.
- Pour approximately ¾ cup batter into a hot waffle iron and bake until browned and crispy.

Waffle Flash

2 eggs

1 cup milk

½ teaspoon vanilla

8 slices stale bread

- Heat waffle iron according to directions.
- Beat eggs and slowly add milk and vanilla; beat well.
- Remove crust from bread and butter both sides of bread.
- When waffle iron is ready, dip bread in egg mixture and place in waffle iron. Close lid. Grill until lightly brown. Serve with syrup.

 # Light and Crispy Waffles

2 cups biscuit mix

1 egg

½ cup oil

1⅓ cups club soda

- Preheat waffle iron.
- Combine all ingredients in a mixing bowl and stir by hand.
- Pour just enough batter to cover waffle iron.

To have waffles for a "company weekend", make up all waffles in advance. Freeze separately on baking sheet and place in large baggies. To heat, warm at 350° for about 10 minutes.

Praline Toast

1 stick butter, softened

1 cup packed brown sugar

⅓ cup finely chopped pecans

Bread slices

- Combine butter, sugar and pecans.
- Spread on bread slices.
- Toast in broiler until brown and bubbly.

French Toast

4 eggs

1 cup whipping cream

2 thick slices bread, cut into 3 strips each

Powdered sugar

- Place a little oil in a skillet. Beat together eggs, cream and a pinch of salt.
- Dip bread into batter allowing batter to soak in.
- Fry bread in skillet until brown; turn and fry on the other side.
- Transfer to baking sheet. Bake at 325° for about 4 minutes or until puffed. Sprinkle with powdered sugar.

Cinnamon Toast

⅔ cup sugar

1 heaping tablespoon cinnamon

Bread

Margarine, softened

- Make cinnamon sugar by mixing sugar with cinnamon. Place in large salt or sugar shaker.
- Place bread on baking sheet and toast top by broiling in oven until light brown.
- Remove baking sheet and spread soft margarine on the toasted side. Sprinkle with cinnamon mixture.
- Return to oven and broil until tops are bubbly. Watch closely because sugar burns easily.

Sunrise Tacos

4 eggs, scrambled, divided

½ cup grated cheddar cheese, divided

½ cup salsa, divided

2 flour tortillas, divided

- For each taco, spread ½ scrambled eggs, ¼ cup cheese and ¼ cup salsa on the tortilla and roll up.

Bacon and Egg Burrito

2 slices bacon, cooked, chopped

2 eggs, scrambled

¼ cup shredded cheddar cheese

1 flour tortilla

- Sprinkle bacon, eggs and cheese in the middle of a tortilla. (Also add taco sauce or salsa, if you like.)
- Fold tortilla sides over and place seam-side down on a dinner plate.
- Microwave for 30 seconds or just until heated thoroughly.

Hot Cheese Melt

1 (12 ounce) can whole jalapeno peppers, drained

1 (15 ounce) can Mexican stewed tomatoes

1 (2 pound) box Velveeta cheese

4 slices bacon, cooked crisp, crumbled

- Cut peppers in half and remove the seeds. Chop the peppers and place them in the bottom of a 9-inch pie plate.
- Spoon the stewed tomatoes over the peppers. Cut the Velveeta cheese into chunks and place them over the tomatoes.
- Bake at 300° for about 15 minutes or until cheese melts. Let cheese set until room temperature. When ready to serve, sprinkle bacon over top.

Serve with tortilla chips.

Blueberry Coffee Cake

1 (16 ounce) package blueberry muffin mix with blueberries

⅓ cup sour cream

1 egg

⅔ cup powdered sugar

- Stir together the muffin mix, sour cream, egg and ½ cup water.
- Rinse blueberries and gently fold into batter. Pour into a non-stick vegetable-sprayed 7 x 11-inch baking dish.
- Bake at 400° for about 25 minutes.
- Mix powdered sugar and 1 tablespoon water and drizzle over coffee cake.

Sticky Pecan Rolls

1 (12 count) package brown and serve dinner rolls

4 tablespoons margarine

⅔ cup packed brown sugar

24 pecan halves

- Place 1 roll in each of 12 well greased muffin cups.
- Cut an "x" in top of each roll.
- Combine the sugar and margarine together and melt, mixing well. Spoon mixture over rolls.
- Tuck two pecan halves in the "x" on each roll. Bake at 350° for 50 minutes or until slightly brown.

Corned Beef Hash Bake

2 (15 ounce) cans corned beef hash, slightly warmed

Margarine

6-8 eggs

⅓ cup half-and-half

- Spread corned beef hash in a greased 9 x 13-inch pan. Pat down with the back of a spoon and make 6 to 8 deep hollows in the hash large enough to accommodate an egg.
- Fill hollows with tiny dab of margarine.
- Pour eggs into each hollow and cover the eggs with a tablespoon or so of the cream.
- Bake uncovered at 350° for 15 to 20 minutes or until eggs are set as desired. Divide into squares to serve.

Dog Gones

1 (10 count) can biscuits

1 cup shortening

1 cup sugar

1 teaspoon cinnamon

- Remove biscuits from can and put on piece of wax paper.
- Cut each biscuit into 4 pieces.
- Heat shortening in skillet and drop biscuits in hot oil a few pieces at a time until golden brown. Remove and place on paper towels to drain.
- Dip in the mixture of sugar and cinnamon. Serve warm.

Cheese Enchiladas

1 dozen corn tortillas

1 (8 ounce) package shredded cheddar cheese, divided

½ cup chopped onion, divided

2 (10 ounce) cans enchilada sauce

- Wrap tortillas in a slightly damp paper towel. Put between two salad plates and microwave on high for 45 seconds.
- Place ⅓ cup cheese and a sprinkle of onions on each tortilla; roll up. Place seam-side down in a 9 x 13-baking dish. Repeat with remaining tortillas.
- Pour enchilada sauce over enchiladas. Sprinkle with remaining cheese and onions.
- Cover and microwave on medium high for 5 to 6 minutes.

Pineapple-Brunch Slices

1 cup cooked ground ham

1 teaspoon mustard

2 tablespoons mayonnaise

5 slices pineapple, drained

- Combine ham, mustard and mayonnaise, mixing well.
- Spread on pineapple slices.
- Bake in an ungreased baking pan at 375° for about 15 minutes or until heated thoroughly.

Chili Rellenos

2 (7 ounce) cans chopped green chilies, drained

1 (16 ounce) package shredded monterey jack cheese, divided

4 eggs, beaten

½ cup milk

• In a 7 x 11-inch baking dish, layer half the green chilies, half the cheese, then the remaining green chilies and cheese.

• Combine the eggs, milk and a little salt and pepper in a small bowl; mix well.

• Pour over the layers of cheese and green chilies.

• Bake uncovered at 350° for 30 minutes or until light brown and set. Cool for 5 minutes before cutting into squares.

Spiced Pears

1 (15 ounce) can pear halves

⅓ cup packed brown sugar

¾ teaspoon ground nutmeg

¾ teaspoon ground cinnamon

• Drain pears, reserving syrup. Set pears aside.

• Place syrup, brown sugar, nutmeg and cinnamon in a saucepan and bring to a boil. Reduce heat and simmer uncovered for 5 to 8 minutes stirring frequently.

• Add pears and simmer 5 minutes longer or until heated thoroughly.

Melon Boats

2 cantaloupes, chilled

4 cups red and green seedless grapes, chilled

1 cup mayonnaise

⅓ cup frozen concentrated orange juice, undiluted

- Prepare each melon in 6 lengthwise sections, removing seeds and peel. Place on separate salad plates on lettuce leaves.

- Heap grapes over and around the cantaloupe slices.

- Combine mayonnaise and juice concentrate; mixing well. Ladle over fruit.

 # Apricot Bake

4 (15 ounce) cans apricot halves, drained

1 (16 ounce) box light brown sugar, divided

2 cups Ritz cracker crumbs, divided

1 stick margarine, sliced

- Grease a 9 x 13-inch baking dish and line bottom with 2 cans of drained apricots.

- Sprinkle half the brown sugar and half the cracker crumbs over apricots. Dot with half the margarine.

- Repeat layers.

- Bake at 300° for 1 hour.

Mini-Apricot Bake

2 (15 ounce) cans apricot halves, drained

¾ cup packed brown sugar

1 cup Ritz cracker crumbs

1 stick margarine, melted

- Butter a 2-quart casserole and layer apricots, sugar and cracker crumbs until all ingredients are used.

- Melt margarine and pour over casserole.

- Bake at 325° for 35 minutes or until cracker crumbs are slightly brown. Serve hot or room temperature.

Treasure-Filled Apples

6 tart apples

½ cup sugar

¼ cup cinnamon candies

¼ teaspoon ground
cinnamon

- Cut tops off apples and set tops aside. Core apples to within ½-inch of bottom.
- Place in a greased 8-inch baking dish.
- In a bowl, combine sugar, candies and cinnamon; spoon 2 tablespoons into each apple. Replace the tops.
- Spoon any remaining sugar mixture over the apples.
- Bake, uncovered, at 350° for 30 to 35 minutes or until apples are tender, basting occasionally.

Peachy Fruit Dip

1 (15 ounce) can sliced
peaches, drained

½ cup marshmallow cream

1 (3 ounce) package
cream cheese, cubed

⅛ teaspoon ground nutmeg

- In a blender or food processor, combine all ingredients. Serve with assorted fresh fruit.

Gingered Cream Spread

1 (8 ounce) package
cream cheese, softened

1 stick unsalted
margarine, softened

2 tablespoons milk

3 tablespoons finely
chopped crystallized
ginger

- Combine all ingredients in mixer. Beat until creamy.
- Spread on your favorite fruit or nut breads.

Peach Bake

2 (15 ounce) cans peach halves, drained

1 cup packed brown sugar

1 cup Ritz cracker crumbs

1 stick margarine, melted

- Butter a 2-quart casserole and layer peaches, sugar and cracker crumbs until all ingredients are used.
- Pour melted margarine over casserole. Bake at 325° for 35 minutes or until cracker crumbs are slightly brown. Serve hot or at room temperature.

Bacon-Cheese Stromboli

1 (10 ounce) tube refrigerated pizza dough

¾ cup shredded cheddar cheese

¾ cup shredded mozzarella cheese

6 bacon strips, cooked and crumbled

- On an ungreased baking sheet, roll the dough into a 12-inch circle.
- On one half of the dough, sprinkle cheeses and bacon to within ½-inch of edge.
- Fold dough over filling; pinch edges to seal.
- Bake at 400° for about 10 minutes or until golden. Serve with salsa.

Cut in pie slices.

Honey Butter

1 stick butter, softened

¼ cup honey

2 tablespoons lemon juice

1 tablespoon brown sugar

- With a hand mixer, cream the butter until fluffy and add honey in a fine stream.
- Add lemon juice and brown sugar, stirring until all ingredients are evenly blended.
- Chill until ready to serve.

Wonderful with hot biscuits!

Pineapple Coffee Cake

1 box butter cake mix

½ cup oil

4 eggs, slightly beaten

1 (20 ounce) can
   pineapple pie filling

• In mixer, combine cake mix, oil and eggs. Beat until well mixed. Pour batter into a greased, floured 9 x 13-inch baking pan.

• Bake at 350° for 45 to 50 minutes. Test with toothpick to make sure cake is done.

• With a knife, punch holes in cake about 2 inches apart. Spread pineapple pie filling over cake while cake is still hot.

SOUPS, SALADS & SANDWICHES

Spicy Tomato Soup

2 (10 ounce) cans tomato
soup

1 (16 ounce) can Mexican
stewed tomatoes

Sour cream

½ pound bacon, fried,
drained, crumbled

- In a saucepan, combine soup and
stewed tomatoes and heat.

- To serve, place a dollop of sour cream
on each bowl of soup and sprinkle
crumbled bacon over sour cream.

Navy Bean Soup

3 cans navy beans,
undrained

1 cup chopped ham

1 large onion, chopped

½ teaspoon garlic powder

- In large saucepan, combine beans, ham,
onion and garlic powder.

- Add 1 cup water and bring to a boil.
Simmer until onion is tender crisp.

Serve hot with cornbread.

Cream of Turkey Soup

1 (10½ ounce) can cream
of celery soup

1 (10½ ounce) can cream
of chicken soup

2 (10½ ounce) cans milk
or cream

1 cup finely diced leftover
turkey

- Combine all ingredients in a large
saucepan.

- Serve hot.

Swiss Vegetable Soup

1 (1.5 ounce) package dry vegetable soup mix

3 cups water

1 cup half-and-half

1½ cups shredded Swiss cheese

• Combine soup mix and water in a saucepan and boil.

• Lower heat and simmer about 10 minutes.

• Add half-and-half and cheese; serve hot.

Chili Soup Warmer

1 (10½ ounce) can tomato bisque soup

1 (10 ounce) can chili

1 (10½ ounce) can fiesta chili beef soup

1 (15 ounce) can chicken broth

• In a saucepan combine all soups and broth. Depending on how thick you want the soup you can add 1 can of water.

• Heat and serve hot with crackers.

Supper Gumbo

1 (10½ ounce) can condensed pepper pot soup

1 (10½ ounce) can condensed chicken gumbo soup

1 (6 ounce) can white flaked crabmeat

1 (6 ounce) can tiny shrimp

• Combine all ingredients and include 1½ soup cans water. (You might want to add a ¼ teaspoon salt.)

• Cover and simmer for 15 minutes.

Bacon-Potato Soup

2 (14 ounce) cans
  chicken broth
  seasoned with garlic

2 potatoes, peeled, cubed

1 onion finely chopped

6 strips bacon, cooked,
  crumbled

• In a large saucepan, combine broth,
  potatoes and onion. Bring to a boil;
  reduce heat to medium high and boil
  about 10 minutes or until potatoes are
  tender.

• Season with pepper.

• Ladle into bowls and sprinkle with
  crumbled bacon.

Cheesy Chicken Soup

1 (10½ ounce) can fiesta
  nacho cheese soup

1 (10½ ounce) can cream
  of chicken soup

1 soup can milk

1 chicken bouillon cube
  or 1 teaspoon bouillon
  granules

• Mix all ingredients in saucepan and stir
  until smooth. Serve hot.

Tomato-French Onion Soup

1 (10½ ounce) can tomato
  bisque soup

2 (10½ ounce) cans
  French onion soup

Grated parmesan cheese

Croutons

• In saucepan combine soups and 2 soup
  cans of water. Heat thoroughly.

• Serve in bowls topped with croutons and
  a sprinkle of cheese.

Speedy Taco Soup

1 (12 ounce) can chicken, undrained

1 (14 ounce) can chicken broth

1 (16 ounce) jar mild thick and chunky salsa

1 (15 ounce) can ranch-style beans

• In large saucepan combine chicken, broth, salsa and beans. (A 15-ounce can of whole kernel corn could also be added.)

• Bring to a boil, reduce heat and simmer 15 minutes.

Spiked Crab Soup

1 package dry onion soup mix

1 (6 ounce) can crabmeat, including liquid, flaked

1 (8 ounce) carton whipping cream

½ cup white wine

• Dissolve soup mix in 2 cups water.

• Add crabmeat, crab liquid and whipping cream. Season with salt and pepper.

• Heat, but not to the boiling stage, and simmer for 20 minutes.

• Stir in wine; heat. Serve warm.

Crunchy Peanut Soup

2 (10½ ounce) cans cream of chicken soup

2 soup cans milk

1¼ cups crunchy peanut butter

½ teaspoon celery salt

• In a saucepan on medium heat, blend together the soup and milk.

• Stir in peanut butter and celery salt and heat until well blended.

New England Clam Chowder

1 (10½ ounce) can New England clam chowder

1 (10½ ounce) can cream of celery soup

1 (10½ ounce) can cream of potato soup

½ cup whole milk

• Combine all ingredients in saucepan.
• Heat and stir.

Asparagus Chiller

1 (10½ ounce) can condensed cream of asparagus soup

⅔ cup sour cream

½ cup finely chopped cucumber

2 tablespoons chopped red onion

• Blend soup, sour cream and 1 soup can water.
• Add cucumber and onion.
• Chill at least 4 hours and serve in chilled bowls.

Yellow Squash Soup

2 pounds fresh, yellow squash, thinly sliced

1 onion, chopped

1 (14 ounce) can chicken broth

1 (8 ounce) carton sour cream

• In a saucepan simmer squash and onions in the broth until very tender.
• Chill.
• Just before serving, add sour cream and a little salt and pepper.
• Serve chilled.

Red and Green Salad

2 (10 ounce) packages
fresh spinach

1 quart fresh
strawberries, halved

½ cup slivered almonds,
toasted

Poppy seed dressing

• Tear spinach into smaller pieces and add the strawberries and almonds.

• Refrigerate until ready to serve.

• Toss with poppy seed dressing.

Sesame-Romaine Salad

1 large head romaine
lettuce

2 tablespoons sesame
seeds, toasted

6 strips bacon, fried,
crumbled

½ cup grated Swiss
cheese

• Wash and dry lettuce. Tear into bite-size pieces.

• When ready to serve, sprinkle sesame seeds, bacon and cheese over lettuce and toss with a creamy Italian dressing.

Salad Surprise

1 (10 ounce) bag fresh
spinach, washed,
stemmed

1 pint fresh strawberries,
stemmed, halved

1 large banana, sliced

⅔ cup chopped walnuts

• Place all salad ingredients in a large bowl.

• When ready to serve, toss with poppy seed dressing.

Strawberry-Spinach Salad

1 (10 ounce) package
  fresh spinach, washed,
  stemmed

1 small jicama, peeled,
  julienned

1 pint fresh strawberries,
  stemmed, halved

2½ cups fresh bean
  sprouts

- Combine spinach, jicama, strawberries and bean sprouts in a large bowl.
- Toss with poppy seed dressing just before serving.

Mandarin Salad

1 head red-tipped lettuce

2 (11 ounce) cans
  mandarin oranges,
  drained

2 avocadoes, peeled,
  diced

1 small red onion, sliced

- Combine all ingredients.
- When ready to serve, toss with a poppy seed dressing.

Crunchy Salad

¼ cup sesame seeds

½ cup sunflower seeds

½ cup almonds

1 head red leaf lettuce

- Toast the sesame seeds, sunflower seeds and almonds in a 300° oven for about 15 minutes or until lightly browned.
- Tear lettuce into bite-size pieces and add seed mixture.
- Toss with creamy Italian dressing.

Oriental Spinach Salad

1 (10 ounce) package
fresh spinach

1 (16 ounce) can bean
sprouts, drained

8 slices bacon, cooked
crisp

1 (11 ounce) can water
chestnuts, chopped

• Combine spinach and bean sprouts.
• When ready to serve add the crumbled
bacon and toss with a vinaigrette salad
dressing made from 3 parts olive oil and
1 part red wine vinegar.

Swiss Salad

1 large head romaine
lettuce

1 bunch fresh green
onions with tops,
chopped

1 (8 ounce) package of
shredded Swiss cheese

½ cup toasted sunflower
seeds

• Tear the lettuce into bite-size pieces.
• Add onions, cheese, sunflower seeds
and toss.
• Serve with a vinaigrette dressing.

Vinaigrette for Swiss Salad

⅔ cup oil

⅓ cup red wine vinegar

1 tablespoon seasoned
salt

• Mix all ingredients and refrigerate.

Spinach-Bacon Salad

1 (10 ounce) package
   fresh spinach

3 hardcooked eggs,
   chopped

8 mushroom caps, sliced

1 (11 ounce) can water
   chestnuts, chopped

- Mix all ingredients together and serve with hot bacon dressing.

Hot Bacon Dressing for Spinach Bacon Salad

½ pound bacon, chopped

1 cup sugar

1⅓ cups white vinegar

5 teaspoons cornstarch

- To make dressing fry the bacon until crisp. Remove bacon to drain and leave bacon drippings in skillet.
- Add the sugar and vinegar to the skillet, stirring well. Add one cup water and bring to a boil.
- Mix cornstarch with ⅔ cup water and stir until dissolved. Pour cornstarch mixture into the skillet with the dressing. Return to a boil; simmer for 5 minutes.
- Remove from heat and toss salad with warm bacon dressing.

Orange-Almond Salad

1 head green leaf lettuce

4 slices bacon, fried,
   crumbled

⅓ cup slivered almonds,
   toasted

1 (11 ounce) can
   mandarin oranges,
   drained, chilled

- Combine all ingredients in a salad bowl.
- When ready to serve toss with a vinaigrette dressing.

Spinach-Orange Salad

1 (10 ounce) package spinach, stems removed

2 (10 ounce) cans mandarin oranges, drained

⅓ small jicama, peeled, julienned

⅓ cup slivered almonds, toasted

- In a large bowl, combine spinach, oranges, jicama and almonds.
- Toss with vinaigrette dressing.

Spinach Salad Oriental

1 (10 ounce) package fresh spinach

2 hardboiled eggs, sliced

1 (14 ounce) can bean sprouts, drained

1 (8 ounce) can water chestnuts, chopped

- Combine all four ingredients. Top with dressing.

Dressing for Spinach Salad Oriental

¾ cup olive oil

⅓ cup sugar

¼ cup ketchup

3 tablespoons red wine vinegar

- Combine all ingredients mixing well.
- You do not need all of this dressing for this salad. Refrigerate remaining salad dressing.

Red Hot Onions

3 large purple onions

2 tablespoons Tabasco

3 tablespoons olive oil

3 tablespoons red wine
vinegar

- Slice onions thinly. Pour a cup of boiling water over onions and let stand 1 minute; drain.
- Mix Tabasco, oil and vinegar and pour over onion rings in a shallow bowl with a lid.
- Refrigerate and let stand at least 3 hours.
- Drain to serve.

  Good with barbecue.

Special Spinach Salad

1 (10 ounce) package
fresh spinach

1 (16 ounce) can bean
sprouts, drained

8 slices bacon, cooked
crisp

1 (11 ounce) can water
chestnuts, chopped

- Combine spinach and bean sprouts.
- When ready to serve add the crumbled bacon and toss with a vinaigrette salad dressing made from 3 parts olive oil and 1 part red wine vinegar.

Red Cabbage Slaw

1 large head red cabbage

2 onions, chopped

½ cup cole slaw dressing

½ cup French dressing

- Slice cabbage and combine with onions.
- Combine dressing and toss with cabbage and onions.
- Refrigerate.

Hawaiian Slaw

2 envelopes unflavored
  gelatin
3 cups orange juice,
  divided
1 (8 ounce) can crushed
  pineapple, undrained
2 cups finely shredded
  cabbage

- Sprinkle gelatin over 1 cup orange juice in a saucepan. Heat until gelatin is dissolved.
- Stir in remaining orange juice and chill until slightly thickened.
- Fold in pineapple and cabbage; blend well.
- Pour into a 8 x 8-inch dish and refrigerate until set.

Deviled Eggs

6 hardcooked eggs
2 tablespoons sweet
  pickle relish
3 tablespoons
  mayonnaise
½ teaspoon mustard

- Peel eggs and cut in half lengthwise. Take yolks out and mash with fork.
- Add relish, mayonnaise and mustard to yolks. Place this yolk mixture back into the egg white halves.
- Sprinkle with paprika, if you like.

Broccoli and Pepperoni Salad

Editor's Choice

1 pound bunch broccoli
½ pound fresh
  mushrooms, sliced
6 ounces Swiss cheese,
  diced
1 (3 ounce) package
  sliced pepperoni,
  chopped

- Cut off broccoli flowerets; combine broccoli, mushrooms, cheese, pepperoni.
- Toss with an Italian dressing.
- Refrigerate at least 8 hours before serving.

Bean and Onion Salad

1 (15 ounce) can whole green beans

1 (15 ounce) can yellow wax beans

½ cup finely chopped red onion

¼ cup slivered almonds

• Combine all ingredients and mix with dressing recipe below.

Dressing for Bean and Onion Salad

¼ cup oil

1 tablespoon white vinegar

1 teaspoon sugar

2 teaspoons dijon mustard

• Combine all ingredients adding ½ teaspoon salt and ½ teaspoon black pepper.

• Pour over bean and onion salad.

• Refrigerate at least 1 hour before serving.

Cashew-Pea Salad

1 (16 ounce) package frozen green peas, thawed

¼ cup diced celery

1 bunch fresh green onions with tops, chopped

1 cup chopped cashews

• Combine the peas, celery, onions and cashews.

• Toss with ½ cup mayonnaise seasoned with ½ teaspoon seasoned salt and black pepper.

Marinated Brussel Sprout Medley

2 (10 ounce) boxes frozen brussel sprouts

1 cup Italian dressing

1 cup chopped green bell pepper

½ cup chopped onion

- Pierce box of brussel sprouts and cook in microwave for 7 minutes.
- Mix together the Italian dressing, bell pepper and onion.
- Pour over brussel sprouts and marinate for at least 24 hours.
- Drain to serve.

Marinated Brussel Sprouts

2 (10 ounce) packages brussel sprouts, cooked

½ cup salad oil

¼ cup white wine vinegar

¼ cup sugar

- Mix all ingredients and marinate over-night.
- Serve cold.

Fusilli Pasta Salad

1 (16 ounce) package fusilli or corkscrew pasta

1 (16 ounce) package frozen broccoli-cauliflower combination

1 (8 ounce) package mozzarella cheese, cut in small chunks

1 (8 ounce) bottle Catalina salad dressing

- Cook pasta according to package directions. Drain and cool.
- Cook vegetables in microwave according to package directions. Drain and cool.
- In a large bowl, combine pasta, vegetables and cheese chunks.
- Toss with catalina dressing. Refrigerate several hours before serving.

Sunshine Salad

2 (15 ounce) cans mexi-corn, drained

2 (15 ounce) cans peas, drained

1 (15 ounce) can kidney beans, rinsed, drained

1 (8 ounce) bottle Italian dressing

• In a large bowl, combine corn, peas and beans.

• Pour salad dressing over vegetables and chill several hours.

Sour Cream Potato Salad

12 medium red potatoes, unpeeled

1¼ cups mayonnaise

1 cup sour cream

1 cup fresh green onions and tops, chopped

• Boil red potatoes until done, about 20 minutes. Slice potatoes.

• Combine mayonnaise, sour cream and 1 teaspoon salt.

• When potatoes are cool toss with sour cream mixture (1 tablespoon horseradish can be added if you like horseradish). Add green onion.

Carrot Salad

3 cups finely grated carrots

1 (8 ounce) can crushed pineapple, drained

4 tablespoons coconut

1 tablespoon sugar

• Combine all ingredients. Toss with ⅓ cup mayonnaise, mixing well.

• Refrigerate.

Cucumber Salad

1 (3 ounce) package lime
  gelatin

2 medium cucumbers

1 tablespoon minced
  onion

½ cup mayonnaise, ½ cup
  sour cream

• Dissolve gelatin in ¾ cup boiling water; mixing well. Bring to room temperature.

• Slice cucumber in half and remove seeds. Grate cucumber and add to cooled gelatin along with the onion, mayonnaise and sour cream.

• Pour into a square dish.

• Refrigerate until set.

Chilled Cucumbers

2 cucumbers, peeled,
  sliced

½ onion, sliced

¼ cup vinegar

⅓ cup sugar

• Place cucumbers and onion in a bowl with a lid.

• Combine vinegar and sugar. Pour over cucumbers and onions.

• Cover and chill for 2 to 3 hours before serving.

Marinated Cucumbers

⅓ cup vinegar

2 tablespoons sugar

1 teaspoon dried dill weed

3 cucumbers, peeled,
  sliced

• Combine the vinegar, sugar, 1 teaspoon salt, dill weed and about ¼ teaspoon black pepper. Pour over the cucumbers.

• Refrigerate one hour before serving.

You could add onion to the cucumbers if you like.

Stuffed Cucumber Slices

3 cucumbers, peeled

2 (3 ounce) packages
cream cheese, softened

¼ cup stuffed green
olives, chopped

½ teaspoon seasoned salt

- Halve cucumbers lengthwise and scoop out seeds.
- Beat cream cheese with mixer, until creamy. Add olives and seasoned salt.
- Fill hollows with cream cheese mixture, press halves together and wrap tightly in plastic wrap; chill.
- Cut crosswise in ⅓-inch slices to serve.

Nutty Grape-Pineapple Salad

1 pound seedless green
grapes, halved

½ cup chopped pecans

⅔ cup shredded cheddar
cheese

1 (15 ounce) can
pineapple tidbits,
drained

- Combine grapes, pecans, cheese and pineapple. Fold in about ½ cup of mayonnaise.
- Serve on lettuce leaves.

Marinated Onion Rings

2 pounds white onion,
thinly sliced

1 cup sugar

2 cups white vinegar

½ teaspoon salt

- Cover onions with boiling water and let stand for five minutes. Drain.
- Combine sugar, vinegar and salt; pour over onion.
- Refrigerate.

Broccoli Salad

5 cups cut broccoli, florets (no stems)

1 sweet red bell pepper, julienned

1 cup chopped celery

8-12 ounces monterey jack cheese, cubed

- Combine all ingredients and mix well.
- Toss with Italian or your favorite dressing. Refrigerate.

Green Beans With Tomatoes

2 pounds frozen, cut green beans

4 tomatoes, chopped, drained

1 bunch green onions, chopped

1 cup Italian salad dressing

- Place beans in a saucepan and cover with water; bring to a boil. Cook uncovered for 8 to 10 minutes or until tender crisp; drain, chill.
- Add the tomatoes, green onions and salad dressing; toss to coat.

Green and White Salad

1 (16 ounce) package frozen green peas, thawed, uncooked

1 head cauliflower, cut into bite-size pieces

1 (8 ounce) carton sour cream

1 envelope dry ranch-style salad dressing

- In a large bowl, combine the peas and cauliflower.
- Combine sour cream and salad dressing. Toss with the vegetables.
- Refrigerate.

Salad is even better if you add half of a purple onion, chopped.

Color-Coded Salad

1 (16 ounce) package tri-colored macaroni, cooked, drained

1 red bell pepper, julienned

1 cup chopped zucchini

1 cup broccoli flowerets

- Combine all ingredients.
- Toss with about 1 cup of Caesar salad dressing.
- Refrigerate.

Snicker Salad

6 large delicious apples, unpeeled, chopped

6 (2 ounce) Snicker candy bars, chopped

½ cup chopped pecans, optional

1 (12 ounce) carton whipped topping

- In a large bowl, combine apples, candy bars and pecans; mixing well.
- Fold in whipped topping.
- Refrigerate.

It is better served the same day.

Cool Apricot Salad

1 (15 ounce) can crushed pineapple, undrained

1 (6 ounce) package apricot gelatin

2 cups buttermilk

1 (12 ounce) carton whipped topping

- Bring pineapple and juice to a boil. Add the gelatin and stir until well dissolved. Cool completely.
- When mixture begins to thicken, add buttermilk and fold in the whipped topping.
- Pour into a 9 x 13-inch glass dish and refrigerate.
- Cut into squares and serve.

Pineapple-Ginger Salad

1 (20 ounce) can pineapple tidbits, reserve juice

1 (6 ounce) package lime gelatin

1 cup ginger ale

¼ teaspoon ground ginger

- Heat ½ cup pineapple juice (if not enough juice, add water to make ½ cup). Pour boiling juice over gelatin, mixing well.
- Add ginger ale and ginger. Chill until slightly thickened.
- Fold in pineapple tidbits and spoon into a 7 x 11-inch shallow dish.
- Refrigerate.

Cold Cola Salad

1 (6 ounce) package cherry gelatin

1 (10 ounce) bottle maraschino cherries, drained

1 cup cola soda

1 cup chopped pecans

- Add gelatin in ¾ cup boiling water.
- Chop cherries into four slices each. Add cherries, cola and pecans.
- Pour into an 8-cup gelatin mold.
- Refrigerate until firm.

Salad Berry Dream

1 (6 ounce) package
blackberry gelatin

1 (15 ounce) can crushed
pineapple, juice
reserved

1 (15 ounce) can
blueberries, drained

Whipped topping, optional

- Add enough water to the pineapple juice to make 2 cups. Put in saucepan and bring to a boil. Pour hot liquid over the gelatin and mix until dissolved.
- Chill until this mixture begins to thicken. Stir in pineapple and blueberries.
- Pour into a 7 x 11-inch dish. Refrigerate.

Topping for Salad Berry Dream

1 (8 ounce) package
cream cheese, softened

1 (8 ounce) carton sour
cream

½ cup sugar

½ cup chopped pecans

- In mixer beat together the cream cheese, sour cream and sugar. Beat until smooth and fluffy.
- Spoon over congealed salad.
- Sprinkle pecans over congealed salad.
- Refrigerate.

Cherry Crush

1 (6 ounce) box cherry
gelatin

1 (8 ounce) package
cream cheese, softened

1 (20 ounce) can cherry
pie filling

1 (15 ounce) can crushed
pineapple, undrained

- Dissolve gelatin with ¾ cup of boiling water.
- With electric mixer beat in the cream cheese, beating very slowly at first. Fold in pie filling and crushed pineapple.
- Pour into a 9 x 13-inch casserole dish. Refrigerate.

Mincemeat-Cherry Salad

1 (6 ounce) package
  cherry gelatin

1 cup prepared
  mincemeat

1 rib celery, chopped

⅔ cup chopped pecans

- Dissolve the gelatin in ¾ cup of boiling water.
- Fold in mincemeat, celery and chopped pecans.
- Pour into an 8-inch mold and refrigerate.

Holiday Salad

1 (15 ounce) can whole
  cranberry sauce

1 (15 ounce) can crushed
  pineapple, drained

2 (15 ounce) cans fruit
  cocktail, drained

1 (8 ounce) carton sour
  cream

- Combine all ingredients and freeze in the cranberry can and another can of equal size.
- When ready to serve, cut upper end of the can and push salad out. Slice and serve on a lettuce leaf.

Watergate Salad

1 (20 ounce) can crushed
  pineapple, undrained

2 (3.4 ounce) packages
  pistachio instant
  pudding mix

¾ cup chopped pecans

1 (12 ounce) carton
  whipped topping

- Mix pineapple with instant pudding mix until slightly thickened; add pecans.
- When mixed well, fold in whipped topping.
- Pour into a pretty crystal bowl and refrigerate.

One cup of miniature marshmallows may be added.

Cashew Cocktail Salad

1 (6 ounce) package
  lemon gelatin
1 quart vanilla ice cream
1 (15 ounce) can fruit
  cocktail, drained
1¼ cups chopped cashew
  nuts

• Dissolve gelatin in 1-cup boiling water and stir in ice cream. Blend until ice cream is melted.

• Add fruit cocktail and cashew nuts; mix well.

• Pour into an 8 x 11-inch glass dish. Refrigerate overnight.

Cranberry Salad

1 (6 ounce) package
  cherry gelatin
1 can whole cranberry
  sauce
1 pint sour cream
¾ cup chopped pecans

• Dissolve gelatin in 1¼ cups of boiling water. When well mixed, add cranberry sauce.

• Mix well and refrigerate until it begins to congeal, then add sour cream and pecans, mixing well.

• Pour into a 7 x 11-inch casserole. Refrigerate for several hours before serving.

Cherry-Cranberry Salad

1 (6 ounce) package
  cherry gelatin
1 cup boiling water
1 (20 ounce) can cherry
  pie filling
1 (16 ounce) can whole
  cranberry sauce

• In mixing bowl, combine cherry gelatin and boiling water; mixing until gelatin is dissolved.

• Mix pie filling and cranberry sauce into gelatin.

• Pour into a 7 x 11-inch dish and refrigerate.

Creamy Cranberry Salad

1 (6 ounce) package cherry gelatin

1 (8 ounce) carton sour cream

1 (16 ounce) can whole cranberry sauce

1 (8 ounce) can crushed pineapple, undrained

- Dissolve gelatin in 1-cup boiling water, mixing well.
- Stir in remaining ingredients and pour into a 7 x 11-inch glass dish.
- Refrigerate until firm.

Frozen Cranberry-Pineapple Salad

1 (20 ounce) can crushed pineapple, drained

2 (16 ounce) cans whole cranberry sauce

1 (8 ounce) carton sour cream

¾ cup chopped pecans

- In large bowl, combine all ingredients.
- Pour into a greased loaf pan.
- Freeze several hours before serving.

Luscious Strawberry Salad

1 (6 ounce) package strawberry gelatin

2 (10 ounce) boxes frozen strawberries, thawed

3 bananas, sliced

1 (8 ounce) carton sour cream

- Dissolve gelatin in 1 cup boiling water, mixing well. Add strawberries and bananas.
- Pour half mixture in a 9 x 13-inch dish, leaving all the bananas in the bottom layer. Chill until firm.
- Spread sour cream over firm gelatin.
- Add remaining gelatin over sour cream. Refrigerate until firm.

Tropical Mango Salad

2 (15 ounce) cans
  mangoes, reserve juice
1 (6 ounce) package
  orange gelatin
1 (8 ounce) package
  cream cheese, softened
½ (8 ounce) carton
  whipped topping

- Place all mango slices on a dinner plate and with a knife and fork, cut slices into bite-size pieces. Place 1½ cups of the mango juice (if not that much juice, add water to make 1½ cups) in a saucepan and bring to boiling point.
- Pour over gelatin in mixer bowl and mix well.
- Add cream cheese and start mixer very slowly. Gradually increase speed until cream cheese is mixed into gelatin. Pour in mango pieces.
- Place in refrigerator until it is lightly congealed. Fold in whipped topping. Pour into a 7 x 11-inch dish. Chill.

Cream Cheese and Mango Salad

2 (15 ounce) cans
  mangoes
1 (6 ounce) package
  lemon gelatin
2 (8 ounces) cream
  cheese, softened
1 (8 ounce) can crushed
  pineapple, undrained

- Drain juice from mangoes. Combine juice and enough water to make ¾ cups liquid. Bring to a boil and add gelatin. Stir until well dissolved.
- In mixing bowl, cream together the mangoes and cream cheese. Fold in pineapple.
- Mix into hot gelatin and pour into muffin tins or a mold.

Salad Supreme

1 (6 ounce) package
  orange gelatin

1 (8 ounce) package
  cream cheese, softened

2 (15 ounce) cans
  mangoes, undrained

2 (10 ounce) cans
  mandarin oranges,
  drained

- Place gelatin in mixing bowl and pour ¾ cup boiling water over gelatin and mix well. Let partially cool and add cream cheese.
- At a very slow speed at first, beat in the cream cheese until will mixed.
- Fold in mangoes and mandarin oranges. Pour into 8-cup molds.
- Chill several hours.

Pineapple Salad

1 (20 ounce) can crushed
  pineapple, undrained

1 (6 ounce) package
  lemon gelatin

1 (8 ounce) package
  cream cheese, softened
  and cubed

1 (8 ounce) carton
  whipped topping,
  thawed

- Heat pineapple to boiling. Pour over gelatin in mixing bowl and stir to dissolve.
- Combine pineapple mixture and cream cheese; whip slowly until well combined.
- Chill until partially set.
- Fold in the whipped topping and pour into an 8-cup mold.

Apple-Pineapple Salad

1 (6 ounce) package lemon gelatin

1 (15 ounce) can pineapple tidbits, undrained

1 cup diced apples, unpeeled

1 cup chopped pecans

- Dissolve gelatin in one cup boiling water. Add pineapple and place in refrigerator until slightly thickened.
- Fold in apples and pecans.
- Pour into a solid mold or into a 7 x 11-inch dish. Chill until firm.

(Editor's Choice) Stained Glass Fruit Salad

2 (20 ounce) cans peach pie filling

3 bananas, sliced

1 (16 ounce) package frozen unsweetened strawberries, drained

1 (20 ounce) can pineapple tidbits, drained

- Drain all fruits except peach pie filling.
- Mix all fruits together; chill and place in a pretty crystal bowl.
- Chill overnight.

  If you like you could use 1 can peach pie filling and 1 can apricot pie filling.

Pineapple-Banana Salad

1 (6 ounce) package lime gelatin

1 (8 ounce) can crushed pineapple, undrained

½ cup sour cream

1 large banana, sliced

- Dissolve gelatin in 1 cup boiling water; mixing well. Stir in pineapple.
- Place in refrigerator until mixture begins to thicken.
- Fold in sour cream and banana and pour into an 8-inch mold.

  A ½ cup chopped pecans could be added.

Orange Glow

1 (6 ounce) package orange gelatin

1 cup finely grated carrots

1 (15 ounce) can crushed pineapple, undrained

¾ cup chopped pecans

- Mix gelatin in 1 cup boiling water; mixing well.
- Add carrots, pineapple and pecans.
- Pour into a 7 x 11-inch glass dish. Refrigerate until congealed.

Orange Sherbet Salad

1 (3 ounce) package orange gelatin

1 (3 ounce) package lemon gelatin

1 pint orange sherbet

2 (11 ounce) cans mandarin oranges

- Place gelatin in a bowl and pour 1 cup boiling water over gelatin, mixing well.
- Fold in sherbet; stir until well mixed.
- Add oranges and pour into an 8-inch ring mold or 7 x 11-inch dish. Refrigerate.

Glazed Fruit Salad

2 (11 ounce) cans mandarin oranges, drained

1 (15 ounce) can pineapple chunks, drained

3 bananas, sliced

1 (18 ounce) carton creamy glaze for bananas

- In a large bowl combine fruit and glaze.
- Toss to coat fruit.
- Serve immediately.

  Grapes, apples or marshmallows could also be added to this salad.

Lime-Cherry Salad

1 (6 ounce) package lime gelatin

1 (10 ounce) bottle maraschino cherries, drained, halved

1 cup diced apples, unpeeled

1 cup chopped pecans

- Dissolve gelatin in 1½ cups boiling water; mixing well.
- Add the drained cherries and place in refrigerator until slightly congealed.
- Add apples and pecans and pour into a 7 x 11-inch dish. Chill until firm.

Orange-Pear Salad

1 (15 ounce) can sliced pears, reserve juice

1 (16 ounce) package orange gelatin

1 (8 ounce) package cream cheese, softened

1 (8 ounce) carton whipped topping

- Drain pears and reserve juice. Boil juice and ½ cup water. Then add gelatin and dissolve. Mix thoroughly and refrigerate until partially set.
- Blend pears and cream cheese in blender. Fold in pear mixture and whipped topping into gelatin mixture. Blend well.
- Pour into a 7 x 11-inch shallow dish.

Applesauce Salad

2 cups applesauce

1 (6 ounce) package lime gelatin

2 (12 ounce) cans lemon lime carbonated drink

1 (8 ounce) can crushed pineapple, drained

- Heat applesauce in a large saucepan.
- Add gelatin to the hot applesauce and stir until dissolved. Add lemon lime drink and pineapple.
- Pour into an 8-inch mold. Refrigerate.

Peaches and Cream

1 (29 ounce) can sliced peaches

1 (6 ounce) package peach gelatin

1 quart vanilla ice cream, softened

1 (11 ounce) can mandarin oranges, drained

- Drain peaches, reserving 1 cup liquid. Cut peach slices into cubes.
- Heat peach liquid and ½ cup water until boiling. Add gelatin and mix well.
- Fold in vanilla ice cream, stirring well.
- Add peaches and mandarin oranges and pour into a mold until set.

Coconut-Orange Salad

1 (6 ounce) package orange gelatin

1 pint vanilla ice cream, softened

½ cup coconut

1 (11 ounce) can mandarin oranges, drained

- Dissolve gelatin in 1 cup boiling water. Let cool slightly. Fold in ice cream, coconut and oranges.
- Pour into a 7 x 11-inch dish and refrigerate.

Cinnamon-Apple Salad

1 cup cinnamon red hot candies

1 (6 ounce) package cherry gelatin

1 (16 ounce) jar applesauce

1 cup chopped pecans

- Heat cinnamon red hots in 1¼ cups boiling water until candy melts.
- While mixture is still hot, pour over gelatin and mix well. Add applesauce and chopped pecans, mixing well.
- Pour into 7 x 11-inch glass dish and refrigerate until firm. When serving, cut in squares.

Coconut Bananas

4 bananas

4 tablespoons lemon juice

1 (16 ounce) carton sour cream

1¼ cups flaked coconut

- Cut bananas into fourths.
- Place lemon juice, sour cream and coconut in separate bowls.
- Dip bananas into lemon juice, roll in sour cream and then in coconut. Cover thoroughly.
- Place in covered bowl and refrigerate several hours or overnight.

Grapefruit-Avocado Salad

2 (15 ounce) cans grapefruit sections, drained

2 ripe avocados, peeled, sliced

½ cup chopped slivered almonds

Prepared poppy seed dressing

- Combine grapefruit, avocados and almonds.
- Toss with the poppy seed dressing. Serve on a bed of lettuce.

Crunchy Fruit Salad

2 red apples, chopped

⅓ cup sunflower seeds

½ cup green grapes

⅓ cup vanilla yogurt

- In a bowl, combine the apples, sunflower seeds, grapes and yogurt. Stir to coat salad. Refrigerate until serving.

Cranberry Mousse

1 (15 ounce) can jellied cranberry sauce

1 (8 ounce) can crushed pineapple, drained

1 (8 ounce) carton sour cream

1 tablespoon mayonnaise

- In a saucepan place the cranberry sauce and crushed pineapple. Cook until cranberry sauce is liquid.
- Fold in the sour cream and mayonnaise.
- Pour into molds or muffin tins and freeze.

Nutty Cranberry Relish

1 pound fresh cranberries

2¼ cups sugar

1 cup chopped pecans, toasted

1 cup orange marmalade

- Wash and drain cranberries and mix with sugar. Place in 1-quart baking dish. Cover dish and bake at 350° for one hour.
- Add marmalade and pecans to cranberry mixture.
- Mix well and pour into a container. Chill before serving.

Chicken Caesar Salad

4 boneless skinless chicken breasts, grilled

1 (10 ounce) package romaine salad greens

½ cup shredded parmesan cheese

1 cup seasoned croutons

- Cut chicken breasts into strips.
- Combine chicken, salad greens, cheese and croutons in a large bowl.
- When ready to serve, toss with about ¾ cup Caesar Italian dressing.

Ginger Dressing for Fruit Salad

1 cup vanilla yogurt

2 tablespoons honey

1 teaspoon sugar

2 tablespoons finely minced, crystallized ginger

• Combine all ingredients; mixing well. Cover and refrigerate. This may be served over any fruit salad.

Mexican Chicken Salad

3-4 boneless skinless chicken breasts, cooked, cubed

1 (15 ounce) can chick peas (garbanzo beans), drained

1 red bell pepper, 1 green bell pepper, seeded, diced

1 cup chopped celery

• Combine all ingredients and serve with the following dressing.

Dressing for Mexican Chicken Salad

1½ cups sour cream

2 tablespoons chili sauce

2 teaspoons ground cumin

1 small bunch cilantro, finely chopped

• Combine all ingredients for the dressing. Add a little salt and black pepper.

• Pour over chicken salad and toss. Chill before serving.

Tarragon-Chicken Salad

1 cup chopped, toasted pecans

3-4 boneless, skinless chicken breasts, cooked, cubed

1 cup chopped celery

¾ cup peeled chopped cucumbers

- Place pecans in a shallow pan; toast at 300° for 10 minutes.
- Combine the chicken, celery and cucumbers.

Dressing for Tarragon Chicken Salad

⅔ cup mayonnaise

1 tablespoon lemon juice

2 tablespoons tarragon vinegar

1¼ teaspoons crumbled, dried tarragon

- Mix all dressing ingredients together. When ready to serve toss with the chicken mixture, add pecans.

Pear Mousse

2 (15 ounce) cans sliced pears, reserve juice

1 (6 ounce) package lemon gelatin

1 (8 ounce) package cream cheese, softened

1 (8 ounce) carton whipped topping

- Drain pears, reserving juice. Heat juice and add water to make ¾ cup. Heat juice to boiling point. Add gelatin. Mix well and cool.
- Place pears and cream cheese in blender and blend until smooth. Place into a large bowl and fold in cooled but not congealed gelatin mixture and whipped topping. Mix until smooth.
- Pour into individual dessert dishes. Cover with a piece of saran wrap and refrigerate.

To garnish place a slice of kiwi on top of the mousse.

Apple-Walnut Chicken Salad

3-4 boneless, skinless chicken breasts, cooked, cubed

2 tart green apples, peeled, chopped

½ cup chopped pitted dates

1 cup finely chopped celery

- Mix all ingredients together.
- Toss with dressing.

Dressing

½ cup chopped, toasted walnuts

⅓ cup sour cream

⅓ cup mayonnaise

1 tablespoon lemon juice

- Toast walnuts at 300° for 10 minutes.
- Mix together sour cream, mayonnaise and lemon juice.
- Mix with walnuts.
- Pour over chicken salad and toss. Refrigerate.

Broccoli-Chicken Salad

3-4 boneless, skinless chicken breasts, cooked, cubed

2 cups fresh broccoli flowerets

1 sweet red bell pepper, seeded, chopped

1 cup chopped celery

- Combine chicken, broccoli, bell pepper and celery.
- Toss with a honey mustard dressing. Refrigerate.

Black Bean Chicken Salad

3-4 boneless, skinless chicken breasts, cooked, cubed

1 (15 ounce) can black beans, drained

1 bunch green onions, chopped

1 cup chopped celery

• Blend all ingredients together and toss with the Cumin Dressing below.

Cumin Vinaigrette

¾ cup virgin olive oil

¼ cup lemon juice

2 teaspoons dijon mustard

2 teaspoons ground cumin

• Combine all ingredients together.

• Toss with black bean and chicken salad. Refrigerate.

Derby Chicken Salad

3-4 boneless, skinless chicken breasts, cooked, cubed

¼ pound bacon, cooked, crumbled

2 avocados, peeled, diced

2 tomatoes, diced, drained

• Combine all ingredients.

• When ready to serve pour Italian salad dressing over salad and toss. Refrigerate.

Savory Chicken Salad

4 boneless, skinless chicken breasts, cooked

1 cup chopped celery

1 red bell pepper, seeded, chopped

⅔ cup slivered almonds, toasted

- Slice chicken breasts into long thin strips.
- Combine chicken, celery, bell pepper and almonds. Toss and refrigerate.

For dressing use a flavored mayonnaise (½ cup mayonnaise with 1 tablespoon lemon juice).

Simply Sweet Pickles

1 gallon whole dill pickles

5 pounds sugar

Tabasco as needed

5 garlic cloves, chopped

- Drain pickles completely. Slice pickles.
- Return pickles to the original jar in five layers in the following order: pickles, sugar, Tabasco and garlic. Pack firmly into the original jar and close lid tightly.
- Let stand at room temperature for six days, turning the jar upside down once a day.
- After the sixth day, store in refrigerator.

Sweet and Sour Pickles

1 quart dill pickles, sliced, reserve juice

1½ cups sugar

½ cup white vinegar

¾ teaspoon mustard seeds

- Set aside juice and pickle jar. Place pickles in a bowl and cover with sugar. Let soak overnight.
- Place pickles back in jar.
- Heat juice, vinegar and mustard seeds to a boiling point and pour over pickles. Let set overnight.

Good Night Onions

1 pound purple onions, sliced

1 cup tarragon vinegar

½ cup sugar

½ teaspoon salt and pepper

- Place onion rings in a large jar.
- Pour in the vinegar, sugar, ½ teaspoon pepper, ½ teaspoon salt and 1 cup water.
- Cover tightly and shake well until the sugar is dissolved. Store in refrigerator overnight before serving.

Fun-to-Make Sweet Pickles

1 quart whole sour pickles

3¼ cups sugar

1 clove garlic, finely chopped

½ teaspoon ground cloves

- Pour off liquid from pickles; discard.
- Slice pickles in ¼-inch slices and place in large bowl. Add sugar, garlic and cloves. Mix and leave at room temperature until sugar is dissolved.
- Spoon all back into jar. Seal and refrigerate. Ready to eat after 3 days.

Cream Cheese Sandwiches

2 (8 ounce) packages
  cream cheese, softened

1 (4 ounce) can black
  olives, chopped

¾ cups finely chopped
  pecans

Pumpernickel rye bread

- Beat the cream cheese until creamy. Fold in olives and pecans.
- Trim crusts on bread.
- Spread cream cheese on bread.
- Slice sandwich into 3 finger strips.

Luncheon Sandwich

1 loaf thinly sliced,
  sandwich bread

2 sticks butter, softened

1 (5 ounce) jar cheese
  spread, softened

½ teaspoon
  worcestershire sauce

- Trim crust on the bread.
- With mixer, beat together the butter and cheese spread until smooth and creamy, adding worcestershire sauce.
- Spread mixture on three slices of bread making a triple decker sandwich.
- Place fourth slice of bread on top. Cut into finger sandwiches.

  These sandwiches can be served cold or warmed at 300° for 5 or 10 minutes.

Party Sandwiches

1 pound bacon, cooked,
  crumbled

½ cup ripe olives,
  coarsely chopped

½ cup chopped pecans

1¼ cups mayonnaise

- Mix all ingredients together.
- Spread on thin sliced white bread.
- Cut sandwiches into three strips.

Watercress Tea Sandwiches

1 small bunch of watercress

5 hard boiled eggs, peeled

6 tablespoons mayonnaise

1 tablespoon dijon mustard

- Trim ½ of the watercress stems. Save the rest for garnish.
- In a food processor, coarsely chop the eggs; add mayonnaise, mustard and a little salt. Process until smooth.
- Fold in the chopped watercress and chill.
- Add mixture on thinly sliced white bread that has the crust trimmed. Cut into finger sandwiches.

Cream Cheese Tea Sandwiches

1 (8 ounce) package cream cheese, softened

½ pound bacon, fried and finely chopped

12-14 slices whole wheat bread

1 (12 ounce) package bean sprouts

- With a mixer, beat the cream cheese until smooth. Add the finely chopped bacon (or you can chop the cream cheese and bacon together in a food processor).
- On 6 to 8 slices of bread, spread the bacon-cream cheese mixture. Add a layer of bean sprouts.
- On the other 6 to 8 slices, spread either mayonnaise or butter and place on top of the bean sprouts making 6 or 8 sandwiches.
- With a sharp knife remove crust and cut each sandwich in 3 finger shapes. Refrigerate.

Cream Cheese Sandwich Spread

2 (8 ounce) packages cream cheese, softened

1 (2½ ounce) jar dried beef, finely chopped

1 bunch fresh green onions and tops, chopped

¾ cup mayonnaise, 1 teaspoon seasoned pepper

- Combine all ingredients together until the mixture will spread smoothly.
- Trim crust of whole wheat bread and spread cream cheese mixture on bread.
- Top with another slice of bread and slice into 3 strips or 4 quarters.

Green Chili Grilled Cheese

4 slices bread

4 slices cheddar cheese

1 (4 ounce) can chopped green chilies, drained

3 tablespoons margarine, softened

- On 2 slices of bread, place a slice of cheese on each slice. Sprinkle with green chilies.
- Top with the two remaining slices of cheese; then with remaining two slices of bread.
- Butter the outside of the sandwiches.
- In a large skillet over medium heat brown sandwiches on both sides until golden brown and cheese has melted.

Confetti Sandwiches

1 tablespoon lemon juice

1 (8 ounce) package cream cheese, softened

½ cup grated carrots

¼ cup each grated cucumber, purple onion and bell pepper

- Combine lemon juice with cream cheese; adding enough mayonnaise to make cheese into spreading consistency.
- Fold in grated vegetables and spread on bread for sandwiches. Refrigerate.

Hot Bunwiches

8 hamburger buns

8 slices Swiss cheese

8 slices ham, 8 slices turkey

8 slices American cheese

- Lay out all 8 buns. On the bottom bun, place the slices of Swiss cheese, ham, turkey and American cheese.
- Place the top bun over the American cheese.
- Wrap each bunwich individually in foil and place in freezer.
- When ready to serve, take out of freezer 2 to 3 hours before serving. Heat at 325° for about 30 minutes. Serve hot.

Reubens on a Bun

1 pound smoked frankfurters (8 per pound)

8 hot dog buns

1 (8 ounce) can sauerkraut, well drained

Caraway seeds

- Pierce each frankfurter and place into split buns.
- Arrange two tablespoons sauerkraut over each frank. Sprinkle with caraway seed.
- Place in a 9 x 13-inch shallow pan and drizzle with Thousand Island dressing.
- Heat just until hot dogs are thoroughly heated.

Italian Sausage Sandwiches

1 pound sweet Italian sausage, cooked, casing removed

1 red bell pepper, chopped

1 onion, chopped

1⅔ cups Italian-style spaghetti sauce

- In a skillet over medium heat, cook sausage, bell pepper and onion until sausage is brown and no longer pink.
- Stir in spaghetti sauce and heat until boiling. Simmer for 5 minutes stirring constantly.
- Pour mixture over split hoagie rolls.

Pizza Burger

1 pound lean ground beef

½ teaspoon salt

½ cup pizza sauce

4 slices mozzarella cheese

- Combine beef, salt and ½ pizza sauce.
- Mold into 4 patties and pan fry over medium heat for 5 to 6 minutes on each side.
- Just before burgers are done, top each with a spoonful of pizza sauce and a slice of cheese.
- Serve on a hamburger bun.

Marshmallow Sandwiches

1 jar marshmallow cream

Chunky peanut butter

White bread or whole wheat bread

Vanilla wafers, optional

- On one slice of bread, spread marshmallow cream.
- On a second slice of bread, spread the peanut butter.
- Put the marshmallow and the peanut butter sides together.

Ranch Cheeseburgers

1 packet ranch-style salad dressing mix

1 pound lean ground beef

1 cup shredded cheddar cheese

4 large hamburger buns, toasted

- Combine dressing mix with beef and cheese.
- Shape into four patties.
- Cook on charcoal grill until thoroughly cooked and browned.

Barking Dogs

10 wieners
5 slices cheese
10 corn tortillas
Oil

- Slice wieners lengthwise and halfway through.
- Cut each cheese slice in half and place inside each wiener.
- Wrap tortillas around wiener and secure with a toothpick.
- Heat several inches of oil in frying pan. Fry dogs in oil until tortilla is crisp. Serve hot.

Cheese Doggies

Sliced frankfurters
Cheddar cheese slices
Bacon slices
Hot dog buns

- Use 1 bacon slice for each frankfurter. Place bacon on paper towel or paper plate and cover with a paper towel and microwave for 45 seconds or until almost crisp.
- Cut lengthwise pocket in the frankfurter and stuff with a strip of cheese.
- Wrap bacon around the doggie and secure with toothpick.
- Place in split hot dog bun and micro- wave for about 30 seconds or until the hot dog is warm.

Dog Wrap

8 wieners
8 slices cheese
1 (8 ounce) package refrigerated crescent rolls

- Split wieners lengthwise and fill with a folded cheese slice.
- Wrap in a crescent dough roll and bake at 375° for about 12 minutes. Serve with mustard.

Hot and Sweet Mustard

4 ounces dry mustard

1 cup vinegar

3 eggs

1 cup sugar

- Soak dry mustard in vinegar overnight.

- Beat eggs and sugar together; then add to vinegar-mustard mixture.

- In top of double boiler, cook over low heat for about 15 minutes, stirring constantly. Mixture will resemble a custard consistency. Pour immediately into jars. Store in refrigerator. Serve with ham.

  Great to keep in the refrigerator for ham sandwiches.

Avocado Butter

2 large avocados, peeled

2 tablespoons lime juice

1 pound butter, softened

¼ teaspoon ginger

- Combine all ingredients in electric blender or food processor. Blend until smooth.

- Serve on crackers or make party sandwiches on white or rye bread.

VEGETABLES
&
SIDE DISHES

Posh Squash

8 medium yellow squash, sliced

½ green bell pepper, seeded, chopped

1 small onion, chopped

1 (8 ounce) package Mexican Velveeta cheese, cubed

- Combine squash, bell pepper and onion in a large saucepan and just barely cover with water.
- Cook just until tender – about 10 to 15 minutes.
- Drain and add cheese; stir until cheese is melted and pour into a buttered 2-quart baking dish.
- Bake at 350° for 15 minutes.

Squash on the Run

5 yellow squash, sliced

2 potatoes, thinly sliced

1 onion, chopped

2 cans cream of chicken soup

- In a buttered 2-quart casserole dish, layer the squash, potatoes and onion.
- In a saucepan, combine soup and ¾ can water; heat just enough to mix well. Pour over vegetables.
- Cover and bake at 350° for 45 minutes.

Seasoned Squash and Onion

8 yellow squash, sliced

2 onions, chopped

½ stick margarine

1 cup grated American cheese

- Cook squash and onion in a small amount of water until tender; drain.
- Add margarine and cheese and toss. Serve hot.

Dilled Zucchini

1 stick butter

8 medium zucchini, grated

1½ tablespoons dried dill weed

Salt and pepper

• In a skillet melt the butter and saute the zucchini and dill weed. Cook on medium heat for 5 minutes or just until tender.

Add salt and pepper and serve hot.

Stuffed Yellow Squash

5 large yellow squash

1 (16 ounce) package frozen chopped spinach

1 (8 ounce) package cream cheese, cubed

1 packet dry onion soup mix

• Steam squash whole until tender.

• Slit squash lengthwise and remove the seeds with a spoon.

• Cook spinach according to package directions. Drain well. When spinach is cooked add the cream cheese and stir until it melts. Do not let this boil as the heat will be too hot for the cream cheese. Add soup mix, blending well.

• Fill scooped out squash shells with spinach mixture and top with a few sprinkles of cheddar cheese.

• Place on a baking sheet and bake at 325° for about 15 minutes.

Baked Squash

5 cups squash, cooked, drained

¾ cup grated monterey jack cheese

1 (10 ounce) can cream of chicken soup

1 (16 ounce) box herb dressing mix

• Place cooked squash in a mixing bowl and season with salt to taste. Add the cheese and soup, blending well. Mix the dressing according to direction on box.

• Place half the dressing in a 9 x 13-greased baking dish. Spoon the squash mixture on top and sprinkle the remaining dressing on top.

• Bake uncovered at 375° for 30 minutes.

Sunny Yellow Squash

6-8 medium yellow squash

1 (8 ounce) package cream cheese, softened, cubed

2 tablespoons margarine

1 teaspoon sugar

• In saucepan, cut up squash, add a little water and boil until tender. Drain.

• Add cream cheese, margarine, sugar and a little salt and pepper.

• Cook over low heat, stirring until cream cheese has melted.

Fried Zucchini

3 large zucchini, grated

5 eggs

1 pack Ritz crackers (⅓ of a 12 ounce box), crushed

½ cup grated parmesan cheese

• Combine the zucchini, eggs and cracker crumbs mixing well. Add cheese and a little salt and pepper.

• Drop by spoonfuls into a skillet with a little oil. Fry for about 15 minutes. Brown on each side.

Zucchini Patties

1½ cups grated zucchini

1 egg, beaten

2 tablespoons flour

⅓ cup finely minced onion

- Mix all ingredients together, adding ½ teaspoon seasoned salt.
- Heat a skillet with about 3 tablespoons oil.
- Drop zucchini mixture by tablespoons onto the skillet at medium high heat. Turn and brown both sides. Remove and drain on paper towels.

Stir-Fry Zucchini

¼ stick margarine

6-8 zucchini, grated

1 teaspoon seasoned salt

¼ cup grated parmesan cheese

- Heat margarine in large skillet and add zucchini. Cook on medium heat about 8 minutes; stir frequently.
- If zucchini gets too dry, add a table-spoon or so of water. Toss with sea-soned salt and parmesan cheese.

Serve hot.

Zucchini Beau Monde

6-8 medium zucchini, sliced

1 teaspoon beau monde seasoning

1 (8 ounce) carton sour cream

¼ cup grated parmesan cheese

- Saute zucchini in 2 tablespoons of margarine. Cook on low for about 5 minutes.
- Stir in seasoning, sour cream and cheese. Heat but do not boil.

Walnut Zucchini

6-8 zucchini, julienned

½ red bell pepper, julienned

½ stick margarine

1 cup chopped walnuts

- Saute zucchini and bell pepper in margarine until tender, shaking the pan and tossing the zucchini to cook evenly. Pour off any excess margarine.
- Add the chopped walnuts, some salt and pepper. When walnuts are well blended and heated, serve hot.

Mushrooms and Corn

4 ounces fresh mushrooms, sliced

3 chopped green onions and tops

2 tablespoons margarine

1 (15 ounce) package frozen whole kernel corn

- Place all ingredients in a 2-quart saucepan and cook on medium heat for 5 to 10 minutes. Add salt and pepper to taste.

Italian Corn

1 (16 ounce) package frozen whole kernel corn

2 slices bacon, cooked and diced

1 onion, chopped

1 (16 ounce) can Italian stewed tomatoes

- Place all ingredients in a 2-quart pan.
- Cook until most of the liquid in the tomatoes has cooked out. Add a little salt and pepper. Serve hot.

Stuffed Corn

1 (15 ounce) can cream-
style corn

1 (15 ounce) can whole
kernel corn, drained

1 stick margarine, melted

1 (6 ounce) package
chicken stuffing mix

• Combine all ingredients together plus
seasoning packet and ½ cup water and
mix well.

• Spoon into a buttered 9 x 13-baking
pan. Bake at 350° for 30 minutes.

Corn Au Gratin

3 (15 ounce) cans
mexicorn, drained

1 (4 ounce) can sliced
mushrooms, drained

1 (10½ ounce) can cream
of mushroom soup

1 cup shredded cheddar
cheese

• Mix all ingredients together in a saucepan and heat slowly until cheese is
melted. Serve hot.

Super Corn Casserole

1 (15 ounce) can whole
kernel corn

1 (15 ounce) can cream-
style corn

1 stick margarine, melted

1 (8 ounce) carton sour
cream

1 (6 ounce) package
jalapeno cornbread mix

• Mix all ingredients together and pour
into a greased 9 x 13-inch baking dish.

• Bake uncovered at 350° for 35 minutes.

Wild West Corn

3 (15 ounce) cans whole kernel corn, drained

1 (10 ounce) can tomatoes and green chilies, drained

1 (8 ounce) package shredded monterey jack cheese

1 cup cheese cracker crumbs

- In a large bowl, combine the corn, tomatoes and green chilies and cheese; mix well.
- Pour into a buttered 2½-quart baking dish.
- Sprinkle cracker crumbs over casserole. Bake uncovered at 350° for 25 minutes.

Calico Corn

1 (16 ounce) package frozen whole kernel corn

1 bell pepper, chopped

⅓ cup chopped celery

1 (10½ ounce) can cream of cheddar cheese soup

- Cook corn in microwave according to package directions; drain well.
- To the corn add the bell pepper and celery. Stir in soup; mixing well.
- Pour into a buttered 2-quart casserole and bake covered at 350° for 30 minutes.

 # Corn Pudding

1 (8 ounce) package corn muffin mix

1 (15 ounce) can cream-style corn

½ cup sour cream

3 eggs, slightly beaten

- Combine all ingredients and pour into a buttered 2-quart baking dish.
- Bake uncovered at 350° for about 35 minutes.

Vegetables

Corn Maize

½ stick margarine, melted

1 (3 ounce) package cream cheese, softened

2 (15 ounce) cans whole kernel corn, drained

⅓ cup salsa

- Mix margarine and cream cheese together. Add corn and salsa sauce.
- Pour into a 2-quart buttered baking dish.
- Bake covered at 350° for about 25 minutes. Serve hot.

 # Shoepeg Corn

1 (8 ounce) package cream cheese, softened

1 stick butter, softened

3 (15 ounce) cans shoepeg corn

1 (4 ounce) can chopped green chilies

- With mixer or fork, combine the butter and cream cheese. Add corn and green chilies, mixing well.
- Spoon into a 7 x 11-inch greased casserole.
- Bake covered at 350° for 30 minutes.

Hot Corn Bake

3 (15 ounce) cans whole kernel corn, drained

1 (10 ounce) can cream of corn soup

1 cup salsa

1 (8 ounce) package shredded Mexican-cheese blend, divided

- Combine corn, corn soup, salsa and ½ the cheese and mix well.
- Pour into a buttered 3-quart baking dish and sprinkle remaining cheese on top.
- Bake at 350° for 20 to 30 minutes.

Baked Beans and Corn

1 (15 ounce) can ranch-style beans

1 (15 ounce) can pork and beans

1 (15 ounce) whole kernel corn, drained

1 (15 ounce) can chili without beans

• Combine all ingredients. Spoon into a lightly greased 3-quart baking dish.

• Bake at 300° for one hour.

Classic Baked Bean Stand-By

3 (18 ounce) cans Bush's baked beans

½ cup chili sauce

⅓ cup packed brown sugar

4 slices bacon, cooked, crumbled

• In a buttered 3-quart baking dish, combine baked beans, chili sauce and brown sugar.

• Bake 325° for 40 minutes.

• When ready to serve, sprinkle bacon on top.

Chili Baked Beans

2 (16 ounce) cans pork and beans

1 (15 ounce) can chili with beans

¼ cup molasses

1 teaspoon chili powder

• Pour visible liquid out of can of pork and beans.

• In a 2-quart casserole combine pork and beans, chili, molasses and chili powder. Heat until bubbly.

Italian-Broiled Tomatoes

4 medium tomatoes
Salt and pepper
½ teaspoon dried oregano
Italian salad dressing

- Core tomatoes and cut in half crosswise.
- Make a shallow crisscross cut on the surface of the tomatoes. Season the cut surface with salt, pepper and oregano; drizzle with salad dressing.
- Broil, cut side up for about 5 minutes or until heated thoroughly.

Stewed Tomato Casserole

2 (15 ounce) cans
  Mexican-style stewed
  tomatoes
2 onions, sliced
1¼ cups cracker crumbs
1 cup shredded cheddar
  cheese

- In a 2-quart casserole layer the tomatoes, onions, cracker crumbs and cheese; repeat layers.
- Sprinkle a little salt and pepper. Bake at 350° for 45 minutes.

Tasty Turnips

6 medium turnips
2 teaspoons sugar
1 teaspoon salt
½ stick butter (not
  margarine), melted

- Peel and dice turnips. Boil with sugar and salt until tender. Drain.
- Add butter to turnips and mash. Serve hot.

Lima Beans

1 (16 ounce) package
   frozen baby lima beans

1 cup chopped celery

3 tablespoons margarine

2 teaspoons lemon juice

- Place lima beans, celery, margarine and lemon juice in a 2-quart saucepan and add ⅓ cup water.
- Cook until vegetables are tender crisp. You may add salt and pepper if you like.

Sesame Peas

1 (10 ounce) package
   frozen green peas

2 tablespoons sesame
   seeds

1 teaspoon sugar

½ stick margarine

- Cook peas as directed on package; drain.
- In a saucepan, heat remaining ingredients. Pour over peas. Serve hot.

Tasty Black-Eyed Peas

2 (10 ounce) packages
   frozen black-eyed peas

1¼ cups chopped green
   pepper

¾ cup chopped onion

1 (15 ounce) can Mexican
   stewed tomatoes,
   undrained

- Cook black-eyed peas according to package directions; drain.
- Saute green pepper and onion in 3 tablespoons margarine. Add peas, tomatoes and a little salt and pepper; cook over low heat until thoroughly heated, stirring often.

Swiss Cheesy Peas

3 (15 ounce) cans green peas and onions, drained

1 (8 ounce) carton sour cream

8 ounces Swiss cheese, grated

2 cups crushed corn flakes

- In a large bowl, combine the peas, onions, sour cream, Swiss cheese and salt to taste.
- Spoon into a buttered 3-quart baking dish. Sprinkle corn flakes over top.
- Bake uncovered at 350° for 35 minutes.

Parmesan Peas

2 (10 ounce) packages frozen green peas

3 tablespoons margarine, melted

1 tablespoon lemon juice

⅓ cup grated parmesan cheese

- Microwave peas in 2 tablespoons water for 3 minutes; rotate bowl ½ turn and cook another 3 minutes. Leave in oven several minutes. Serve hot.

Sauteed Celery with Water Chestnuts

1 bunch celery, chopped diagonally

1 (8 ounce) can water chestnuts, drained and chopped

¼ cup almonds, toasted

½ stick margarine, melted

- Boil celery in salted water just until tender crisp. Drain.
- Saute the water chestnuts and almonds in the melted margarine.
- Toss together the celery and the water chestnuts-almond mixture. Serve hot.

Black-Eyed Peas and Okra

3 (15 ounce) cans black-eyed peas, drained

¾ cup shredded ham

1 onion, chopped

1 pound small fresh whole okra pods

- In a large saucepan, combine the peas, ham and onion; bring to a boil.
- Place all the okra on top of the pea-onion mixture; do not stir.
- Bring to a boil again; lower heat and simmer about 5 to 10 minutes until okra is tender. Serve hot

Fried Okra

Small, fresh garden okra

Milk or buttermilk

Corn meal

Salt and pepper

- Thoroughly wash and drain okra. Cut off top and ends and slice.
- Toss okra with a little milk or buttermilk (just enough to make the cornmeal stick). Sprinkle cornmeal over okra and toss.
- Heat 2 or 3 tablespoons of oil in skillet. Fry okra, turning several times until okra is golden brown and crisp.

Carrots and Peas

1 (15 ounce) can sliced carrots, drained

1 (15 ounce) can green peas, drained

½ stick margarine

⅓ cup chopped cashew nuts

- In a saucepan, combine carrots, peas, margarine and cashew nuts.
- Heat until the margarine melts; mix well. Serve hot.

Tangy Carrot Coins

2 (15 ounce) cans sliced carrots

¼ stick margarine

2 tablespoons brown sugar

1 tablespoon dijon mustard

- Place all ingredients in a saucepan. Cook and stir over medium heat for about 2 minutes. Serve hot.

Creamy Carrots with Toasted Almonds

2 (15 ounce) cans sliced carrots

1 (10 ounce) can cream of celery soup

½ cup milk

⅓ cup chopped almonds, toasted

- In a saucepan, combine carrots, soup and milk. Over medium heat stir to mix and heat throughout.
- Stir almonds in just before serving. Serve hot.

Dilled Baby Carrots

1 (12 ounce) package fresh baby carrots

3 chicken bouillon cubes or 2 teaspoons bouillon granules

¾ stick butter

2 teaspoons dill weed

- Boil carrots in water with dissolved bouillon cubes until tender (about 8 minutes). Drain.
- Place in a skillet with melted butter. Cook on low heat for only a few minutes making sure the butter coats all carrots.
- Sprinkle dill weed over carrots and shake to make sure dill is on all carrots. Place in serving dish and serve immediately.

Glazed Carrots

1 (16 ounce) package
  frozen baby carrots

¼ cup apple cider

¼ cup apple jelly

1½ teaspoons dijon
  mustard

- In saucepan place carrots and apple cider and bring to boil. Reduce heat. Cover and simmer about 8 minutes until carrots are tender.

- Remove cover and cook on medium heat until liquid evaporates; stir in jelly and mustard. Cook until jelly melts and the carrots are glazed.

Brown Sugar Carrots

2 (15 ounce) cans carrots

½ stick margarine

3 tablespoons brown
  sugar

½ teaspoon ground ginger

- Drain carrots but reserve 2 tablespoons liquid.

- Combine the 2 tablespoons liquid with the margarine, brown sugar and ginger. Heat thoroughly.

- Add carrots, stirring gently and cook 3 minutes. Serve hot.

Speedy Cabbage

1 head cabbage, shredded

¼ stick margarine

3 tablespoons sour cream

½ teaspoon black pepper

- Saute cabbage in margarine and about 2 tablespoons water until tender (about 3 to 4 minutes) stirring constantly.

- Stir in sour cream and about ½ teaspoon salt, ½ teaspoon sugar and pepper. Serve hot.

Creamy Cabbage Bake

1 head cabbage, shredded

1 (10½ ounce) can cream of celery soup

⅔ cup milk

1 (8 ounce) package shredded cheddar cheese

- Place cabbage in a 2-quart buttered baking dish.
- Pour celery soup diluted with milk over top of cabbage. Bake covered at 325° for 30 minutes.
- Remove from oven, sprinkle with cheese and bake uncovered another 5 minutes.

Fried Cabbage

1 small head cabbage, finely chopped

½ teaspoon salt

3 tablespoons oil

2 tablespoons Italian salad dressing

- Sprinkle cabbage with salt and set aside for 30 minutes.
- Heat oil in skillet until very hot. Add the cabbage and stir fry about 5 minutes.
- Remove and add Italian dressing.

Cheesy Baked Eggplant

1 eggplant

½ cup mayonnaise

⅔ cup seasoned breadcrumbs

¼ cup grated parmesan cheese

- Peel eggplant and slice ½-inch thick.
- Spread both sides with mayonnaise and dip in mixture of crumbs and cheese. Coat both sides well.
- Place in a single layer in a shallow baking dish. Bake at 400° for 20 minutes.

Eggplant Casserole

1 large eggplant

1 cup cracker crumbs

1 cup shredded cheddar cheese, divided

1 (10 ounce) can tomatoes and green chilies

- Peel and slice eggplant.
- Place in a saucepan and cover with water. Cook 10 minutes or until tender. Drain well on paper towels.
- Mash eggplant. Stir in crackers, ¾ cup of the cheese and tomatoes; mix well.
- Spoon eggplant in a 1-quart buttered baking dish. Sprinkle with remaining cheese. Bake at 350° for about 30 minutes.

Spicy Hominy

1 (15 ounce) can yellow hominy, drained

1 (8 ounce) carton sour cream

1 (4 ounce) can chopped green chilies

1¼ cups grated cheddar cheese

- Combine all ingredients, adding a little salt. Pour into a one-quart baking dish and bake at 350° for about 20 minutes.

Baked Eggplant

1 medium eggplant

½ stick butter, melted

1 (5 ounce) can evaporated milk

1½ cups cracker crumbs

- Peel, slice and boil eggplant until easily mashed; drain. Season with a little salt and pepper.
- Add all other ingredients.
- Pour into a 2-quart buttered baking dish. Bake at 350° for 25 minutes.

Hominy

1 (8 ounce) jar jalapeno processed cheese spread

2 (15 ounce) cans of golden yellow hominy

1 (8 ounce) carton sour cream

1 teaspoon seasoned salt

- Heat processed cheese spread in microwave (lid off) just enough for cheese to mix with hominy. Combine hominy, sour cream and processed cheese spread.

- Pour into a 2-quart casserole dish and bake at 350° for about 30 minutes or until bubbly and lightly brown on top.

Baked Onions

4 large onions, thinly sliced

1½ cups crushed potato chips

1 cup shredded cheddar cheese

1 (10½ ounce) can cream of chicken soup

- In a 9 x 13-inch baking dish alternate layers of onion, potato chips and cheese.

- Spoon soup over the last layer and pour ¼ cup milk or ¼ cup water on top. Sprinkle with a little red or black pepper.

- Bake at 300° for 1 hour.

Cheesy Baked Onions

4 yellow onions, peeled, sliced

1 stick margarine

25 Ritz crackers, crushed

⅓ cup grated parmesan cheese

- Saute onions in margarine until transparent.

- Spread ½ of the onions in a 2-quart buttered casserole dish. Top with ½ of the crackers, ½ of the cheese. Repeat layers.

- Bake uncovered at 325° for 30 minutes.

Onion Casserole

5-6 medium mild onions, thinly sliced

3 tablespoons margarine

1 cup milk

4 eggs

• Saute onions in margarine in covered skillet for about 30 minutes. Cool.

• In bowl beat together milk and eggs. Stir in onions and transfer to greased baking dish. Bake at 325° for 45 to 50 minutes or until light golden.

Easy Onions

6 medium white onions, peeled and cored

6 beef bouillon cubes

Worcestershire

½ stick margarine, melted

• Place each onion in a piece of heavy-duty aluminum foil.

• Place a bouillon cube in each onion cavity and several drops of worcestershire. Fill cavity up with margarine and wrap tightly in foil. Place on grill and cook 40 to 45 minutes. (Onion can be baked in the oven at 350° for 30 to 40 minutes.)

Cheesy Onion Casserole

5 sweet onions, sliced

1 stick margarine

1 cup shredded cheddar cheese

22 saltine crackers, crushed

• Saute onion in margarine until soft.

• In a buttered 2-quart casserole layer half the onions, half the cheese, half the crackers. Repeat layers.

• Bake at 325° for 35 minutes.

Spinach To Like

2 (10 ounce) packages
   frozen, chopped
   spinach

1 (8 ounce) carton sour
   cream

½ package dry onion soup
   mix

⅔ cup seasoned
   breadcrumbs

- Cook spinach according to package directions; drain well. Add sour cream and onion soup mix to the spinach.

- Pour into a 2-quart casserole. Sprinkle breadcrumbs on top. Bake at 350° for 35 minutes.

Creamed Spinach Bake

1 (16 ounce) package
   frozen chopped spinach

2 (3 ounce) packages
   cream cheese, softened

3 tablespoons margarine

1 cup Italian-style
   seasoned breadcrumbs

- In a saucepan, cook spinach, with ¾ cup water for 6 minutes; drain. Add cream cheese and margarine to the spinach; heat until cream cheese and margarine are melted and mixed well with the spinach.

- Pour into a greased 2-quart baking dish. Sprinkle a little salt over spinach; then cover with the breadcrumbs.

- Bake uncovered at 350° for 15 to 20 minutes.

Baked Tomatoes with Basil

3 large tomatoes

1½ cups seasoned
   breadcrumbs

4 tablespoons butter

Dried basil

- Cut tomatoes in half or slice tomatoes in ½ to 1-inch thick slices and place on baking sheet.

- Sprinkle slices generously with breadcrumbs and top with butter and basil. Bake at 350° for 10-15 minutes until lightly brown on top.

Herbed Spinach

2 (16 ounce) packages
  frozen chopped spinach

1 (8 ounce) package
  cream cheese, softened

½ stick margarine, melted

1 (6 ounce) package herb-
  seasoned stuffing

• Cook spinach as directed on package.
Drain and add the cream cheese and ½
of the margarine. Season with a little
salt and pepper.

• Pour into a buttered casserole dish.
Spread the herb stuffing on top and
then drizzle with the remaining margarine.

• Bake at 350° for 25 minutes.

 # Favorite Spinach

2 (10 ounce) packages
  frozen chopped
  spinach, thawed, well
  drained

1 package dry onion soup
  mix

1 (8 ounce) carton sour
  cream

⅔ cup shredded monterey
  jack cheese

• Combine the spinach, onion soup mix
and sour cream. Pour into a buttered
2-quart baking dish. Bake at 350° for
20 minutes.

• Take out of oven and sprinkle cheese
over the top and place casserole back in
oven for 5 minutes.

Cheezy Peas Please

1 (10½ ounce) can cream
  of mushroom soup

1 (6 ounce) roll garlic
  cheese

2 (15 ounce) cans green
  peas, drained

⅛ teaspoon red pepper

• In a saucepan heat soup and cheese
until the cheese has melted. Add peas
and red pepper. Heat.

Spinach Bake

2 (8 ounce) packages
cream cheese, softened

1 (10½ ounce) can cream
of chicken soup,
undiluted

2 (16 ounce) packages
frozen chopped
spinach, thawed, well
well drained

1 cup crushed Ritz
crackers

• In mixing bowl, beat the cream cheese
until smooth. Add soup; mix well.

• Stir in spinach. Spoon into a well
greased 3-quart baking dish.

• Sprinkle cracker crumbs over top of
casserole. Bake uncovered at 325° for
35 minutes.

Creamed Peas and Potatoes

2 pounds small new
potatoes, quartered

1 (10½ ounce) can cream
of mushroom soup

⅓ cup milk

1 (10 ounce) package
frozen peas with pearl
onions

• Cook new potatoes about 25 minutes or
until tender.

• Add soup, milk, ½ teaspoon black
pepper and the peas, stirring occasionally.

Seasoned Green Beans

4 slices bacon, chopped

1 medium onion, chopped

2 (15 ounce) cans green
beans, drained

1 teaspoon sugar

• Saute bacon and onion in skillet. Drain.

• Add green beans and sugar and heat
thoroughly.

Italian Green Beans

1 (16 ounce) package
frozen Italian green
beans

3 green onions and tops,
chopped

2 tablespoons margarine

1 teaspoon mixed Italian
seasoning

• Mix all ingredients in a 2-quart saucepan and cook according to package
directions.

Green Beans

1 pound fresh green
beans

2 tablespoons soy sauce

¼ teaspoon ground
nutmeg

½ cup toasted sesame
seeds

• Cook green beans until tender crisp,
about 10 minutes.

• Combine the soy sauce, nutmeg and 2
tablespoons margarine. Cook over
medium heat for a few minutes.

• Add to green beans and toss lightly.

• Add sesame seeds, toss again.

Crunchy Green Beans

3 (15 ounce) cans whole
green beans

2 (10 ounce) cans cream
of mushroom soup

2 (11 ounce) cans water
chestnuts, chopped

2 (2.8 ounce) cans french
fried onion rings

• Combine green beans, mushroom soup,
water chestnuts, ½ teaspoon of salt and
a little pepper.

• Pour into a 2-quart casserole. Bake
covered at 350° for 30 minutes.

• Remove casserole from oven and
sprinkle onion rings over top and bake
10 minutes longer.

Green Beans and Almonds

2 (16 ounce) packages frozen french cut green beans

¼ stick margarine

2 (8 ounce) cans water chestnuts, chopped

½ cup slivered almonds, toasted

- Cook beans according to the package directions.
- Drain, add margarine and heat just until margarine melts. Fold in water chestnuts.
- Place in serving dish and sprinkle almonds over the top.

Souper Cauliflower

1 (16 ounce) package frozen cauliflower, cooked, drained

1 (10½ ounce) can cream of celery soup

¼ cup milk

1 cup shredded cheddar cheese

- Place cauliflower in a 2-quart greased baking dish.
- In a saucepan, combine soup, milk and cheese; heat just enough to mix well. Pour over cauliflower.
- Bake at 350° for 15 minutes.

Savory Cauliflower

1 head cauliflower

1 (1.25 ounce) cnvclope hollandaise sauce mix

Fresh parsley to garnish

Lemon slices to garnish, optional

- Cut cauliflower into small flowerets. Cook in salted water until barely tender. Do not overcook.
- Mix sauce as directed on package.
- Drain cauliflower, top with sauce and a sprinkling of parsley.

169

Cauliflower Whiz

1 head cauliflower

1 jar jalapeno processed
cheese spread, melted

- Place cauliflower on a microwaveable plate. Cover with plastic wrap leaving a 1-inch vent opening. For each pound of cauliflower, microwave on high for 7 minutes.

- When done remove plastic wrap and pour melted processed cheese spread over top.

Best Cauliflower

1 (16 ounce) package
frozen cauliflower

1 (8 ounce) carton sour
cream

1½ cups grated American
or cheddar cheese

4 teaspoons sesame
seeds, toasted

- Cook cauliflower as directed on package.

- Drain and place half of cauliflower in a 2-quart baking dish. Sprinkle a little salt and pepper on cauliflower. Spread one half of the sour cream and one half of the cheese. Top with 2 teaspoons sesame seed. Repeat layers.

- Bake at 350° for about 15 to 20 minutes.

Shrimp and Almond Sauce for Broccoli

1 (10½ ounce) can cream
of shrimp soup

1 (3 ounce) package
cream cheese

1 tablespoon lemon juice

⅓ cup slivered almonds,
toasted

- Cook a 16-ounce package of broccoli flowerets.

- Combine in saucepan the shrimp soup, cream cheese and lemon juice. Heat slowly until cream cheese is melted.

- When ready to serve pour over cooked broccoli and sprinkle almonds over top of sauce.

Lemon Broccoli

2 (16 ounce) packages
broccoli flowerets

½ stick butter

1 tablespoon lemon juice

½ teaspoon seasoning
salt

- Cook broccoli according to package directions; drain.
- Melt butter and stir in lemon juice and seasoned salt.
- Pour over broccoli and toss to coat.

Crunchy Broccoli

2 (10 ounce) packages
frozen broccoli florets

1 (8 ounce) can sliced
water chestnuts,
drained, chopped

1 stick margarine, melted

1 packet dry onion soup
mix

- Place broccoli in a microwave dish; cover and microwave 5 minutes. Turn dish and cook another 4 minutes.
- Add the water chestnuts. Combine the melted margarine and soup mix, blending well. Toss with the cooked broccoli.

 # Cheddar-Broccoli Bake

1 (10½ ounce) can
cheddar cheese soup

½ cup milk

1 (16 ounce) bag frozen
broccoli flowerets,
cooked

1 (2.8 ounce) can french-
fried onion rings

- In 2-quart casserole, mix soup, milk, and broccoli.
- Bake at 350° for 25 minutes.
- Stir. Sprinkle onions over broccoli mixture.
- Bake 5 more minutes or until onions are golden.

Broccoli Stuffed Tomatoes

4 medium tomatoes

1 (10 ounce) package frozen chopped broccoli

1 (6 ounce) roll garlic cheese, softened

½ teaspoon garlic salt

- Cut tops off tomatoes and scoop out pulp.
- Cook broccoli according to package instruction; drain well.
- Combine broccoli, cheese and garlic salt. Heat just until cheese is melted. Stuff broccoli mixture into tomatoes and place on baking sheet.
- Bake at 375° for about 10 minutes.

Asparagus Caesar

3 (15 ounce) cans asparagus spears, drained

½ stick margarine, melted

3 tablespoons lemon juice

½ cup grated parmesan cheese

- Place asparagus in a 2-quart baking dish. Drizzle on margarine and lemon juice. Sprinkle with cheese (and a little paprika if you like).
- Bake at 400° for 15 to 20 minutes.

Almond Asparagus

⅓ cup margarine

1-1½ pounds fresh asparagus

⅔ cup slivered almonds

1 tablespoon lemon juice

- Melt margarine in skillet, add the asparagus and almonds. Saute 3 to 4 minutes.
- Cover and steam about 2 minutes or until tender crisp.
- Sprinkle lemon and a little salt and pepper over asparagus. Serve hot.

Sesame Asparagus

6 fresh asparagus spears, trimmed

1 tablespoon margarine or butter

1 teaspoon lemon juice

1 teaspoon sesame seeds

- Place asparagus in a skillet. Sprinkle with salt if desired. Add ¼ cup water; bring to a boil. Reduce heat. Cover and simmer about 4 minutes.

- Melt the butter and add lemon juice and sesame seed.

- Drain asparagus; drizzled with the butter mixture.

Asparagus Bake

2 (15 ounce) cans cut asparagus spears, reserve liquid

3 hardcooked eggs, chopped

½ cup chopped pecans

1 (10 ounce) can cream of asparagus soup

- Arrange asparagus spears in buttered 2-quart baking dish.

- Top with eggs and pecans.

- Heat asparagus soup, adding the reserved liquid from the asparagus spears.

- Spoon over eggs and pecans. Bake covered at 350° for 25 minutes.

Vegetable Medley

1 (16 ounce) package frozen broccoli, cauliflower and carrots

1 (16 ounce) package frozen corn

2 (10½ ounce) cans fiesta nacho cheese soup

½ cup milk

- Combine broccoli mixture and corn in a 2-quart greased baking dish.

- Combine fiesta nacho cheese soup and milk in a saucepan, heat just enough to mix well.

- Pour over vegetables.

- Cover and bake at 350° for about 30 minutes.

Roasted Vegetables

1½ pounds assorted fresh vegetables such as squash, carrots, red bell peppers, zucchini, cauliflower or broccoli

1 (11 ounce) can water chestnuts, drained

1 envelope savory herb with garlic soup mix

¼ stick margarine, melted

• Cut all vegetables in uniform 2-inch pieces and place in a greased 2-quart casserole dish with water chestnuts.

• Combine melted margarine and soup mix and drizzle over vegetables, stirring well.

• Cover and bake vegetables at 400° for 20 to 25 minutes or until tender, stirring once.

Buttered Vegetables

1 stick butter

2 yellow squash, sliced

1 (16 ounce) package broccoli flowerets

1 (10 ounce) box frozen corn

• Melt butter in large skillet and add all vegetables.

• Saute vegetables for about 10 to 15 minutes or until tender-crisp. Add a little salt if you like. Serve warm.

Herb Seasoned Vegetables

1 (14 ounce) can seasoned chicken broth with Italian herbs

½ teaspoon garlic powder

1 (16 ounce) package frozen vegetables (broccoli, cauliflower, etc.)

½ cup grated parmesan cheese

• Heat broth, garlic and vegetables to a boil. Cover and cook over low heat for 5 minutes or until tender-crisp. Drain.

• Place in serving dish and sprinkle cheese over vegetables.

Creamy Vegetable Casserole

1 (16 ounce) package frozen broccoli, carrots and cauliflower

1 (10½ ounce) can cream of mushroom soup, undiluted

1 (8 ounce) carton spreadable garden vegetable cream cheese

1 cup seasoned croutons

- Cook vegetables according to package directions; drain and place in a large bowl.

- In a saucepan, place the soup and cream cheese; heat just enough to mix easily.

- Pour into the vegetable mixture, mixing well.

- Pour into a 2-quart baking dish. Sprinkle with croutons. Bake uncovered at 375° for 25 minutes or until bubbly.

Veggies To Love

1 (16 ounce) package frozen broccoli, cauliflower and carrot combination

1 can cream of celery soup

⅓ cup milk

1 (2.8 ounce) can french-fried onions

- Cook vegetables according to package directions. Add soup and milk, mixing well.

- Pour into a buttered 2-quart baking dish and sprinkle french-fried onions over top.

- Bake at 350° for about 30 minutes or until bubbly.

Potatoes Supreme

1 (32 ounce) package frozen hash browned potatoes, thawed

1 onion, chopped

2 (10½ ounce) cans cream of chicken soup

1 (8 ounce) carton sour cream

• In a large bowl, combine potatoes, onion, soup and sour cream. Pour into a greased 9 x 13-inch baking dish.

• Bake covered at 350° for 1 hour.

This recipe is also good with ½ cup parmesan or cheddar cheese sprinkled on top about the last 5 minutes of baking.

Potatoes with a Zip

1 (32 ounce) bag frozen hash brown potatoes

1 (16 ounce) box Velveeta cheese, cubed

2 cups mayonnaise

1 (7 ounce) can chopped green chilies

• In a large bowl, combine hash browns, cheese, mayonnaise and green chilies.

• Spoon into a buttered 9 x 13-inch baking dish. Cover and bake at 325° for 1 hour.

• Stir twice during baking to prevent burning.

Creamy Cheesy Potatoes

1 (32 ounce) bag frozen hash brown potatoes

1 (16 ounce) box Velveeta cheese, cubed

1 (10½ ounce) can cream of chicken soup

1 (8 ounce) carton sour cream

• In a large bowl, combine hash browns, cheese, soup and sour cream. (You may want to add ½ teaspoon salt.)

• Spoon into a buttered 9 x 13-inch baking dish. Cover and bake at 325° for 1 hour.

• Stir twice during baking to prevent burning.

Creamy Potato Bake

6-8 baked potatoes

1 (8 ounce) carton sour cream

1 (8 ounce) package cream cheese, softened

1½ cups shredded cheddar cheese

- Cut potatoes in half lengthwise. Scoop meat out of potatoes and place in mixing bowl.

- Add salt to taste, sour cream and cream cheese and whip until mixed well. Spoon mashed potatoes back into potato skins; place in a hot oven until potatoes have reheated. Sprinkle cheddar cheese on top of potatoes.

Baked Potato Toppers

1 cup grated cheddar cheese

½ cup sour cream

¼ cup soft margarine, softened

4 tablespoons chopped green onion

- Mix all ingredients and serve on baked potato.

Golden Potato Casserole

1 (2 pound) bag frozen hash brown potatoes, thawed

1 pint sour cream

1 (8 ounce) bag shredded cheddar cheese

1 bunch chopped fresh green onions with tops, chopped

- Combine potatoes, sour cream, cheese and onion in a large bowl and thoroughly mix.

- Pour into a 9 x 13-inch buttered casserole dish. Sprinkle a little paprika on top.

- Cover and bake at 325° for 55 minutes.

Loaded Baked Potatoes

6 medium to large
  potatoes

1 (1 pound) hot sausage

1 (1 pound) box Velveeta
  cheese

1 (10 ounce) can
  tomatoes and green
  chilies, drained

- Wrap potatoes in foil and bake at 375°
  for 1 hour or until done.

- Brown sausage and drain.

- Cube cheese and add to sausage.

- Heat until cheese is melted; add the
  tomatoes and green chilies.   Serve the
  sausage-cheese mixture over baked
  potatoes.

Vegetable Stuffed Potatoes

2 (10 ounce) cans fiesta
  nacho cheese soup

1 (16 ounce) bag frozen
  assorted vegetables,
  cooked, drained

8 large potatoes, baked

Black pepper

- In saucepan, heat nacho cheese and
  vegetables.

- Cut a lengthwise slice in the top of each
  potato.

- Slightly mash the pulp in each potato.

- Spoon sauce mixture onto each potato.
  Sprinkle with black pepper.

Broccoli Potatoes

5 baking potatoes

Margarine

1 (9 ounce) package
  frozen broccoli and
  cheese sauce

Paprika to garnish,
  optional

- Put the potatoes in a 400° oven for 1
  hour. (Potatoes are thoroughly cooked
  when you can stick a fork in the center
  and potato is soft.)

- Just before serving, slit each potato
  lengthwise.

- Fluff potato up with a fork, adding
  margarine.

- Heat broccoli and cheese sauce in
  saucepan and pour over each potato.

Oven-Roasted Potatoes

2 pounds potatoes, unpeeled

1 envelope dry onion soup mix

⅓ cup oil

½ teaspoon black pepper

- Wash potatoes and cut into medium-size chunks.
- In a large plastic bag, add all ingredients. Shake until potatoes are evenly coated.
- Empty coated potatoes into a greased 9 x 13-inch baking pan.
- Bake uncovered at 425°, stirring twice, 40 minutes or until golden brown. Serves 8.

Philly Potatoes

4½ cups instant mashed potatoes, prepared, hot

2 tablespoons freeze-dried chives

1 (8 ounce) package cream cheese, softened

1 egg slightly beaten

- Mix all ingredients, blending well.
- Place in a greased 3-quart casserole.
- Bake covered at 350° for 30 minutes.
- Uncover and bake for 15 minutes more.

Company Potatoes

5 potatoes, peeled and sliced

2 (8 ounce) cartons whipping cream

2 tablespoons dijon mustard

⅓ cup grated parmesan cheese

- In a greased 9 x 13-inch baking dish, layer potatoes and add a little salt and pepper.
- In a saucepan, combine the cream, mustard, 2 tablespoons margarine and a little garlic powder; heat to boiling. Pour over potatoes.
- Cover and bake at 350° for 1 hour.
- Uncover and top with parmesan cheese. Bake 10 minutes longer or until potatoes are tender.

Cheddar Potatoes

1 (10½ ounce) can cheddar cheese soup

⅓ cup sour cream

2 fresh green onions, chopped

3 cups instant seasoned mashed potatoes, prepared

- In a saucepan, heat soup; add sour cream, onion and little black pepper.
- Stir in potatoes until well blended.
- Pour into a buttered 2-quart casserole.
- Cook at 350° for about 25 minutes.

Ranch Mashed Potatoes

4 cups instant, unsalted mashed potatoes, prepared

1 packet ranch-style dressing mix

½ stick margarine

½ cup sour cream

- Combine all ingredients in saucepan.
- Heat on low until potatoes are thoroughly heated.

Potato Puff

3 eggs, separated

2 cups instant mashed potatoes, prepared, hot

½ cup sour cream

2 teaspoons dried parsley

- Beat egg whites until stiff but still moist. Set aside.
- Beat yolks until smooth and add to potato mixture.
- Fold in the beaten egg whites, sour cream, parsley, 1 teaspoon seasoned salt and ½ teaspoon white pepper.
- Pour into a buttered 2-quart casserole. Bake uncovered at 350° for 45 minutes.

Cheesy Potatoes

10-12 new potatoes

1 (8 ounce) carton sour cream

½ stick margarine, melted

1 (1 pound) box Velveeta cheese, sliced

- Rinse and scrub potatoes well but do not peel. Cut into ¼-inch slices and place in a large saucepan; cover with water. Cook about 25 minutes until slightly tender. Drain.
- Place ½ of potatoes in a 9 x 13-inch baking dish. Sprinkle with salt and pepper.
- Spread half of sour cream and half of the melted margarine over top of potatoes. Put half the sliced cheese on top.
- Repeat layer. Bake at 400° about 20 minutes or until bubbly.

Baked New Potatoes

1 pound new potatoes, unpeeled

1 clove garlic, minced

1 large onion coarsely chopped

1 stick butter or margarine

- Par-boil new potatoes. Drain and quarter.
- In large skillet, saute onion and garlic with butter until onions start to become translucent. Add potatoes. Toss to coat.
- Place in large casserole dish. Add 1 teaspoon seasoned salt.
- Bake at 350°, basting occasionally, for 25 to 30 minutes until potatoes are fork tender.

Grilled New Potatoes

1 pound new potatoes

3 tablespoons orange
   marmalade

1 teaspoon brown sugar

2 tablespoons melted
   butter or margarine

- Cook new potatoes covered in boiling water until crisp-tender.
- Drain and cut in half. Thread on skewers.
- Combine next 3 ingredients and brush mixture over potatoes.
- Grill over medium hot coals until potatoes are browned, about 5 minutes each side. Salt and pepper to taste. Baste frequently. Can be baked at 400° for 20 minutes.

Mashed Red Potatoes

3 pounds red potatoes,
   quartered, unpeeled

⅓ cup whole milk

⅔ stick margarine

¼ teaspoon white pepper

- Place potatoes in a large saucepan and cover with water; adding 1 teaspoon salt. Cover and bring to a boil.
- Reduce heat; cook for 25 minutes or until very tender.
- Drain potatoes well and place in a large mixing bowl. Add the milk, butter, pepper and a little salt.
- Beat until potatoes are light and fluffy.

Potato Souffle

2⅔ cups instant mashed
   potatoes

2 eggs, beaten

1 cup shredded cheddar
   cheese

1 can french-fried onion
   rings

- Prepare mashed potato mix according to package directions.
- Add eggs, cheese and stir until blended.
- Spoon mixture into a lightly greased 2-quart dish. Sprinkle with onion rings.
- Bake uncovered at 325° for 25 minutes.

Potato Pancakes

3 pounds white potatoes, peeled, grated

1 onion, finely minced

3 eggs, beaten

½ cup seasoned dry breadcrumbs

- In a large bowl, combine the potatoes, onions, eggs, a little salt and pepper and breadcrumbs and mix well.

- In a skillet, drop by spoonfuls in hot oil and brown on both sides.

Ham-Baked Potatoes

4 potatoes, baked

1 cup diced cooked ham

1 (10½ ounce) can cream of mushroom soup

1 cup shredded cheddar cheese

- Place the hot potatoes on a microwave-safe plate. Cut in half lengthwise.

- Fluff up the potatoes with fork. Top each potato with ¼ of the ham.

- In saucepan, heat the soup with ¼ cup water, heating just until spreadable. Spoon soup over potatoes and top with cheese.

- Microwave on high for 4 minutes or until hot.

Broccoli-Topped Potatoes

4 hot baked potatoes, halved

1 cup diced, cooked ham

1 (10½ ounce) can cream of broccoli soup

½ cup shredded cheddar cheese

- Place hot baked potatoes on a micro-wave-safe plate.

- Carefully fluff up potatoes with fork. Top each potato with ham.

- Stir the soup in the can until smooth. Spoon soup over potatoes and top with cheese.

- Microwave on high for 4 minutes.

Whipped Sweet Potatoes

2 (15 ounce) cans sweet potatoes

½ stick margarine, melted

¼ cup orange juice

1 cup miniature marshmallows

- Combine sweet potatoes, margarine, orange juice and ½ teaspoon salt in mixing bowl.
- Beat until fluffy. Fold in marshmallows.
- Spoon into a buttered 2-quart casserole.
- Bake uncovered at 350° for 25 minutes.

  You might sprinkle additional marshmallows and broil until lightly browned.

Sweet Potato Casserole

1 (28 ounce) can sweet potatoes

½ cup chopped pecans

1 ½ cups packed light brown sugar

1 stick margarine

- Slice sweet potatoes into a two-quart casserole dish. Sprinkle pecans over sweet potatoes.
- Make a syrup of the brown sugar and margarine with just enough water to make it pourable.
- Bring to a boil and pour syrup over sweet potatoes.
- Bake at 350° for about 30 minutes until the potatoes are browned.

Sweet Potatoes and Pecans

2 (17 ounce) cans sweet potatoes, drained, divided

1½ cups packed brown sugar

½ stick margarine, melted

1 cup chopped pecans

- Slice half of the sweet potatoes and place in a buttered, 2-quart baking dish.
- Mix together brown sugar, margarine and pecans and sprinkle half of mixture over sweet potatoes. Repeat layer. Bake uncovered at 350° for 30 minutes.

Tasty Rice Bake

1½ cups uncooked rice

1 stick margarine, melted

1 (10 ounce) can French onion soup

1 (8 ounce) can sliced water chestnuts, drained

- Combine rice, margarine, soup, water chestnuts and 1¼ cups water.
- Pour into a buttered, 2-quart baking dish. Bake covered at 350° for 1 hour.

Baked Rice

2 cups uncooked rice

1 stick margarine, melted

1 (10½ ounce) can cream of celery soup

1 (10½ ounce) can cream of onion soup

- Combine the rice, margarine, soups and 1½ cup water.
- Pour into a buttered 3-quart baking dish.
- Bake at 350° covered for 1 hour.

Broccoli and Wild Rice

2 (10 ounce) packages frozen chopped broccoli

1 (6 ounce) box long grain and wild rice

1 (8 ounce) jar Cheez Whiz

1 (10½ ounce) can cream of chicken soup

- Cook broccoli and rice according to package directions.
- Combine all ingredients and pour into a buttered 2-quart casserole dish.
- Bake at 350° for 25 to 30 minutes or until bubbly.

Tasty Rice

½ stick margarine

1 cup raw white rice

2 (10 ounce) cans beef broth

¼ cup parmesan cheese

- Melt margarine in a 3-quart casserole dish.
- Add the rice and pour the beef broth over rice.
- Sprinkle with parmesan cheese.
- Cover and bake at 350° for 45 minutes.

Brown Rice

1 cup rice (not instant)

1 can French onion soup

1 can beef broth

3 tablespoons margarine, melted

- Put rice in bottom of casserole dish.
- Pour soups and margarine on top.
- Bake covered at 350° for 45 minutes.

Spanish Rice

¾ stick margarine, melted

1 onion, chopped

2 cups cooked rice

1 (10 ounce) can chopped tomatoes and green chilies

- In large bowl, combine margarine, onion, rice, tomatoes and green chilies and salt to taste.
- Spoon mixture into a buttered 3-quart baking dish.
- Cover and bake at 350° for 30 minutes.

Mushroom Rice

1 (5.9 ounce) package
  chicken rice-a-roni

1 (4 ounce) can sliced
  mushrooms, drained

⅓ cup slivered almonds

1 (8 ounce) carton sour
  cream

• Prepare rice as directed on package.

• Fold in mushrooms, almonds and sour cream. Place in a 3-quart greased casserole.

• Bake covered at 350° for 25 to 30 minutes.

Dinner Rice

2 cups cooked white rice

1 onion, chopped

½ stick margarine,
  melted

1 (8 ounce) package
  shredded Mexican
  Velveeta cheese

• Combine all ingredients and mix well.

• Spoon mixture into a buttered 2-quart baking dish.

• Bake covered at 325° for 30 minutes.

Hoppin' John

4 slices bacon

1 onion, chopped

1 cup raw rice

1 (15 ounce) can black-
  eyed peas, undrained

• Fry bacon; drain.

• Saute onion in the bacon grease.

• In a large saucepan, combine the onion, bacon grease, salt, rice and 2½ cups water. Bring to a boil. Cover. Lower heat and simmer for 30 minutes.

• Add bacon and black-eyed peas; simmer 5 more minutes. Remove from heat and allow to stand for 5 more minutes until liquid is absorbed.

Rice 'N Beans

4 cups cooked rice

1 (15 ounce) can pinto beans, undrained

1 cup shredded cheddar cheese

3 tablespoons margarine, melted

- Mix all ingredients together in a saucepan.
- Cook over low heat until cheese is melted. Serve hot.

Easy Rice

1 onion, finely chopped

2 tablespoons margarine

1 cup raw white rice

2 (14 ounce) cans chicken broth

- Saute onion in the margarine until transparent.
- In a 2-quart casserole combine the onion, rice and broth. Cover and bake at a 350° oven for 55 minutes.

Chili-Rice Bake

1 cup instant rice

1 pint sour cream

1 (7 ounce) can chopped green chilies

1 (8 ounce) package shredded Monterey Jack cheese

- Cook rice according to directions.
- Add remaining ingredients plus ½ teaspoon salt.
- Place in a buttered casserole dish.
- Bake covered at 325° for 15 to 20 minutes until thoroughly heated.

Spinach Fettuccine

1 (6 ounce) can tomato paste

1 (5 ounce) can evaporated milk

1 stick margarine or butter

1 (12 ounce) package spinach fettuccine

- In a saucepan, combine the tomato paste, milk and heat until margarine is melted.
- Season with a little salt and pepper.
- Cook fettuccine according to directions on package. Serve sauce over fettuccine.

Creamy Fettuccine

1 (8 ounce) package fettuccine

1 pound Italian sausage

1 (10½ ounce) can cream of mushroom soup

1 (16 ounce) carton sour cream

- Cook fettuccine and drain.
- Cut up sausage into 1-inch pieces and brown over medium heat cooking for about 8 minutes. Drain.
- Mix all ingredients together and place in a 2-quart greased baking dish.
- Bake at 325° for 30 minutes.

Creamy Pasta

1 (8 ounce) jar roasted red peppers, drained

1 (15 ounce) can chicken broth

1 (3 ounce) package cream cheese

8 ounces pasta

- Combine red peppers and broth in a blender, mixing well.
- Pour into a saucepan. Heat to boiling.
- Turn heat down and whisk in cream cheese. Serve over your favorite pasta.

Special Macaroni and Cheese

1 (8 ounce) package small macaroni shells

1 (15 ounce) can stewed tomatoes

1 (8 ounce) package Velveeta cheese, cubed

3 tablespoons margarine, melted

- Cook shells according to package directions; drain.
- In a large bowl, combine shells, tomatoes, cheese cubes and margarine.
- Pour into a 2-quart buttered baking dish.
- Bake covered at 350° for 35 minutes.

Macaroni and Cheese

1 cup uncooked macaroni

1½ cups small curd cottage cheese

1½ cups shredded cheddar cheese or American cheese

4 tablespoons grated parmesan cheese

- Cook macaroni according to package directions; drain.
- Combine cottage cheese and both cheeses. Combine macaroni with the cheese mixture.
- Spoon into a greased 2-quart baking dish.
- Bake covered at 350° for 35 minutes.

 # Carnival Couscous

1 (5.7 ounce) box herbed chicken couscous

½ stick margarine

1 red bell pepper, 1 yellow squash, both cut in tiny pieces

¾ fresh broccoli flowerets, finely chopped

- Cook couscous as package directs, leaving out the butter.
- With margarine in saucepan, saute the bell pepper, squash, and broccoli, cooking about 10 minutes or until vegetables are almost tender.
- Combine couscous and vegetables. Serve hot.

MAIN DISHES

Bacon-Wrapped Chicken

6 boneless, skinless chicken breast halves

1 (8 ounce) carton whipped cream cheese with onion and chives

Margarine

6 bacon strips

- Flatten chicken to ½-inch thickness. Spread 3 tablespoons cream cheese over each.
- Dot with margarine and a little salt.
- Roll up. Wrap each with a bacon strip.
- Place seam-side down in a greased 9 x 13-inch baking dish.
- Bake uncovered at 375° for 40-45 minutes or until juices run clear. To brown, broil 6 inches from heat for about 3 minutes or until bacon is crisp.

Saucy Chicken

5-6 boneless, skinless chicken breasts

2 cups thick and chunky salsa

⅓ cup packed light brown sugar

1½ tablespoons dijon-style mustard

- Place chicken breasts in a greased 9 x 13-inch baking dish.
- Combine salsa, sugar and mustard and pour over chicken.
- Cover and bake at 350° for 45 minutes. Serve over rice.

Golden Chicken

6 boneless, skinless chicken breasts

½ stick margarine

1 (10½ ounce) can golden mushroom soup

½ cup sliced almonds

- Place chicken breasts in a greased 9 x 13-inch baking pan.
- In a saucepan, combine margarine, soup, almonds and ¼ cup water. Heat and mix just until margarine is melted.
- Pour mixture over chicken.
- Cover and bake at 350° for 1 hour.

Spicy Chicken and Rice

3 cups cooked chicken, sliced

2 cups cooked brown rice

1 (10 ounce) can fiesta nacho cheese soup

1 (10 ounce) can chopped tomatoes and green chilies

• Combine chicken, rice, cheese soup, tomatoes and green chilies and mix well.

• Spoon mixture into a buttered 3-quart baking dish.

• Cook covered at 350° for 45 minutes.

Chicken Crunch

4-6 boneless, skinless chicken breasts

½ cup Italian salad dressing

½ cup sour cream

2½ cups corn flakes, crushed

• Place chicken in a zip-top plastic bag; add salad dressing and sour cream. Seal, refrigerate 1 hour.

• Remove chicken from marinade, discarding marinade.

• Dredge chicken in corn flakes; place in a 9 x 13-inch non-stick sprayed baking dish.

• Bake uncovered at 375° for 45 minutes.

Chili Pepper Chicken

5 boneless, skinless chicken breasts

1 envelope hot and spicy recipe Shake'N Bake coating mixture

1 (4 ounce) can chopped green chilies

Chunky salsa

• Dredge chicken in coating mixture and place in a greased 9 x 13-inch baking dish.

• Bake at 375° for 25 minutes.

• Remove from oven and spread green chilies over the 5 chicken breasts and return to oven for 5 minutes. Serve with the salsa over each chicken breast.

Catalina Chicken

6-8 boneless, skinless
chicken breast halves

1 (8 ounce) bottle
Catalina dressing

1 teaspoon black pepper

1½ cups crushed cracker
crumbs

• Marinate chicken breasts in Catalina dressing for 3-4 hours, then discard marinade.

• Combine pepper and cracker crumbs.

• Dip each chicken breast in crumbs and place in a large, greased baking dish.

• Bake uncovered at 350° for 1 hour.

Cola Chicken

4-6 boneless, skinless
chicken breasts

1 cup ketchup

1 cup cola

2 tablespoons
worcestershire sauce

• Place chicken in a 9 x 13-inch casserole dish. Sprinkle with salt and pepper.

• Mix ketchup, cola and worcestershire and pour over chicken.

• Cover and bake at 350° for 50 minutes.

Asparagus Chicken

1 package hollandaise
sauce mix

2 large boneless chicken
breasts, cut into strips

1 tablespoon lemon juice

1 (15 ounce) can
asparagus spears

- Prepare hollandaise sauce according to directions on package.

- In a large skillet with a little oil, cook chicken strips for 12 to 15 minutes or until brown, stirring occasionally.

- Add hollandaise sauce and lemon juice.

- Cover and cook another 10 minutes, stirring occasionally. Serve over hot cooked noodles. When ready to serve, place chicken strips over the noodles, then add the heated asparagus spears.

Peachy Chicken

½ cup Italian dressing

2 teaspoons ground
ginger

4 boneless, skinless
chicken breasts

⅓ cup peach preserves

- In a large plastic bag combine Italian dressing and ginger.

- Place chicken in bag and turn several times to coat chicken. Marinate in refrigerator (turning occasionally) 4 hours or overnight.

- When ready to bake remove chicken reserving ⅓ cup of the marinade.

- In a small saucepan bring reserved marinade to boil and boil for one minute. Remove from heat and stir in preserves; set aside.

- In oven broil chicken until chicken is no longer pink, brushing with preserved mixture the last 5 minutes of cooking.

Wine and Chicken

6-8 boneless, skinless
  chicken breasts

1 (10½ ounce) can cream
  of mushroom soup

1 (10½ ounce) can cream
  of onion soup

1 cup white wine

- In skillet brown chicken in a little bit of oil. Place in a 9 x 13-inch baking dish.
- Combine soups and wine; pour over chicken.
- Bake covered at 325° for 35 minutes.
- Uncover and bake another 25 minutes.

Baked Chicken

6 boneless, skinless
  chicken breasts

1 stick margarine, melted

Cornbread stuffing mix,
  crushed (plus
  seasoning)

- Dip chicken breast in melted margarine.
- Roll in cornbread stuffing mix to coat.
- Bake uncovered at 350° for 45 minutes.

Glazed Chicken and Rice

4 boneless, skinless
  chicken breasts, cubed

1 (20 ounce) can
  pineapple chunks,
  undrained

½ cup honey mustard
  grill and glaze sauce

1 red bell pepper,
  chopped

- In a skillet with a little oil, brown chicken and cook on low heat for 15 minutes. Add the pineapple, honey mustard and bell pepper.
- Bring to a boil, then reduce heat to low and simmer for 10 to 15 minutes or until sauce is slightly thickened.
- Serve over hot cooked rice.

Rosemary Chicken

1 tablespoon dried
  rosemary, divided

½ cup flour

Italian dressing

3-5 boneless, skinless
  chicken breasts

- Combine the flour and ½ the rosemary together.

- Place a little Italian dressing in a shallow bowl and dip chicken breasts in dressing.

- Dredge chicken in the flour mixture. Place in a 9 x 13-inch shallow baking dish.

- Bake uncovered at 350° for 40 minutes. Remove from oven and sprinkle remaining rosemary over breasts and cook another 10 minutes.

Chicken Dipping

1½ cups cornbread
  stuffing mix, plus ½ of
  the seasoning packet

4 tablespoons oil

4 boneless, skinless
  chicken breasts

Dipping Sauce

- Place stuffing mix in a plastic bag and crush with a rolling pin.

- Add oil to the center of a 9 x 13-inch baking pan and spread it around the entire pan.

- Cut chicken breasts into three or four pieces; dip in stuffing mix and place in the baking pan. Arrange chicken making sure the pieces are not touching.

- Bake at 350° uncovered for 25 minutes. Remove from oven and turn pieces over and bake another 15 minutes or until brown.

Dipping Sauce for Chicken

4 tablespoons honey

3 tablespoons spicy
  brown mustard

- To serve, dip chicken in dipping sauce and enjoy.

Lemonade Chicken

6 boneless, skinless
chicken breast halves

1 (6 ounce) can frozen
lemonade, thawed

⅓ cup soy sauce

1 teaspoon garlic powder

- Place chicken in a greased 9 x 13-inch baking dish.

- Combine the lemonade, soy sauce and garlic powder and pour over the chicken.

- Cover with foil and bake at 350° for 45 minutes.

- Uncover. Pour juices over chicken and cook another 10 minutes uncovered.

Classy Chicken

4 boneless, skinless
chicken breasts

¼ cup lime juice

1 envelope Italian salad
dressing mix

½ stick butter, melted

- Season chicken with salt and pepper; place in shallow baking dish.

- Mix lime juice, salad dressing mix and melted butter and pour over chicken.

- Cover and bake at 325° for 1 hour. Remove cover for the last 15 minutes of cooking time.

Wild Rice and Chicken

1 (6.2 ounce) package
long grain and wild rice
mix

4 boneless, skinless
chicken breasts

4 tablespoon margarine,
divided

1 large red pepper,
chopped

- Prepare rice according to package directions.

- In a large skillet cook chicken in 2 tablespoons of the margarine making sure each chicken breast is browned on both sides. Remove chicken and keep warm.

- Add remaining margarine to pan drippings; saute red pepper until tender. Add to the rice. Serve with the cooked chicken breast.

Mozzarella Cutlets

4 boneless, skinless chicken breast halves

1 cup Italian seasoned dry breadcrumbs

1 cup prepared spaghetti sauce

4 slices mozzarella cheese

- Pound each chicken breast to flatten slightly.
- Coat well in breadcrumbs. Arrange chicken breasts in a greased 9 x 13-inch baking dish.
- Place ¼ of the sauce over each portion. Place slice of cheese over each and garnish with remaining breadcrumbs.
- Bake uncovered at 350° for 45 minutes.

Crispy Nutty Chicken

⅓ cup dry roasted peanuts, minced

1 cup corn flake crumbs

½ cup ranch-style buttermilk salad dressing

5-6 chicken breasts

- Combine peanuts and corn flake crumbs on piece of wax paper.
- Pour salad dressing into a pie plate.
- Dip each piece of chicken in the salad dressing and roll in crumb mixture to coat.
- Arrange chicken in a 9 x 13-inch shallow baking dish.
- Bake uncovered at 350° for 50 minutes until lightly brown.

Sunday Chicken

5-6 boneless, skinless chicken breast halves

½ cup sour cream

¼ cup soy sauce

1 (10½ ounce) can French onion soup

- Place chicken in a greased 9 x 13-inch baking dish.
- In saucepan, combine the sour cream, soy sauce and soup; heat just enough to mix well. Pour over chicken breasts.
- Bake covered at 350° for 55 minutes.

Chicken and Beef

1 (4 ounce) jar sliced dried beef, separated

6 strips bacon

6 boneless, skinless chicken breasts

1 (10½ ounce) can cream of chicken soup

- Place dried beef in greased 9 x 13-inch baking dish.
- Wrap bacon strip around each chicken breast and place over beef.
- In a saucepan heat chicken soup and ¼ cup water just until it can be poured over chicken.
- Bake covered at 325° for 1 hour and 10 minutes.

Seasoned Chicken

4-5 boneless, skinless chicken breasts

1 tablespoon oregano

¾ teaspoon garlic powder

1 stick margarine, melted

- Place chicken breasts in a baggie and add the oregano, garlic and margarine.
- Marinate in refrigerator for 3 or 4 hours.
- Place chicken and marinade in a shallow baking dish.
- Bake covered at 325° for 1 hour.

Ritzy Chicken

6 boneless, skinless chicken breasts

½ cup sour cream

1 stack Ritz crackers, crushed into fine crumbs

¼ teaspoon pepper

- Dip chicken in sour cream and roll in cracker crumbs with pepper mixed in.
- Place chicken in a greased shallow baking dish.
- Bake uncovered at 350° for 55 minutes.

Chicken and Noodles

1 package chicken
   flavored instant ramen
   noodles

1 (16 ounce) package
   frozen broccoli,
   cauliflower and carrots

⅔ cup sweet and sour
   sauce

3 boneless, skinless
   chicken breasts,
   cooked, cut into thin
   strips

- Reserve seasoning packet from noodles. In a saucepan cook noodles and vegetables in 2 cups of boiling water for 3 minutes, stirring occasionally; drain.

- Combine noodle-vegetable mixture with seasoning packet, sweet and sour sauce and a little salt and pepper. (You may want to also add 1 tablespoon of soy sauce.)

- Add chicken and heat thoroughly.

Jiffy Chicken

8 boneless, skinless
   chicken breasts

¾ cup mayonnaise

2 cups crushed corn flake
   crumbs

½ cup grated parmesan
   cheese

- Sprinkle chicken breasts with salt and pepper.

- Dip chicken in mayonnaise and spread mayonnaise over chicken with a brush.

- Combine corn flakes and parmesan cheese. Dip mayonnaise-covered chicken in the cornflake mixture (get plenty of the crumbs on chicken) and place on a non-stick vegetable sprayed 9 x 13-inch glass baking dish.

- Bake uncovered at 325° for 1 hour.

Chicken Parmesan

1½ cups biscuit mix

⅔ cup grated parmesan cheese

6-8 boneless, skinless chicken breast halves

1 stick margarine, melted

- In a shallow bowl, combine biscuit mix and parmesan cheese.
- Dip chicken in margarine and then in biscuit-cheese mixture.
- Place in a large buttered, baking dish. Bake uncovered at 325° for 1 hour or until lightly browned.

Skillet Chicken and Stuffing

1 (6 ounce) box stuffing mix for chicken

1 (16 ounce) package frozen whole kernel corn

½ stick margarine

4 boneless, skinless chicken breast halves, cooked

- In a large skillet combine contents of the seasoning packet in the stuffing mix, corn, 1⅔ cups water and the margarine. Bring to a boil. Reduce heat, cover and simmer for 5 minutes.
- Stir in stuffing mix just until moistened.
- Cut chicken into thin slices. Mix with the stuffing-corn mixture.
- Cook on low heat just until thoroughly heated.

Chicken Curry

2 (10 ounce) cans cream of mushroom soup

2 teaspoons curry powder

⅓ cup chopped almonds, toasted

4 skinless chicken breast halves, cooked, cubed

- In a large saucepan combine the soup, 1 can water, curry powder, almonds and cubed chicken.
- Heat, while stirring frequently.
- When ready to serve, spoon over cooked white rice.

Chicken Bake

8 boneless, skinless chicken breast halves

8 slices swiss cheese

1 (10 ounce) can cream of chicken soup

1 (8 ounce) box chicken stuffing mix

- Flatten each chicken breast with rolling pin and place in greased 9 x 13-inch baking dish.
- Place cheese slice over chicken. Combine chicken soup and ½ cup water and pour over chicken.
- Mix stuffing mix as directed on box and sprinkle over chicken. Bake uncovered at 325° for hour.

Oven-Glazed Chicken

4 boneless, skinless chicken breasts

1 (10 ounce) can Italian tomato soup

2 tablespoons white wine worcestershire

2 tablespoons packed brown sugar

- Place chicken breasts in a greased, 7 x 11-inch baking dish.
- In small bowl, combine tomato soup, worcestershire and brown sugar, and mix well. Spoon over chicken.
- Bake at 350° for 1 hour.

Chicken Supper

5 boneless, skinless chicken breasts

5 slices onion

5 potatoes, peeled and quartered

1 (10½ ounce) can cream of celery soup

- Place chicken breasts in a 9 x 13-inch greased baking dish.
- Top chicken with onion slices, placing potatoes around chicken.
- Heat soup with ¼ cup water just enough to be able to pour the soup over chicken and vegetables.
- Bake covered at 325° for 1 hour and 10 minutes.

Apricot-Ginger Chicken

2 teaspoons ground
  ginger
½ cup Italian dressing
4 boneless, skinless
  chicken breasts
⅔ cup apricot preserves

- Combine ginger and Italian dressing; place in a large baggie. Add chicken to the bag and marinate in refrigerator overnight, turning occasionally.

- When ready to cook, remove chicken, reserving ¼ cup of the marinade. Place chicken in a shallow baking dish.

- Pour the ¼ cup of marinade in saucepan, bring to a boil and cook 1 minute. Remove from heat and stir in preserves. Set aside.

- Bake chicken on 350° for 45 minutes; brush with marinade mixture the last 10 minutes of cooking.

Chicken Quesadillas

3 boneless, skinless
  chicken breasts, cubed
1 (10½ ounce) can
  cheddar cheese soup
⅔ cup chunky salsa
10 flour tortillas

- Cook chicken in skillet until juices evaporate, stirring often.

- Add soup and salsa and heat thoroughly.

- Spread about ⅓ cup soup mixture on half of each tortilla to within ½ inch of edge. Moisten edge with water, fold over and seal. Place on 2 baking sheets.

- Bake at 400° for 5 to 6 minutes.

Chicken Oriental

1 (6 ounce) jar sweet and sour sauce

1 envelope dry onion soup mix

1 (16 ounce) can whole cranberry sauce

6-8 boneless, skinless chicken breasts

- In a bowl combine the sweet and sour sauce, onion soup mix and cranberry sauce.
- Place chicken breasts in a Pam sprayed 9 x 13-inch shallow baking dish.
- Pour cranberry mixture over chicken breasts.
- Bake covered at 325° for 30 minutes. Uncover and bake 25 minutes longer.

Reuben Chicken

4 boneless, skinless chicken breasts

4 slices Swiss cheese

1 (15 ounce) can sauerkraut, drained

1 (8 ounce) bottle Catalina salad dressing

- Arrange chicken breasts in a greased shallow baking pan.
- Place cheese over chicken and then the sauerkraut. Cover with Catalina dressing.
- Bake covered at 350° for 30 minutes. Uncover and cook another 15 minutes.

Best Ever Meatloaf

2 pounds ground turkey

1 (6¼ ounce) package stuffing mix for beef plus seasoning

2 eggs, beaten

½ cup ketchup, divided

- Combine the ground turkey, stuffing mix, eggs and ¼ cup of the ketchup. Mix well.
- Shape meat into an oval loaf into the center of a 9 x 13-inch baking dish.
- Spread remaining ¼ cup of ketchup on top of loaf.
- Bake at 350° for 1 hour.

Honey Mustard Chicken

⅓ cup dijon mustard

½ cup honey

2 tablespoons dried dill

1 (2½ pound) chicken, quartered

- Combine mustard, honey and dill.
- Arrange chicken quarters in a 9 x 13-inch baking dish.
- Pour mustard mixture over chicken. Turn chicken over and make sure the mustard mixture covers the chicken.
- Bake covered at 350° for 35 minutes. Uncover and bake another 10 minutes.

Nacho Chicken

2 chickens, quartered

2 (10 ounce) cans fiesta nacho cheese soup

¾ cup milk

3 tablespoons white wine worcestershire

- Place chicken quarters in large baking pan with sides.
- In saucepan, combine nacho cheese soup, milk and worcestershire and spread over chicken.
- Cover and bake at 350° for 1 hour.

Fried Chicken Breasts

4 boneless, skinned chicken breasts

20 saltine crackers, crushed

2 eggs, beaten

¼ teaspoon black pepper

- Pound chicken breasts to ¼-inch thickness.
- Combine eggs, pepper and 2 tablespoons water.
- Dip chicken in egg mixture and then in crushed crackers, coating well.
- Deep fry until golden brown. Drain well.

One-Dish Chicken Bake

1 (6 ounce) package
    chicken stuffing mix
4 skinless, boneless
    chicken breasts halves
1 (10 ounce) can cream of
    mushroom soup
½ cup sour cream

- Toss contents of vegetable-seasoning packet, stuffing mix and 1⅔ cups water into bowl and set aside. Place chicken in a greased 9 x 13-inch baking dish.

- Mix soup and sour cream in a saucepan and heat just enough to pour over chicken. Spoon stuffing evenly over top. Bake uncovered at 375° for 40 minutes.

Sunshine Chicken

1 chicken, quartered
Flour
1 cup barbecue sauce
½ cup orange juice

- Place chicken in a bowl of flour, coating well.

- In skillet, brown chicken and place in a greased shallow baking pan.

- Combine barbecue sauce and orange juice. Pour over chicken.

- Bake covered at 350° for 45 minutes. Remove from oven and spoon sauce over chicken; bake uncovered another 20 minutes.

 # Company Chicken

2 chickens, quartered
2 (10½ ounce) cans cream
    of mushroom soup
1 pint sour cream
1 cup sherry

- Place chickens in a large shallow baking dish.

- In a saucepan combine soup, sour cream and sherry. Pour mixture over chicken. (You might sprinkle a little paprika on top.)

- Bake covered at 300° for 1 hour and 15 minutes.

Good served over rice.

Sweet 'N Spicy Chicken

1 pound boneless skinless chicken breasts, cut into ½-inch cubes

3 tablespoons taco seasoning

1 (11 ounce) jar chunky salsa

1 cup peach preserves

- Place the chicken in a large resealable plastic bag; add taco seasoning and toss to coat.
- In a skillet, brown the chicken in a little oil.
- Combine salsa and preserves. Stir into the skillet.
- Bring to a boil. Reduce heat and cover and simmer until the juices run clear.

Serve over rice or noodles.

Chicken Broccoli Skillet

3 cups cubed, cooked chicken

1 (16 ounce) package frozen broccoli florets

1 (8 ounce) package Velveeta cheese, cubed

⅔ cup mayonnaise

- In a skillet, combine the chicken, broccoli, cheese and ¼ cup water. Cover and cook over medium heat until broccoli is crisp-tender and cheese is melted.
- Stir in mayonnaise; heat through, but do not boil.

Serve over hot cooked rice.

Tempting Chicken

3 boneless, skinless chicken breasts

3 boneless, skinless chicken thighs

1 (16 ounce) jar tomato-alfredo sauce

1 (10 ounce) can tomato bisque soup

- In a large skillet, brown chicken pieces in a little oil.
- Pour tomato-alfredo sauce, tomato bisque soup and ½ cup water over chicken pieces.
- Cover and simmer about 30 minutes.

Italian Chicken and Rice

3 boneless chicken
breasts, cut into strips

1 (14 ounce) can chicken
broth seasoned with
Italian herbs

¾ cup uncooked rice

¼ cup grated parmesan
cheese

• Cook chicken in a non-stick skillet until brown, stirring often. Remove chicken.

• To the skillet add the broth and rice. Heat to boiling point. Cover and simmer over low heat for 25 minutes (check to see if it needs more water).

• Stir in cheese. Return chicken to pan. Cover and cook for 5 minutes or until done.

Chicken and Sauerkraut

6 large , boneless,
skinless chicken
breasts

1 (16 ounce) can sliced
potatoes, drained

1 (16 ounce) can
sauerkraut, drained

¼ cup pine nuts or ½
teaspoon caraway
seeds

• In a prepared large skillet, season the chicken with black pepper to taste and cook over medium heat until chicken is brown on both sides, about 15 minutes.

• Add potatoes to the skillet. Spoon sauerkraut over the potatoes. Cover and cook over low heat until chicken is done, about 35 minutes. Toast pine nuts in a dry skillet on medium heat, stirring constantly, until golden brown. Sprinkle the chicken and sauerkraut with toasted pine nuts or caraway seeds and serve. *Option: Serve with sour cream.*

Sweet and Sour Chicken

2-3 pounds chicken
  pieces

Oil

1 package dry onion soup
  mix

1 (6 ounce) can frozen
  orange juice
  concentrate, thawed

• In a skillet, brown chicken in a little oil. Place chicken in a 9 x 13-inch baking dish.

• In a small bowl, combine onion soup mix, orange juice and ⅔ cup water, stirring well. Pour over chicken.

• Bake uncovered at 350° for 50 minutes.

Curried Chicken Casserole

1 (10 ounce) box chicken
  flavor Rice a Roni

2 (5 ounce) cans chunk
  white chicken,
  undrained

1 teaspoon curry powder

⅓ cup raisins (optional)

• In a skillet, prepare the Rice a Roni according to the directions on the box.

• Once the Rice a Roni is cooked, add curry powder and chicken plus liquid and raisins; mix well.

• Cover and remove from heat. Let stand 10 minutes and serve.

El Pronto Chicken

4 boneless, skinless
  chicken breasts

1 stick butter, melted

⅔ cup seasoned
  breadcrumbs

½ cup grated parmesan
  cheese

• Dip chicken in the butter.

• Mix together the crumbs, cheese, some garlic powder, salt and pepper.

• Roll chicken in crumb-cheese mixture. Place in a greased 9 x 13-inch baking dish.

• Cover and bake at 350° for 55 minutes. *Serve over a bed of rice.*

E Z Chicken

6-8 boneless, skinless chicken breasts

1 (10½ ounce) can cream of chicken soup

1 (3 ounce) package cream cheese

1 (8 ounce) carton sour cream

- Place chicken breast in a 9 x 13-inch shallow baking dish.
- In saucepan, combine soup, cream cheese, and sour cream. Heat on low just until cream cheese is melted and all three are mixed well.
- Pour mixture over chicken breasts and sprinkle chicken breasts with lemon pepper.
- Cover and bake at 300° for 60 minutes. Uncover and bake another 15 minutes.

Serve over cooked rice.

Turkey Casserole

1 (7 ounce) package herb seasoned stuffing

1 cup whole cranberry sauce

1 (12 ounce) can turkey

1 (10 ounce) can turkey gravy

- Prepare stuffing according to package directions.
- In medium bowl combine the prepared stuffing and cranberry sauce; set aside.
- In a buttered, 2-quart baking dish place the turkey. Pour gravy over the turkey and spoon stuffing mixture over casserole.
- Bake uncovered at 375° for 15 to 20 minutes or until hot and bubbly.

Chicken for Lunch

4 cooked chicken breast slices from deli (thick sliced)

1 (3 ounce) package cream cheese, softened

3 tablespoons salsa

2 tablespoons mayonnaise

• Place chicken slices on serving platter.

• With mixer, cream together the cream cheese, salsa and mayonnaise. Place a heaping tablespoon on top of chicken slices.

Serve cold.

Sesame Chicken

1 stick margarine, melted

¾ tablespoon chili powder

4 skinless, boneless chicken breast halves

1 cup sesame seeds, lightly toasted

• Combine margarine and chili powder. Dip chicken in margarine mixture then roll in the sesame seeds.

• Place in a buttered, 9 x 13- inch baking dish. Bake uncovered at 325° for 1 hour, turning after 30 minutes.

Turkey and Noodles

2½ cups diced cooked turkey

1 (8 ounce) package noodles

1 package chicken gravy, prepared

2 cups Ritz cracker crumbs

• Boil noodles according to directions on package; drain.

• Arrange alternate layers of noodles, turkey and gravy in greased 2-quart baking dish. Cover with crumbs.

• Bake uncovered at 350° for 35 minutes.

Adobe Chicken

2 cups cooked brown rice

1 (10 ounce) can chopped tomatoes and green chilies, drained

3 cups chopped cooked chicken

4 (8 ounce) package shredded monterey jack cheese, divided

- Combine rice, tomatoes and green chilies, chicken and ½ of the jack cheese.
- Spoon into a buttered, 7 x 11-inch baking dish. Cook covered at 325° for 30 minutes.
- Uncover, sprinkle remaining cheese over casserole and return to oven for 5 minutes.

Duck with Cherry Sauce

1 (4-5 pound) domestic duckling

1 (12 ounce) jar cherry preserves

2 tablespoons red wine vinegar

- Prick skin of duckling. Place breast side down on a rack in a shallow roasting pan.
- Bake uncovered at 325° for 2 hours or when a meat thermometer reads 180°. Drain fat from the pan.
- Cover and let stand for 20 minutes before carving.

For the sauce combine, preserves and vinegar in a small saucepan. Heat and stir over medium heat until heated through. Serve with the duck.

Smothered Steak

1 large round steak

1 (10½ ounce) can golden mushroom soup

1 envelope dry onion soup mix

⅔ cup milk

- Cut steak into serving-size pieces and place in a well greased 9 x 13-inch baking pan.
- In a saucepan mix soup, dry onion soup and milk. Heat just enough to be able to mix well. Pour over steak.
- Seal with foil. Bake at 325° for 1 hour.

Steak Bake Italiano

2 pounds lean round steak

2 teaspoons Italian seasoning

1 teaspoon garlic salt

2 (15 ounce) cans stewed tomatoes

- Cut the steak into serving-size pieces and brown in a skillet.
- Place in a 9 x 13-inch baking dish.
- Combine Italian seasoning, garlic salt and stewed tomatoes. Pour over steak pieces.
- Cover and bake at 325° for 1 hour.

Roasted Garlic Steak

2 (15 ounce) cans tomato with roasted garlic and herb soup

½ cup Italian salad dressing

⅓ cup water

1½ pounds (¾-inch) boneless beef sirloin steak

- In saucepan, combine soups, dressing and water.
- Broil steaks to desired doneness; allow 15 minutes for medium. Turn once and brush often with the sauce.
- Heat remaining sauce to serve with steak.

Savory Rib Roast

1 tablespoon dried thyme

1 tablespoon dried, crushed rosemary

1 teaspoon rubbed sage

1 (4-5 pound) rib roast

- In small bowl, combine the thyme, rosemary and sage and rub over roast. Place roast, fat side up.
- On a rack in a large roasting pan. Bake uncovered at 350° for 2-2½ hours or until meat reaches desired doneness.
- Remove roast to a warm serving platter and let stand 10 minutes before slicing.

Southwestern Steak

½ pound tenderized round steak

1 (15 ounce) can Mexican stewed tomatoes

¾ cup picante sauce

2 teaspoons beef bouillon

- Cut beef into serving-size pieces and dredge in flour.
- In a skillet, brown steak in a little oil.
- Mix tomatoes, picante sauce and beef bouillon and pour over steak.
- Cover and bake at 325° for 1 hour.

Baked Onion-Mushroom Steak

1½ pounds round steak, (½ thick)

Salt and pepper

1 (10½ ounce) can cream of mushroom soup

1 envelope dry onion soup mix

- Place steak in a greased 9 x 13-inch baking dish. Sprinkle with salt and pepper.
- Pour mushroom soup and ½ cup water over steak and sprinkle with onion soup mix.
- Cover and bake at 325° for 2 hours.

Red Wine Round Steak

2 pounds (¾-inch thick) round steak

1 package dry onion soup mix

1 cup dry red wine

1 (4 ounce) can sliced mushrooms

- Remove all fat from steak and cut in serving size pieces. Brown meat in skillet with a little oil on both sides. Place steak in a buttered 9 x 13-inch casserole dish.

- In a frying pan combine the onion soup mix, wine, 1 cup hot water and mushrooms. Pour over browned steak.

- Cover and bake for 1 hour 20 minutes or until steak is tender.

Round Steak Simmer

2 pounds (½-inch thick) round steak

Flour, oil

2 (10½ ounce) cans tomato bisque soup

1 onion, thinly sliced

- Cut steak into serving size pieces. Dust with flour and a little salt and pepper. In a skillet brown meat in a little oil.

- Mix onions and soup with 1 can water and add to steak. Bring to boil.

- Turn heat down and simmer for 1 hour 20 minutes.

Casserole Supper

1 pound lean ground beef

¼ cup uncooked white rice

1 (10 ounce) can French onion soup

1 (2.8 ounce) can french-fried onion rings

- Brown ground beef, drain and place in a buttered 7 x 11-inch baking dish.

- Add the rice, onion soup and ½ cup water. Cover and bake at 325° for 40 minutes.

- Uncover and sprinkle onion rings over top; return to oven for 10 minutes.

Pepper Steak

Seasoning salt

1 (1¼ pound) sirloin
steak, cut into strips

1 (16 ounce) package
frozen bell pepper and
onion strips, thawed

1 (1 pound) box Mexican
Velveeta cheese, cubed

• Sprinkle steak with seasoned salt.

• Coat large skillet with non-stick vegetable spray. Cook steak strips about
10 minutes or until no longer pink.
Remove steak from skillet and set aside.

• Stir in vegetables and ½ cup water.
Simmer vegetables about 5 minutes
until all liquid is cooked out.

• Add the Velveeta cheese. Turn heat to
medium low until cheese is melted. Stir
in steak and serve over hot cooked rice.

Beef and Broccoli

1 pound beef sirloin steak

1 onion, chopped

1 (10 ounce) can cream
of broccoli soup

1 (10 ounce) package
frozen chopped
broccoli, thawed

• Slice beef across the grain into very thin
strips. In a large skillet brown steak
strips and onion in a little oil, stirring
several times.

• Reduce heat and simmer 10 minutes.
Stir in soup and broccoli and heat.

• When ready to serve, spoon beef mixture
over hot, cooked noodles.

Beef and Noodles

3 pounds lean beef, cubed

2 (10½ ounce) cans
golden mushroom soup

½ cup cooking sherry

1 package dry onion soup
mix

• Mix all ingredients adding ¾ cup water.
Pour into a 3-quart baking dish.

• Bake at 325° for about 2 hours.

Serve over noodles.

Easy Roast

1 (4 pound) rump roast

1 (10½ ounce) can cream of mushroom soup

1 envelope dry onion soup mix

½ cup white wine

- Place roast in roaster.
- Combine mushroom soup, onion soup mix and white wine and ⅓ cup water. Pour over roast.
- Cover roast with foil and bake at 325° for about 3 to 4 hours.

Supper-Ready Beef

1 (3-4 pound) rump roast

1 (10 ounce) can French onion soup

1 (14 ounce) can beef bouillon

1 teaspoon garlic powder

- Place roast in a roasting pan.
- Pour soup and bouillon over roast and sprinkle with garlic powder.
- Place lid on roasting pan and bake at 350° for 3½ hours.
- Gravy will be in pan.

Rump Roast

1 (3-4 pound) boneless rump roast

4 medium potatoes, peeled, cut into pieces

2 onions, quartered

1 (10½ ounce) can golden mushroom soup

- Place roast in a roaster; season with seasoned salt and pepper, cover.
- Bake at 350° for about 1 hour.
- Uncover; add potatoes and onions. Continue cooking for another hour.
- In a saucepan combine soup and ½ cup water; heat just to be able to pour over roast and vegetables.
- Place roaster back in oven just until soup is hot.

Easy Salisbury Steak

1¼ pounds lean ground beef

½ cup flour

1 egg

1 (10 ounce) can beef gravy

- In a large bowl, combine beef, flour and egg. Add a little seasoned salt and pepper; mix well.
- Shape into 5 patties and place in a shallow 7 x 11-inch baking dish.
- Bake uncovered at 350° for 20 minutes; drain off any fat.
- Pour beef gravy over patties. Bake another 20 minutes.

  Serve with rice or noodles.

Onion-Beef Bake

3 pounds lean ground beef

1 package dry onion soup mix

½ cup water

2 (10½ ounce) cans condensed French onion soup

- Combine beef, soup mix and water. Stir well and shape into patties about ½-inch thick.
- Cook in a large skillet and brown on both sides.
- Move patties to a 9 x 13-inch baking dish. Pour the soup over the patties.
- Cover and bake at 350° for about 35 minutes.

A Wicked Meatloaf

1 (7 ounce) package stuffing mix, plus seasoning packet

1 egg

½ cup salsa

1½ pounds lean ground beef

- In a bowl combine stuffing mix, seasoning, egg, salsa and ⅓ cup water; mix well.
- Add ground beef to the stuffing mixture.
- Spoon into a 9 x 5-inch loaf pan.
- Bake at 350° for 1 hour.

Smothered Beef Steak

2 pounds lean round
  steak

1 cup uncooked rice

1 (14 ounce) can beef
  broth

1 green bell pepper,
  chopped

- Cut steak into serving-size pieces and brown in a very large skillet.

- Add the rice, beef broth, bell peppers and 1 cup water to the skillet. Bring to a boil. Reduce heat and cover; simmer for 1 hour.

Potato-Beef Bake

1 pound ground beef

1 can sloppy joe sauce

1 (10½ ounce) can fiesta
  nacho cheese soup

1 (32 ounce) package
  frozen hash browned
  potatoes, thawed

- In a skillet cook beef over medium heat until no longer pink; drain.

- Add sloppy joe sauce and fiesta nacho cheese soup.

- Place hash browns in a greased 9 x 13-inch baking dish. Top with the beef mixture.

- Cover and bake at 400° for 25 minutes. Uncover and bake 10 minutes longer.

  This is good sprinkled with a cup of grated cheddar cheese.

Smothered Beef Patties

1½ pounds ground beef

½ cup chili sauce

½ cup buttery cracker
  crumbs

1 (14 ounce) can beef
  bouillon

- Combine beef, chili sauce and cracker crumbs and form into 5 or 6 patties. In a skillet, brown patties and pour beef bouillon over patties.

- Bring to a boil. Reduce heat and cover; simmer for about 40 minutes.

Savory Herb Meat Loaf

1 pound ground round
   beef, browned
1 (10½ ounce) can each
   cream of mushroom
   soup and cream of
   celery soup
1 package dry onion soup
   (savory herb with
   garlic) mix
1 cup cooked rice

- Mix all ingredients together.
- Place into a 9 x 13-inch baking dish
  and form a loaf.
- Bake at 350° for 50 minutes.

Mexican Casserole

1 (13 ounce) bag tortilla
   chips, divided
2 pounds lean ground
   beef
1 (10 ounce) can Mexican
   stewed tomatoes
1 (8 ounce) package
   shredded Mexican
   4-cheese blend

- Partially crush ½ bag of chips and place
  in bottom of a buttered 9 x 13-inch
  baking dish.
- Brown ground beef and drain.
- Add stewed tomatoes and the cheese
  and mix well. Sprinkle finely crushed
  chips over top of casserole.
- Bake uncovered at 350° for 40 minutes.

Beef Patties in Creamy Onion Sauce

1½ pounds lean ground
   beef
⅓ cup salsa
⅓ cup butter cracker
   crumbs
1 (10 ounce) can cream of
   onion soup

- Combine beef, salsa and cracker crumbs
  and form into 5-6 patties. Brown in
  skillet and reduce heat.
- Add ¼ cup water and simmer for 15
  minutes. In a saucepan combine onion
  soup and ½ cup water or milk; heat and
  mix.
- Pour over beef patties.   Serve over hot,
  cooked noodles.

Yummy Creamy Pasta Shells

1¼ pounds lean ground beef

1 onion, chopped

1 (10½ ounce) can cream of celery soup

1 package Velveeta shells and cheese

- In a skillet, brown beef and onion, stirring until beef is crumbly.
- Add a little black pepper and garlic salt. Add soup and mix.
- Prepare shells and cheese according to package directions. Stir into beef mixture.
- Simmer about 20 minutes. Serve hot.

Cheesy Beefy Gnocchi

1 pound lean ground beef

1 (10½ ounce) can cheddar cheese soup

1 (10½ ounce) can tomato bisque soup

2 cups uncooked gnocchi or shell pasta

- In skillet cook beef until brown, drain fat.
- Add the soups, 1½ cups water and the pasta. Bring to a boil.
- Cover and cook over medium heat 10 to 12 minutes or until pasta is done, stirring often.

Next-Day Beef

1 (5-6 pound) trimmed beef brisket

1 packet dry onion soup mix

1 (10 ounce) bottle Heinz 57 sauce

1 (12 ounce) bottle barbecue sauce

- Place brisket, cut side up, in a roasting pan.
- In a bowl, combine onion soup mix, Heinz 57 sauce and barbecue sauce. Pour over brisket.
- Cover and cook at 325° for 4-5 hours or until tender. Remove brisket from pan and pour off drippings. Chill both, separately, overnight.
- The next day, trim all the fat from meat, slice and reheat. Skim fat off the drippings and reheat; serve sauce over brisket.

Easy Breezy Brisket

1 (4-5 pound) brisket

1 envelope dry onion soup mix

2 tablespoons worcestershire

1 cup red wine

- Place brisket in a shallow baking pan.
- Sprinkle onion soup over the brisket.
- Pour worcestershire and red wine in the pan.
- Cover and bake at 325° for 5 to 6 hours.

Slow Cookin', Good Tastin' Brisket

½ cup liquid hickory-flavored smoke

1 (4-5 pound) beef brisket

1 (5 ounce) bottle worcestershire

¾ cup barbecue sauce

- Pour liquid smoke over brisket. Cover and refrigerate overnight.
- Drain. Pour worcestershire sauce over brisket.
- Cover and bake at 275° for 6 to 7 hours.
- Cover with barbeque sauce. Bake uncovered for another 30 minutes. Slice very thin across the grain.

Taste of the Irish Corned Beef

1 (4-5 pound) corned beef brisket

4 large potatoes, peeled, quartered

6 carrots, peeled, halved

1 head cabbage

- Place corned beef in roaster, cover with water. Bring to a boil. Turn heat down and simmer 3 hours, adding water if necessary.
- Add potatoes and carrots. Cut cabbage into eighths and lay over top of other vegetables.
- Bring to a boil; turn heat down and cook another 30 to 40 minutes, until vegetables are done. When slightly cool, slice corned beef across the grain.

Bueno Taco Casserole

2 pounds ground beef

1½ cups taco sauce

2 (15 ounce) cans Spanish rice

1 (8 ounce) package shredded Mexican 4-cheese blend, divided

- In skillet, brown ground beef and drain. Add the taco sauce, Spanish rice and ½ of the cheese. Spoon into a buttered 3-quart baking dish.
- Cover and bake at 350° for 35 minutes. Uncover and sprinkle remaining cheese on top and return to oven for 5 minutes.

Sweet Corned Beef

1 (5 pound) corned beef
brisket

Whole cloves

½ cup maple syrup

¼ teaspoon black pepper

- Place corned beef in a casserole with water to cover beef. Bring to boil. Lower the heat and simmer until done, allowing 50 minutes per pound.

- When corned beef has cooked, place on a rack in a shallow pan. Stick the whole cloves in a crosswise design.

- Pour syrup over meat and sprinkle with black pepper.

- Place in oven at 375° to brown and glaze for about 15 minutes. When ready to serve, slice beef across the grain. Serve hot or at room temperature.

Serve with creamed cabbage.

Cheese 'N Wiener Crescents

8 large wieners

4 slices American cheese,
cut into 6 strips each

1 (8 ounce) can
refrigerated crescent
dinner rolls

- Slit wieners to within ½-inch of end; insert 3 strips of cheese in each slit.

- Separate crescent dough into 8 triangles; wrap dough over wiener keeping cheese side up. Place on cookie sheet.

- Bake at 375° for 12 to 15 minutes or until golden brown.

Meat and Potato Stew

2 pounds beef stew meat

2 (15 ounce) cans new
potatoes, drained

1 (15 ounce) can sliced
carrots, drained

1 (10 ounce) can French
onion soup

• In large pot, cook stew meat with about
2 cups water for 1 hour.

• Add the potatoes, carrots and onion
soup and mix. Heat to boiling, reduce
heat and simmer for 30 minutes.

Chihuahua Dogs

1 (10 ounce) can chili hot
dog sauce

1 (10 count) package
frankfurters

10 preformed taco shells

Shredded cheddar cheese

• Put hot dog sauce in a saucepan.

• Place a frank in each taco shell. Top
with the heated chili sauce and cheese;
onions and tomatoes if you like.

• Place in microwave and heat for 30
seconds or until the frankfurters are
warm.

Slow Cook Stew

2 pounds stew meat

1 envelope dry onion
soup mix

2 (10 ounce) cans golden
mushroom soup

1 (8 ounce) carton sour
cream

- Brown stew meat in a roasting pan.
- Combine soup mix, soup and 2 cans water. Pour over stew meat. Cover tightly.
- Bake at 275° for 6-8 hours. When ready to serve, stir in sour cream. Return mixture to oven until heated thoroughly. Serve over noodles.

This will be great in a slow cooker while you are at work or overnight while you sleep.

Texas Chili Pie

2 (20 ounce) cans chili
without beans

1 (16 ounce) package
small corn chips

1 onion, chopped

1 (16 ounce) package
shredded cheddar
cheese

- Heat chili in saucepan.
- In 9 x 13-inch baking dish, layer the corn chips, chili, onion and cheese ⅓ at a time. Repeat layers with cheese on top.
- Bake at 325° for 20 minutes or until cheese bubbles.

"Giddy-Up" Pork Chops

6 boneless pork chops

½ cup salsa

½ cup honey or packed brown sugar

1 teaspoon soy sauce

- Brown pork chops in an oven-proof pan.
- Combine salsa, honey or brown sugar and soy sauce and heat for 20-30 seconds in microwave oven. Pour salsa mixture over pork chops, cover and bake at 325° for about 45 minutes or until pork chops are tender.

Variation: ¼ teaspoon crushed red pepper flakes

Pork Chops in Cream Gravy

4 (¼-inch thick) pork chops

Flour

Oil

2¼ cups whole milk

- Dip chops in flour with a little salt and pepper. Brown pork chops on both sides in a little oil. Remove chops from skillet.
- Add about 2 tablespoons flour to skillet and brown lightly; stir in a little salt and pepper. Slowly stir in milk to make gravy. Return chops to skillet with the gravy.
- Cover and simmer on low burner for about 40 minutes.

Serve over rice or noodles.

Pork-Potato Chop

6 boneless or loin pork chops, seasoned with salt and pepper

1 (14 ounce) can chicken broth

2 (1 ounce) packages dry onion gravy mix

4 red potatoes, sliced

- Brown pork chops a large skillet.
- Combine chicken broth and gravy mix. Place potatoes with pork chops and pour the gravy mixture over the pork chops and potatoes.
- Heat to boiling, cover and simmer about 45 minutes or until the pork chops and potatoes are fork-tender.

Cranberries and Pork Chops

6-8 thick pork chops

Flour

2 cups fresh or frozen
  cranberries

1 cup sugar

- Coat the pork chops in flour; brown in a small amount of oil in skillet. Place in a shallow baking dish.
- Add the cranberries, sugar and ½ cup water.
- Cover. Bake at 350° for 30 minutes. Uncover and continue baking for another 30 minutes.

Mexicali Pork Chops

1 envelope taco seasoning

4 (½-inch thick) boneless
  pork loin chops

1 tablespoon oil

Salsa

- Rub taco seasoning over pork chops.
- In a skillet, brown pork chops in oil over medium heat.
- Add 2 tablespoons water; turn heat to low and simmer pork chops about 40 minutes. Check to see if a little more water is needed.
- Spoon salsa over pork chops to serve.

Chops and Stuffing

1 (6 ounce) box savory
  herb stuffing mix

6 center-cut pork chops

Oil

3 onions, halved

- Make stuffing according to package directions and set aside.
- Fry pork chops in skillet with a little oil. Brown chops on both sides and place in a greased 9 x 13-inch baking dish.
- Divide stuffing and onions among pork chops and mound on top of each.
- Cover and bake at 350° for about 30 minutes.

Apple-Pork Chops

4 butterflied pork chops

2 apples, peeled and cored

2 teaspoons margarine

2 tablespoons brown
   sugar

- Place pork chops in a non-stick sprayed shallow baking dish. Season with salt and pepper.
- Cover and bake at 350° for 30 minutes. Uncover, and place apple halves on top of pork chops. Add a little butter and a little brown sugar on each of these apples.
- Bake for another 15 minutes.

Pork Chops, Potatoes and Green Beans

6-8 boneless or loin pork
   chops

2 (1 ounce) packets gravy
   mix or 2 (12 ounce) jars
   prepared gravy

2 (15 ounce) cans white
   potatoes, drained

2 (15 ounce) cans cut
   green beans, drained

- Season pork chops with salt and pepper if desired. Brown pork chops in large, non-stick Dutch oven.
- Mix the gravy with water as directed or pour the prepared gravy over the pork chops. Cover and simmer for 30 minutes.
- Add the potatoes and green beans and simmer about 10 minutes or until the pork chops are tender and the green beans and potatoes are heated through.

Baked Pork Chops

¾ cup ketchup

¾ cup packed brown
   sugar

¼ cup lemon juice

4 butterflied pork chops

- Combine ketchup, ½ cup water, brown sugar and lemon juice.
- Place pork chops in a 7 x 11-inch buttered baking dish and pour sauce over pork chops.
- Bake covered at 325° for 50 minutes.

Spicy Pork Chops

4-6 pork chops

1 large onion

1 bell pepper

1 (10 ounce) can diced tomatoes and green chilies

• Brown pork chops in a skillet with a little oil.

• Spray casserole dish with non-stick spray. Place chops in dish.

• Cut onion and bell pepper into large chunks and place on chops. Pour tomato and green chilies over chops; sprinkle 1 teaspoon salt over casserole.

• Bake covered at 350° for 45 minutes.

Pork Chop Dinner

4 medium potatoes, peeled

2 large onions, sliced

4-6 medium thick pork chops

Milk

• Peel and thinly slice potatoes and onions.

• Place a layer of potatoes in the bottom of a 9 x 13-inch baking dish, sprinkle with salt and pepper. Place a layer of onions in dish and sprinkle with salt and pepper.

• Arrange pork chops on top, sprinkle with salt and pepper.

• Carefully pour the milk into dish until it is about ½-inch deep. Cover dish with foil sealing around edges.

• Bake covered at 325° for 1 hour. Uncover and bake 15 minutes more to brown chops.

Sweet and Sour Spareribs

4 pounds pork spareribs

1 (6 ounce) can lemonade concentrate

½ teaspoon garlic salt

⅓ cup soy sauce

- Place ribs, meaty side down in a shallow roasting pan. Cook covered at 350° for 40 minutes.
- Remove cover, drain fat and return ribs to oven. Bake 30 minutes more. Drain fat again.
- Combine remaining ingredients and brush on ribs.
- Reduce temperature to 325°. Cover and bake for 1 more hour or until tender, brushing occasionally with sauce.

Saucy Pork Chops

4 (½-inch thick) pork chops

1 tablespoon oil

1 can cream of onion soup

2 tablespoons soy sauce

- In skillet, brown pork chops in oil and cook about 15 minutes; drain.
- Add soup and soy sauce. Heat to a boil.
- Return chops to pan. Reduce heat to low. Cover and simmer about 20 minutes.

Honey Ham Slice

⅓ cup orange juice

⅓ cup honey

1 teaspoon prepared mustard

1 (1-inch thick) slice fully cooked ham

- Combine orange juice, honey and mustard in a saucepan and cook slowly for 10 minutes, stirring occasionally.
- Place ham in a broiling pan about 3 inches from heat. Brush with orange glaze.
- Broil 8 minutes on first side. Turn ham slice over. Brush with glaze again and broil another 6 to 8 minutes.

Cran-Apple Ham

1 cup apple juice, divided

1 tablespoon cornstarch

1 cup whole cranberry sauce

1 center-cut ham slice or 1 (2-3 pound) smoked, boneless ham

- In a medium saucepan over low heat, pour in ¼ cup apple juice and cornstarch and stir until the cornstarch is smooth. Add the remaining apple juice. Using medium heat, bring to a boil and cook, stirring constantly, until the mixture clears and has thickened.

- Stir in the cranberry sauce and heat 2-3 minutes.

- Place the ham slice in a shallow baking pan. Spread sauce over the ham slice and bake at 350° about 20-30 minutes, basting the ham with the sauce 2-3 times.

- Serve warmed sauce with the ham. (If you use the boneless ham in this recipe, cook 45-60 minutes longer.)

Optional: Add ½ teaspoon lemon juice, pinch of ground cinnamon or dash of ground cloves.

Orange Pork Chops

6-8 medium thick pork chops

½ stick margarine

2¼ cups orange juice

2 tablespoons orange marmalade

- Brown both sides of pork chops in margarine in hot skillet adding salt and pepper.

- Pour orange juice over chops. Cover and simmer until done about one hour but time will vary with the thickness of the pork chops. Add more orange juice if necessary.

- During the last few minutes of cooking add the 2 tablespoons of orange marmalade.

This makes a delicious gravy to serve over rice.

Pork Chop and Fried Rice

4-6 boneless pork chops

1 (11 ounce) can fried rice

⅓ cup frozen peas

3 green onions with tops, sliced

• Dry pork chops and brown over medium heat in a preheated, prepared large skillet. Add ¼ cup water and simmer until tender, adding water if needed.

• Remove the pork chops from the skillet and keep warm.

• In a medium bowl, mix the fried rice and ½ cup water. Add the fried rice to the skillet and heat for 10 minutes.

• Add the peas and green onions to rice and cook an additional 5 minutes or until peas are crisp-tender.

• Serve the pork chops with the fried rice.

Hawaiian Pork

2 pound lean pork tenderloin, cut in 1-inch cubes

1 (15 ounce) can pineapple chunks, undrained

1 (12 ounce) bottle chili sauce

1 teaspoon ground ginger

• In skillet, season pork cubes with salt and pepper.

• Combine meat, pineapple with juice, chili sauce and ginger.

• Simmer covered for 1½ hours.

Serve over rice.

Ham and Sweet Potatoes

3 tablespoons dijon-style mustard, divided

1 (3-4 pound) boneless smoked ham

½ cup honey or packed brown sugar

1 (29 ounce) can sweet potatoes, drained or 4 cooked sweet potatoes, quartered

- Preheat oven at 325°. Spread 2 tablespoons mustard on the ham. Place ham in prepared shallow baking pan and bake for 20 minutes.

- Combine the remaining mustard with the brown sugar or honey and spread over the ham.

- Add the sweet potatoes, baste with the sauce and bake for 20 minutes.

Mustard Ham

1 (1-inch) slice cooked ham

2 teaspoons dry mustard

⅓ cup honey

⅓ cup cooking wine

- Rub ham slice with the dry mustard, using 1 teaspoon mustard for each side. Place in a shallow baking pan.

- Combine honey and wine; pour over ham.

- Bake uncovered at 350° for about 35 minutes.

Supper in a Dish

2 bags instant rice in a bag

1½ cups cubed, cooked ham

1½ cups shredded cheddar cheese

1 (8 ounce) can green peas

- Prepare rice according to directions on package.

- In a large bowl, combine rice, ham, cheese and peas.

- Pour into a 3-quart baking dish and bake at 350° for 15 to 20 minutes.

Ham and Veggies

2 (15 ounce) packages
mixed vegetables

1 (10½ ounce) can cream
of celery soup

2 cups cubed, cooked
ham

½ teaspoon dried basil

- Cook vegetables as directed on package.
- Add soup, ham and basil.
- Cook until thoroughly heated. Serve hot.

Cranberry Sauce

1 (14 ounce) carton
strawberry glaze

1 (12 ounce) package
frozen cranberries

½ cup orange juice

Sugar

- In saucepan combine the glaze, cranberries and juice. Heat to boiling.
- Reduce heat and simmer 10 minutes or until cranberries pop, stirring often.
- Refrigerate several hours before serving.
- Cool and taste. Add sugar if necessary.
  Serve with pork or ham.

Peach-Pineapple Baked Ham

3-4 pound boneless
smoked ham

4 tablespoons dijon-style
mustard, divided

1 cup peach preserves

1 cup pineapple
preserves

- Preheat oven to 325°. Spread 2 tablespoons mustard on the ham.
- Place ham in a prepared, shallow baking pan and bake for 20 minutes.
- Combine the remaining 2 tablespoons mustard and both preserves and heat in the microwave oven for 20 seconds (or in a small saucepan at low heat for 2-3 minutes).
- Pour over the ham and bake for about 15 minutes.

Ham Patties

2 cups ground ham

2 eggs, slightly beaten

1 cup cracker crumbs

- Combine ham, eggs, cracker crumbs and a little pepper. Shape into patties.
- Place a little oil in a heavy skillet and saute patties until golden brown.

This is a great way to use leftover ham.

Spunky Spareribs

5-6 pounds spareribs

1 (6 ounce) can frozen orange juice, undiluted

2 teaspoons worcestershire sauce

½ teaspoon garlic powder

- Place spareribs in a shallow baking pan, meaty side down. Sprinkle with a little salt and pepper.
- Roast at 375° for 30 minutes.
- Turn ribs and roast another 30 minutes. Drain off fat.
- Combine remaining ingredients and brush the mixture on ribs.
- Reduce heat to 300°. Cover ribs and roast 2 hours or until tender, basting occasionally.

Orange Spareribs

4-5 pounds pork spareribs

1 (6 ounce) can orange juice concentrate, thawed

½ teaspoon garlic salt

⅔ cup honey

- Place ribs, meaty side down in a shallow roasting pan. Bake at 350° for 30 minutes. Drain off fat and turn ribs. Bake 30 minutes more.
- Combine remaining ingredients and brush on ribs. Reduce temperature to 325°. Cover pan and bake 1½ hours or until tender, brushing with sauce several times.

Barbecued Spare Ribs

3-4 pounds pork spareribs or country-style pork ribs, trimmed

1 cup hot ketchup or chili sauce

½ cup honey or packed brown sugar

1 teaspoon liquid smoke

- Place spareribs on a prepared broiler pan and bake at 350° for 1½ hours.
- Combine ketchup, honey or brown sugar and liquid smoke in a small saucepan and simmer for 2-3 minutes.
- Baste the spareribs on both sides generously with the ketchup mixture.
- Bake spareribs an additional 1½ hours or until tender, basting generously every 15-20 minutes.

German-Style Ribs and Kraut

3-4 pounds baby-back pork ribs or country-style pork ribs, trimmed

3 potatoes, peeled, cubed or sliced

1 (32 ounce) jar refrigerated sauerkraut, drained

¼ cup pine nuts, toasted

- In a prepared Dutch oven, brown ribs on all sides. Pepper ribs to taste and add 1 cup water.
- Bring to a boil, turn down heat and simmer about 2 hours until ribs are very tender.
- Add potatoes and cook on low heat for 20 minutes. Add jar of sauerkraut and continue cooking until potatoes are done.
- Sprinkle pine nuts or caraway seeds on the ribs and kraut immediately before serving.

Tequila Baby Back Ribs

4 pounds baby back pork ribs

1 (12 ounce) bottle tequila lime marinade, divided

Black pepper

- Cut ribs in lengths to fit in large, resealable plastic bag.

- Place ribs in bag and add ¾ cup marinade; seal bag and shake to coat. Marinate in refrigerator overnight. Place ribs in a shallow baking dish coated with non-stick vegetable spray; discard used marinade.

- Cover ribs with foil and bake at 375° for 30 minutes.

- Remove from oven and spread a little of the extra marinade over ribs. Lower heat to 300° and cook for 1 hour.

- Uncover to let ribs brown; bake 30 minutes longer.

Plum Peachy Pork Roast

1 (4-5 pound) boneless pork loin roast

1 (12 ounce) jar plum jelly

½ cup peach preserves

½ teaspoon ginger

- Place roast in a shallow baking pan and bake at 325° for about 35 minutes. Turn roast to brown the other side and bake another 35 minutes.

- In a saucepan heat the jelly, peach preserves and ginger.

- When roast is finished cooking brush roast generously with preserve mixture.

- Bake and baste another 15 minutes.

Pork Tenderloin

3 pounds pork tenderloin

1 (15 ounce) can stewed tomatoes

1 package savory herb with garlic soup mix

2 tablespoons worcestershire sauce

• Place tenderloin strips in roaster.

• Mix remaining ingredients; spread over meat.

• Bake covered at 325° for 1 hour and 20 minutes.

Tenderloin With Apricot Sauce

3 pounds pork tenderloin

1 cup apricot preserves

⅓ cup lemon juice, ⅓ cup ketchup

1 tablespoon soy sauce

• Place tenderloins in roaster.

• Combine preserves, lemon juice, ketchup and soy sauce.

• Pour over pork and bake covered at 325° for one hour and 20 minutes. Baste once during cooking.

Serve over white rice.

Pork Picante

1 pound pork tenderloin, cubed

2 tablespoons taco seasoning

1 cup chunky salsa

⅓ cup peach preserves

• Toss pork with the taco seasoning and brown with a little oil in a skillet.

• Stir in salsa and preserves. Bring to a boil.

• Lower heat and simmer 30 minutes.

Pour over hot cooked rice.

Apple-Topped Tenderloin

1½ cups hickory
marinade, divided

1 (3-4 pound) pork
tenderloin

1 (20 ounce) can apple pie
filling

¾ teaspoon cinnamon

- In a baggie combine 1 cup marinade and tenderloin; seal bag. Marinade in refrigerator for at least 1 hour.

- Remove tenderloin; discard used marinade.

- Cook tenderloin uncovered at 325° for 1 hour, basting twice with ¼ cup of the marinade. Let stand 10 or 15 minutes before slicing. In a saucepan combine pie filling, the extra ¼ cup marinade and cinnamon; heat.

Serve heated apples over sliced tenderloin.

Italian Sausage and Ravioli

1 pound sweet Italian
pork sausage, casing
removed

1 (1 pound, 10 ounce) jar
extra chunky
mushroom and green
pepper spaghetti sauce

1 (24 ounce) package
frozen cheese-filled
ravioli, cooked, drained

Grated parmesan cheese

- In a roaster pan, over medium heat, cook sausage as directed on package or until browned and no longer pink, stirring to separate meat.

- Stir in spaghetti sauce. Heat to boiling.

- Add ravioli. Heat through, stirring occasionally.

- Pour into serving dish and sprinkle with parmesan cheese.

Sausage Casserole

1 pound pork sausage

2 (15 ounce) cans pork and beans

1 (15 ounce) can Mexican style stewed tomatoes

1 package corn muffin mix

- Brown sausage and drain fat.

- Add beans and tomatoes and blend. Bring to a boil. Pour into a 3-quart greased casserole.

- Prepare muffin mix according to package. Drop by spoonfuls over meat and bean mixture.

- Bake at 400° for 30 minutes or until top is browned.

Tangy Pork Chops

4-6 pork chops

¼ cup worcestershire sauce

¼ cup ketchup

½ cup honey

- In skillet, brown pork chops. Place in a shallow baking dish.

- Combine worcestershire, ketchup and honey. Pour over pork chops.

- Cover and bake at 325° for 45 minutes.

Sweet and Savory Pork Chops

6-8 (¾-1-inch thick) boneless pork chops, trimmed

½ cup grape, apple or plum jelly

½ cup chili sauce or hot ketchup

Soy sauce

- Brown pork chops and season to taste with salt and pepper. Transfer browned pork chops to a shallow baking dish, place in oven and bake at 325° for 30 minutes.

- Combine jelly and chili sauce or ketchup and spread over the pork chops. Cook for 15 minutes, baste with the sauce and cook 15 minutes more or until pork chops are tender. Serve with soy sauce.

Shrimp Newburg

1 (10½ ounce) can condensed cream of shrimp soup

¼ cup water

1 teaspoon seafood seasoning

1 (1 pound) package frozen cooked salad shrimp, thawed

- In a saucepan, combine soup, water and seafood seasoning. Bring to a boil.
- Reduce heat and stir in shrimp. Heat thoroughly.

Serve over hot white rice.

Broiled Lemon-Garlic Shrimp

1 pound shrimp, peeled and deveined

1 teaspoon garlic salt

2 tablespoons lemon juice

2 tablespoons butter

- Place shrimp in a shallow baking pan.
- Sprinkle with garlic salt and lemon juice; dot with butter.
- Broil on one side for 3 minutes. Turn and broil 3 minutes more.

If the shrimp are large, split them down the middle and spread them out like a butterfly, then season.

Skillet Shrimp

2 teaspoons olive oil

2 pounds uncooked shrimp, peeled and deveined

⅔ cup herb and garlic marinade with lemon juice

¼ cup finely chopped green onion with tops

- In large nonstick skillet, heat oil. Add shrimp and marinade.
- Cook, stirring often until shrimp turns pink. Stir in green onions.

Serve over hot, cooked rice or your favorite pasta.

Beer-Batter Shrimp

1 (12 ounce) can beer

1 cup flour

2 teaspoons garlic powder

1 pound shrimp, peeled, veined

- Make batter by mixing beer, flour and garlic powder and stir to a creamy consistency.
- Dip shrimp into batter to cover and deep fry in hot oil.

Boiled Shrimp

3 pounds fresh shrimp

1 teaspoon salt

2 teaspoons seafood seasoning

½ cup vinegar

- Remove heads from shrimp.
- Place shrimp, salt, seasoning and vinegar in large saucepan. Cover shrimp with water and bring to boil.
- Reduce heat and boil for 10 minutes. Remove from heat and drain. Chill in refrigerator.

Creamed Shrimp Over Rice

3 cans frozen cream of shrimp soup

1 pint sour cream

1½ teaspoon curry powder

2 (5 ounce) cans deveined shrimp

- Combine all ingredients in top of double boiler.
- Heat, stirring constantly, but do not boil.

  Serve over hot, cooked rice.

Crab Mornay

2 (6 ounce) cans crabmeat, drained, flaked

1 cup cream of mushroom soup

½ cup shredded swiss cheese

½ cup seasoned breadcrumbs

- Preheat oven to 350°.
- Combine crabmeat, soup and cheese.
- Pour into a prepared 1½-quart casserole dish and sprinkle with breadcrumbs.
- Bake uncovered for 30 minutes or until soup is bubbling and breadcrumbs are lightly browned.

Shrimp Supper

1½ pounds cooked and peeled shrimp

1 small head lettuce, chopped

1 (14 ounce) jar artichokes, quartered, drained

1 avocado, sliced

- Combine all ingredients and serve with a creamy ranch dressing.

Seafood Delight

1 (6 ounce) can shrimp, drained

1 (6 ounce) can crabmeat, drained, flaked

1 (10 ounce) can corn or potato chowder

2-3 cups seasoned breadcrumbs, divided

- Preheat the oven to 350°. Mix the shrimp, crabmeat, chowder and ⅓ cup breadcrumbs.
- Place in a prepared 1½-quart casserole dish. Sprinkle with the remaining breadcrumbs.
- Bake for 30 minutes or until the casserole is bubbling and the breadcrumbs are lightly browned.

Curried Red Snapper

1½ pounds fresh red snapper

2 medium onions, chopped

2 celery ribs, chopped

1 teaspoon curry powder

¼ cup milk

- Place snapper in a greased 9 x 13-inch baking pan.
- In skillet, saute onions and celery in a little margarine. Add curry powder and a little salt, mixing well. Remove from heat; stir in milk. Spoon over snapper.
- Bake, uncovered, at 350° for 25 minutes or until fish flakes easily with a fork.

Tuna-Asparagus Pot Pie

1 (8 ounce) package crescent rolls, divided

1 (6 ounce) can solid white tuna in water, drained, flaked

1 (15 ounce) can cut asparagus, drained

1 cup shredded cheddar cheese

- Preheat oven to 375°. Form a 7-inch square using 4 crescent rolls. Pinch edges together to seal.
- Place in an 8 x 8 x 2-inch square, prepared baking pan. Spread the tuna, then the asparagus, followed by the shredded cheese.
- Form the remaining 4 crescent rolls into a square. Place on the top of the cheese. Bake about 20 minutes or until the top is golden brown and the cheese is bubbling.

Tuna Toast

1 (10½ ounce) can cream of chicken soup

1 (6 ounce) can tuna in water, drained

2 slices thick Texas toast

1 tomato, cut into chunks

- In saucepan, combine soup and tuna; stirring to break up chunks of tuna.
- Toast the Texas toast on both sides. Pour soup mixture over toast.
- Sprinkle tomatoes over soup mixture. Serve immediately.

Tuna Noodles

1 (8 ounce) package wide noodles, cooked, drained

2 (6 ounce) cans white tuna, drained

1 (10 ounce) can cream of chicken soup, ¾ cup milk

¾ cup chopped black olives

- Place half the noodles in a 2-quart buttered casserole.
- In saucepan, combine the tuna, soup, milk and olives. Heat just enough to mix well.
- Pour half the soup mixture over noodles. Repeat layers.
- Cover and bake at 300° for about 20 minutes.

Home Fried Fish

1½ pounds haddock, sole or cod

1 egg beaten

2 tablespoons milk

2 cups corn flake crumbs

- Cut fish into serving-size pieces.
- Combine egg and milk. Dip fish in egg mixture and coat with the crushed corn flakes on both sides.
- Fry in a thin layer of oil in a skillet until brown on both sides.

 # Crispy Flounder

⅓ cup mayonnaise

1 pound flounder fillets

1 cup seasoned breadcrumbs

¼ cup grated parmesan cheese

- Place mayonnaise in a small dish. Coat the fish with mayonnaise and dip in crumbs to coat well.
- Arrange in a shallow baking dish. Bake uncovered at 375° for 25 minutes.

Haddock Fillets

1½ cups lemon lime soda

1 pound haddock fillets

2 cups pancake mix

¼ teaspoon pepper

- Pour soda in a shallow bowl; add fillets and let marinate for 15 minutes.

- In another shallow bowl combine pancake mix and pepper.

- Remove fish from soda and coat with pancake mix.

- In a large skillet heat about ¼-inch of oil. Fry fish for about 3 minutes on each side until fish flakes with a fork. Drain on paper towels.

Chips and Fish

1 cup mayonnaise

2 tablespoons fresh lime juice and lime wedges

3-4 fish fillets, rinsed, dried

1½ cups crushed corn chips

- Preheat oven to 425°. Mix mayonnaise and lime juice. Spread on both sides of the fish fillets.

- Place the crushed corn chips on wax paper and dredge both sides of the fish in the chips. Shake off the excess chips.

- Place the fillets on a foil-covered baking sheet and bake for 15 minutes or until the fish flakes. Serve with lime wedges.

Red Fish Barbecue

2 pounds red fish fillets

1 (8 ounce) bottle Italian dressing

1 (12 ounce) can beer

Several dashes of Tabasco

- Place fish in a glass casserole dish. Pour Italian dressing, beer and Tabasco over fish.

- Cover and marinate in refrigerator at least two hours. When ready to cook, drain the fish and place in a microwave safe container.

- Microwave fish about 4 to 5 minutes per pound.

Orange Roughy With Peppers

1½ pounds orange roughy

2 red bell peppers, cut into julienne strips

1 teaspoon dried thyme leaves

¾ teaspoon seasoned salt

- Cut fish into serving size pieces.
- Heat a little oil in a skillet. Layer the bell pepper and seasoning. Place fish on top.
- Turn burner on high until fish is hot enough to begin cooking.
- Lower heat, cover and cook fish for 15 to 20 minutes or until fish flakes easily.

Baked Halibut

2 pounds halibut steaks (1 inch thick)

1 (8 ounce) carton sour cream

½ cup grated parmesan cheese

¾ teaspoon dill weed

- Place halibut in a greased 9 x 13-inch baking dish.
- Combine the sour cream, parmesan cheese and dill weed; salt and pepper if desired. Spoon over halibut.
- Cover and bake at 325° for 20 minutes.
- Uncover and sprinkle with paprika. Bake another 10 minutes longer or until fish flakes easily with a fork.

Broiled Salmon Steaks

4 (1-inch thick) salmon steaks

Garlic salt

Worcestershire

¼-½ cup melted butter

- Place salmon steaks on baking sheet and sprinkle both sides with garlic salt.
- Splash worcestershire and butter on top of each steak and broil for 2-3 minutes.
- Remove from oven and turn each steak. Splash worcestershire and butter on top and broil for 2-3 minutes. (Do not overcook. Fish will flake, but should not be dry inside.)
- Top with a little melted butter before just before serving.

Crab-Potato Salad

5 potatoes, peeled and cubed

2 (8 ounce) packages imitation crabmeat, chopped

1 cup finely chopped onion

2 cups mayonnaise

- Place potatoes in a saucepan covered with water; bring to a boil and cook for about 20 minutes or until tender. Drain and cool.
- In a large bowl combine the potatoes, crab, onion, salt and pepper. Toss with the mayonnaise.
- Refrigerate for about 3 hours before serving.

Baked Oysters

1 cup oysters, drained, rinsed

2 cups cracker crumbs

½ stick margarine, melted

½ cup milk

- Make alternate layers of oysters, cracker crumbs and margarine in a 7 x 11-inch baking dish.
- Pour warmed milk over layers adding lots of salt and pepper.
- Bake at 350° for about 35 minutes.

Butter Fish

Cod or flounder fillets

1 stick butter

Lemon juice

- Place butter in a shallow baking dish in a very hot oven until butter is melted and slightly browned.
- Place filets in hot butter and cook 10 minutes at 400°.
- Turn and baste with pan juices. Sprinkle fish with lemon juice and a little salt and pepper.
- Bake another 10 minutes or until fish flakes easily.

Salmon Patties

1 (15 ounce) can pink
  salmon, reserve juice

1 egg

½ cup cracker crumbs

1 teaspoon baking
  powder

- Pour off juice from salmon and set aside. Remove the bones and skin.

- Stir in egg and cracker crumbs with salmon.

- In a small bowl add baking powder to ¼ cup of salmon juice. Mixture will foam. After foaming add to salmon mixture.

- Drop by teaspoons in hot oil in skillet. Brown lightly on both sides. Serve hot.

Lemon Baked Fish

1 pound sole or halibut
  fillets

¼ stick margarine

1 teaspoon dried tarragon

2 tablespoons lemon
  juice

- Place fish fillets in a greased, shallow pan. Sprinkle with salt, pepper and a little of the margarine.

- Bake at 375° for about 8-10 minutes. Turn and bake another 6 minutes or until fish is flaky.

- Melt margarine with the tarragon and lemon juice. Serve over warm fish fillets.

DESSERTS

Caramel-Cinnamon Dessert

1 (5 ounce) package
   French vanilla instant
   pudding

3 cups milk

1 (8 ounce) carton
   whipped topping

1 box cinnamon graham
   crackers

- Combine the pudding and milk, mixing well. Fold in whipped topping.
- Line bottom of a 9 x 13-inch glass dish with whole graham crackers.
- Put half the pudding mixture over crackers and top with a second layer of crackers. Spread remaining pudding over top. Top with the remaining crackers (you should have 2 or 3 crackers left over from the box).
- Add a prepared caramel icing over the last layer of graham crackers. Refrigerate.

  Make this a day ahead of time so the pudding can soak into the crackers.

Macaroon Delight

12 soft coconut
   macaroons

1 (8 ounce) carton
   whipping cream,
   whipped

3 pints sherbet: 1 each,
   orange, lime, raspberry,
   softened

- Warm macaroons in a 300° oven for 10 minutes. Then break into pieces and cool.
- Spoon macaroons into the whipped cream.
- Completely line a 9 x 5-inch loaf pan with foil. First spread 1 pint of the orange sherbet in loaf pan.
- Then spread ½ of the whipped cream mixture, next the lime sherbet and the remaining whipped cream mixture. Raspberry sherbet will be on top.
- Freeze overnight. To serve unmold and remove foil and slice.

Caramel-Apple Delight

3 (2.07 ounce) Snickers candy bars, frozen

2 Granny Smith apples, chopped

1 (12 ounce) carton whipped topping

1 (3 ounce) package dry instant vanilla pudding

- Smash frozen candy bars in the wrappers with a hammer.
- Mix all ingredients together.
- Refrigerate.

Place in a pretty crystal bowl or serve in individual sherbet glasses.

Coffee Mallow

3 cups miniature marshmallows

½ cup hot, strong coffee

1 cup whipping cream, whipped

½ teaspoon vanilla

- In large saucepan, combine marshmallows and coffee. On low heat and stirring constantly, cook until marshmallows have melted. Cool this mixture.
- Fold in whipped cream and vanilla.
- Pour into individual dessert glasses. Stir until ready to serve.

Grape Fluff

1 cup grape juice

2 cups miniature marshmallows

2 tablespoons lemon juice

1 (8 ounce) carton whipping cream

- In saucepan heat grape juice to boiling. Add marshmallows. Stir constantly until melted.
- Add lemon juice and cool.
- Fold in whipped cream and spoon into individual serving dishes. Refrigerate.

Ice Cream Dessert

19 ice cream sandwiches

1 (12 ounce) carton whipped topping, thawed

1 (11¾ ounce) jar hot fudge ice cream topping

1 cup salted peanuts

- Cut one ice cream sandwich in half. Place one whole and one half sandwich along a short side of an ungreased 9 x 13-inch pan. Arrange eight sandwiches in opposite direction in the pan.
- Spread with half of the whipped topping.
- Spoon fudge topping by teaspoonfuls onto whipped topping.
- Sprinkle with ½ cup peanuts.
- Repeat layers with remaining ice cream sandwiches, whipped topping and peanuts (pan will be full). Cover and freeze.

To serve, take out of freezer 20 minutes before serving.

Lemon Treat

1 (3 ounce) package lemon pie filling mix (not instant)

⅓ cup sugar

1 egg

½ (8 ounce) carton whipped topping

- Mix pie filling, sugar and egg with ¼ cup water until smooth. Slowly add another 1¾ cup water.
- Cook, stirring constantly, over medium heat until mixture comes to a full boil. Remove from heat and cool completely.
- Fold in whipped topping and spoon into dessert dishes.

Top with a fresh strawberry or a slice of kiwi.

Apricot Pudding

1 (3.4 ounce) package vanilla pudding (not instant)

1 (15 ounce) can apricots, halved, reserve juice

1 (11 ounce) can mandarin oranges, drained

1 (8 ounce) carton whipped topping

- Cook pudding with 1¼ cups apricot juice (adding water to make the 1¼ cups). Cool.
- Add drained oranges and cut-up apricots. Refrigerate until mixture begins to thicken.
- Fold in whipped topping. Spoon into 6 individual sherbet dishes.

Peachy Sundaes

1 pint vanilla ice cream

¾ cup peach preserves, warmed

¼ cup chopped almonds, toasted

¼ cup coconut

- Divide ice cream into 4 sherbet dishes.
- Top with preserves.
- Sprinkle with almonds and coconut.

Mango Cream

2 soft mangoes

½ gallon vanilla ice cream, softened

1 (6 ounce) can frozen lemonade, thawed

1 (8 ounce) carton whipped topping

- Peel the mangoes and cut slices around the seed; then cut into small chunks.
- In a large bowl, mix together the ice cream, lemonade and whipped topping.
- Fold in the mango chunks.
- Quickly spoon mixture into parfait glasses or sherbets; cover with plastic wrap. Place in freezer.

Divinity Heaven

1 pint marshmallow
  cream
3 cups sugar
Pinch salt
⅔ cup chopped pecans

- Put marshmallow cream in a large bowl.
- In saucepan combine ½ cup water with sugar and salt. Bring to a rolling boil and boil exactly 2 minutes.
- Pour the sugar mixture into the marshmallow cream. Stir quickly.
- Add pecans and drop by teaspoonfuls onto wax paper.

Cookies and Cream

25 Oreo cookies, crushed
½ gallon vanilla ice
  cream, softened
1 (5 ounce) can chocolate
  syrup
1 (12 ounce) carton
  whipped topping

- Press crushed cookies in a 9 x 13-inch baking dish. Spread ice cream over cookies.
- Pour syrup over the ice cream and top with the whipped topping.
- Freeze overnight.
- Slice into squares to serve.

Peanut Butter Sundae

1 cup light corn syrup
1 cup chunky peanut
  butter
¼ cup milk
Ice cream or pound cake

- In a mixing bowl, stir together the corn syrup, peanut butter and milk until well blended.
- Serve over ice cream or pound cake. Store in refrigerator.

Strawberry Trifle

1 (5 ounce) package
French vanilla instant
pudding mix

1 (10 ounce) loaf pound
cake

½ cup sherry

2 cups fresh strawberries

• Make pudding as instructed on package.

• Place a layer of pound cake slices in the bottom of an 8-inch crystal bowl. Sprinkle with ¼ cup of the sherry. Add a layer of the strawberries. Next, add a layer of half the pudding. Repeat these layers. Refrigerate overnight or several hours.

• Before serving, top with whipped topping.

Amaretto Ice Cream

1 (8 ounce) carton
whipping cream,
whipped

1 pint vanilla ice cream,
softened

⅓ cup amaretto

⅓ cup chopped almonds,
toasted

• Combine whipped cream, ice cream and amaretto. Freeze in sherbet glasses.

• When ready to serve, drizzle a little additional amaretto over the top of each individual serving and sprinkle with toasted almonds.

Blueberry Fluff

1 (20 ounce) can
blueberry pie filling

1 (20 ounce) can crushed
pineapple, drained

1 can sweetened,
condensed milk

1 (8 ounce) carton
whipped topping

• Mix pie filling, pineapple and condensed milk together.

• Fold in container of whipped topping. (This dessert is even better if you add ¾ cup of chopped pecans).

• Combine all ingredients and pour into parfait glasses. Refrigerate.

Winter Wonder Dessert

28 chocolate cream-filled chocolate cookies, divided

2¾ cup milk

3 (3.4 ounce) packages instant pistachio pudding

1 (8 ounce) carton whipped topping

- Crush the 28 cookies, reserving ⅔ of a cup. Place crushed cookies in a 9 x 13-inch dish.
- In mixing bowl, combine milk and instant pistachio pudding. Mix about 2 minutes until thickened. Pour over crushed cookies.
- Spread whipped topping over pistachio pudding.
- Sprinkle the reserved cookies over the top of whipped topping and refrigerate overnight before serving.

Divine Strawberries

1 quart fresh strawberries

1 (20 ounce) can pineapple chunks, well drained

2 bananas, sliced

2 (18 ounce) cartons strawberry glaze

- Cut strawberries in half (or in quarters if the strawberries are very large.)
- Add pineapple chunks and bananas.
- Fold in the strawberry glaze and chill.

This is wonderful served over pound cake or just served in sherbet glasses.

You can make your own amaretto by following the recipe for amaretto on page 65. It's great.

Amaretto Peaches

4½ cups peeled, sliced fresh peaches

½ cup amaretto

½ cup sour cream

½ cup packed brown sugar

- Lay the peaches in a 2-quart baking dish. Pour amaretto over peaches and spread sour cream over peaches. Sprinkle brown sugar evenly over all.
- Broil mixture until it is heated thoroughly and sugar melts.

Serve over ice cream or pound cake.

Brandied Apples

1 (10 ounce) loaf pound cake

1 (20 ounce) can apple pie filling

½ teaspoon allspice

2 tablespoons brandy

- Slice pound cake and place on dessert plates.
- In saucepan, combine pie filling, allspice and brandy. Heat and stir just until heated thoroughly.
- Place several spoonfuls over cake. Top with a scoop of vanilla ice cream.

Amaretto Sauce for Pound Cake

1 (3.4 ounce) package French vanilla pudding (not instant)

1 cup milk

1 (8 ounce) carton whipping cream, whipped

¼ cup amaretto

- Cook pudding with the milk according to package directions. Cover and cool to room temperature.
- With a wire whisk, stir in whipped cream and amaretto.
- Pour over pound cake or vanilla ice cream.

Boiled Custard

1 (14 ounce) can
  sweetened condensed
  milk

1 quart milk

4 eggs

½ teaspoon vanilla

- Combine the milk and heat in the top of a double boiler.
- In a separate pan, beat the eggs well.
- Slowly pour a little of the milk over the eggs, stirring constantly. Gradually add the eggs to the milk and cook on low for 5 to 10 minutes, stirring constantly, until thickened.
- Stir in vanilla and refrigerate.

  This can be served in custard cups or stemmed glasses.

Chocolate-Coconut Mist

2 (14 ounce) packages
  flaked coconut

2 tablespoons butter,
  optional

1⅓ cups semi-sweet
  chocolate chips, melted

3 quarts mint chocolate
  chip ice cream

- In a bowl, toss coconut, butter and chocolate together until well blended.
- On a baking sheet covered with wax paper, shape about ⅓ cupfuls into 2⅓-inch nests. Chill until firm.

  Just before serving top each nest with ½ cup of ice cream.

Butterscotch Finale

1 (pint) carton whipping cream

¾ cup butterscotch ice cream topping

1 (9½-inch in diameter) angel food cake

¾ pound toffee bars, crushed, divided

- In mixer bowl, whip the cream until it begins to thicken.
- Slowly add butterscotch topping and continue beating until mixture is thick.
- Slice cake into 3 equal horizontal layers.
- With bottom layer on a cake plate, spread with about 1½ cups of the whipped cream mixture. Sprinkle with ¼ of the crushed toffee.
- Repeat layers and frost top as well as sides of the cake.
- Sprinkle toffee over top of cake. Refrigerate at least 8 hours before serving.

Rainbow Sherbet Delight

1 gallon vanilla ice cream, divided

½ gallon each of lime and orange sherbet, divided

1 large chocolate bar, shaved

2 cups chopped pecans

- Melt vanilla ice cream and pour 1 inch into bottom of angel food cake pan. Place in freezer until frozen.
- Scoop half of lime sherbet and half of orange sherbet into balls and place on top of frozen vanilla ice cream, filling cake pan halfway. Leave space around balls and at top of pan.
- Pour half of remaining vanilla ice cream to fill in spaces. Refreeze.
- Make a layer of the shaved chocolate and pecans.
- Repeat process of sherbet balls on top. Cover with remaining melted ice cream. Freeze. Unmold to serve.

Black Forest Cake

1 devil's food cake mix

1 (20 ounce) can cherry
pie filling

1 (3.4 ounce) package
vanilla instant pudding

1 (8 ounce) carton
whipped topping

• Bake cake according to directions in a greased and floured 9 x 13-inch baking pan.

• While cake is still warm poke top with fork and spread cherry pie filling over cake.

• While cake cools, prepare the pudding using 1 cup of milk. Fold in the whipped topping.

• Spread pudding and whipped topping mixture over cake, carefully covering the cherry pie filling. Refrigerate.

Pecan Cake

1 butter pecan cake mix

1 stick margarine, melted

1 egg

1 cup chopped pecans

• Combine cake mix, ¾ cup water, margarine and egg, mixing well. Stir in pecans.

• Pour into a 9 x 13-inch baking dish.

Topping for Pecan Cake

1 (8 ounce) package
cream cheese, softened

2 eggs

1 (1 pound) box powdered
sugar

• With mixer, combine cream cheese, eggs and powdered sugar. Pour over cake mixture.

• Bake at 350° for 40 minutes. Check with toothpick to make sure cake is done.

Oreo Cake

1 package white cake mix

⅓ cup oil

4 egg whites

1¼ cups coarsely chopped Oreo cookies

- In a mixer bowl combine cake mix, oil, 1¼ cup water and egg whites. Blend on low speed until moistened. Then beat two minutes at high speed.
- Gently fold in coarsely chopped cookies. Pour batter into two greased and floured 8-inch round cake pans.
- Bake at 350° for 25 to 30 minutes or until toothpick inserted in center comes out clean.
- Cool for 15 minutes; then remove from pan. Let cool completely and frost.

Frosting for Oreo Cake

4¼ cups powdered sugar

2 sticks butter, softened

1 cup shortening (not butter flavored)

1 teaspoon almond flavoring

- With mixer combine all ingredients. Beat together until creamy.
- Ice the first layer of cake and place second layer on top; ice top and sides.
- Sprinkle with extra crushed Oreo cookies on top.

Favorite Cake

1 butter pecan cake mix

1 cup almond toffee bits

1 cup chopped pecans

Powdered sugar

- Mix cake mix according to package directions. Fold in toffee bits and pecans.
- Pour into a greased and floured bundt cake pan. Bake at 350° for 45 minutes or until toothpick inserted in center comes out clean.
- Allow cake to cool several minutes; then remove cake from pan. Dust with sifted powdered sugar.

Delightful Pear Cake

1 (15 ounce) can pears in light syrup, undrained

1 white cake mix

2 egg whites

1 egg

- Drain pears, reserving the liquid; chop pears.
- Place pears and the liquid in a mixing bowl; add cake mix, egg whites and egg. Beat on low speed for 30 seconds. Beat on high for 4 minutes.
- Grease and flour a 10-inch bundt pan. Pour in batter.
- Bake at 350° for 50 to 55 minutes. Cook until a toothpick inserted in middle comes out clean. Cool in pan for about 10 minutes. Remove cake and dust with sifted powdered sugar.

Miracle Cake

1 lemon cake mix

3 eggs

⅓ cup oil

1 (20 ounce) can crushed pineapple, undrained

- In mixing bowl combine all ingredients.
- Blend on low speed; then beat on medium for 2 minutes.
- Pour batter into a greased and floured 9 x 13-inch baking dish.
- Bake for 30 to 35 minutes until cake tests done with a toothpick.

Miracle Cake Topping

1 (14 ounce) can sweetened condensed milk

¼ cup lemon juice

1 (8 ounce) carton whipped topping

- Blend all ingredients, mixing well. Spread over cake. Refrigerate.

Chocolate Pudding Cake

1 milk chocolate cake mix

1¼ cups milk

⅓ cup oil

3 eggs

- In mixing bowl combine all ingredients. Beat well.
- Pour into a greased and buttered 9 x 13-inch baking pan.
- Bake at 350° for 35 minutes or cake tester comes out clean.

Frosting for Chocolate Pudding Cake

1 can sweetened condensed milk

¾ (16 ounce) can chocolate syrup

1 (8 ounce) carton whipped topping, thawed

⅓ cup chopped pecans

- In a small bowl mix the sweetened condensed milk and chocolate syrup.
- Pour over cake and let soak into cake. Chill for several hours.
- Spread whipped topping over top of cake and sprinkle pecans over the top. Refrigerate.

O'Shaughnessy's Special

1 (10 ounce) pound cake loaf

1 (15 ounce) can crushed pineapple, undrained

1 (3.4 ounce) box pistachio pudding mix

1 (8 ounce) carton whipped topping

- Slice cake horizontally, making 3 layers.
- Combine pineapple and pudding; beat until mixture begins to thicken; fold in whipped topping, blending well. (You may add a few drops of green food coloring if you would like the cake to be a brighter green).
- Spread on each layer and on top. Refrigerate.

Carnival Cake

1 white cake mix

2 (10 ounce) frozen
   sweetened
   strawberries, undrained

1 (3.4 ounce) package
   instant vanilla pudding

1 (8 ounce) carton
   whipped topping

- Make cake mix by following directions on box. Pour into a greased 9 x 13-inch baking dish. Bake according to package directions.

- When cool, poke holes with a knife in the top of the cake and pour strawberries over the top of the cake.

- Make up the package of instant pudding using 1¼ cups milk and when that is set, pour over the strawberries. Cover cake with the whipped topping. Refrigerate.

Apple Cake

1 box spiced cake mix

1 (20 ounce) can apple pie
   filling

2 eggs

⅓ cup chopped walnuts

- Combine all ingredients; mix very thoroughly with a spoon. Make sure all lumps from the cake mix are broken up.

- Pour into a greased and floured bundt pan.

- Bake at 350° for 50 minutes. Check with toothpick for doneness.

  You may substitute any other pie filling for this cake.

Pineapple Angel Cake

1 (1-step) angel food cake
   mix

1 (20 ounce) can crushed
   pineapple, undrained

- Place angel food cake mix in mixing bowl and add pineapple and juice. Beat as directed on cake mix box.

- Pour into an ungreased 9 x 13-inch baking pan. Bake at 350° for 30 minutes.

  This is a good low calorie cake.

Chocolate-Cherry Cake

1 milk chocolate cake mix

1 (20 ounce) can cherry pie filling

3 eggs

- In mixing bowl, combine all ingredients. Mix by hand.
- Pour into a greased and floured 9 x 13-inch baking dish.
- Bake at 350° for 35 to 40 minutes. Test with toothpick for doneness.

Chocolate-Cherry Cake Frosting

5 tablespoons margarine

1¼ cups sugar

½ cup milk

1 (6 ounce) package chocolate chips

- When cake is done, combine margarine, sugar and milk in a medium saucepan. Boil one minute, stirring constantly. Add chocolate chips and stir until chips are melted. Pour over hot cake.

Pink Lady Cake

1 strawberry cake mix

3 eggs

1 teaspoon lemon extract

1 (20 ounce) can strawberry pie filling

- In mixer, beat the cake mix, eggs and lemon extract together.
- Fold in pie filling.
- Pour in a greased and floured 9 x 13-baking pan.
- Bake at 350° for 30 to 35 minutes. Test with a toothpick to make sure that cake is done.

Add a prepared vanilla icing or whipped topping.

Hawaiian Dream Cake

1 yellow cake mix

4 eggs

¾ cup oil

½ (20 ounce) can crushed pineapple with ½ juice

- With mixer beat together all ingredients for 4 minutes.
- Pour into a greased and floured 9 x 13-inch baking pan.
- Bake at 350° for 30 to 35 minutes or until cake tests done with toothpick. Cool.

 ## Hawaiian Dream Cake
Coconut Pineapple Icing

½ (20 ounce) can crushed pineapple with ½ juice

1 stick margarine

1 (16 ounce) box powdered sugar

1 (7 ounce) can coconut

- Heat together the pineapple and margarine. Boil 1½ minutes.
- Add powdered sugar and coconut.
- Punch holes in cake with knife. Pour hot icing over cake.

Pound Cake Deluxe

1 (10 inch) round bakery pound cake

1 (20 ounce) can crushed pineapple, undrained

1 (5.1 ounce) package coconut instant pudding mix

1 (8 ounce) carton whipped topping

- Slice cake horizontally to make 3 layers.
- Mix pineapple, pudding and whipped topping together, blending well.
- Spread on each layer and top of cake. Coconut can be sprinkled on top layer. Refrigerate.

Coconut Angel Cake

1 (14 ounce) 10-inch round angel food cake

1 (20 ounce) can coconut pie filling

1 (12 ounce) carton whipped topping

3 tablespoons coconut

- Cut angel food cake horizontally to make three layers.
- Combine coconut pie filling and whipped topping. Spread ⅓ of mixture on the first layer. Top with second layer.
- Spread ⅓ of mixture on the second layer and top with the third layer. Spread remaining whipped topping mixture on top of cake.
- Sprinkle the coconut on top of mixture. Refrigerate.

Fluffy Orange Cake

1 orange cake mix

4 eggs

⅔ cup oil

½ cup water

- In mixer bowl, combine all ingredients.
- Beat on low speed to blend then beat on medium speed for 2 minutes. Pour into a greased and floured 9 x 13-inch baking pan.
- Bake at 350° for 30 minutes or until cake tests done. Cool.

Topping for Fluffy Orange Cake

1 (14 ounce) can sweetened condensed milk

⅓ cup lemon juice

1 (8 ounce) carton whipped topping

2 (11 ounce) cans mandarin oranges, drained, cut in half, chilled

- In a large bowl blend condensed milk and lemon juice mixing well.
- Fold in whipped topping until blended. Fold in orange slices.
- Pour mixture over cooled cake. Cover and refrigerate.

Basic Pound Cake

3 sticks of butter
3 cups sugar
8 eggs
3 cups sifted flour

- In mixer, cream together butter and sugar, mixing well.
- Add eggs one at a time, beating well after each addition. Add flour stirring in small amounts at a time.
- Pour into a greased and floured 10-inch bundt pan and bake at 300° for 1½ hours.

  Do not open oven door during baking.

Emergency Cheesecake

1 (8 ounce) package cream cheese, softened
1 can sweetened condensed milk
½ cup lemon juice
1 teaspoon vanilla

- Blend all ingredients in mixer.
- Pour into a graham cracker crust. Refrigerate.

  To serve, top with cherry pie filling.

Chiffon Torte

1 round bakery orange chiffon cake
1 (20 ounce) can crushed pineapple, undrained
1 (5.1 ounce) package vanilla instant pudding
1 (8 ounce) carton whipped topping

- Slice cake horizontally to make 3 layers.
- In mixer combine pineapple and pudding, beat by hand until mixture begins to thicken. Fold in whipped topping.
- Spread on each layer and cover top of cake.
- Refrigerate overnight.

  Toasted almonds can be sprinkled on top of cake.

Lemon-Pineapple Cake

1 lemon cake mix

1 (20 ounce) can crushed pineapple, undrained

3 eggs

⅓ cup oil

- In mixing bowl, combine all ingredients. Blend on low speed to moisten, then beat on medium for 2 minutes.
- Pour batter into a greased and floured 9 x 13-inch baking pan.
- Bake at 350° for 30 minutes. Test with toothpick to be sure cake is done. When cake is baking start making the topping for the cake. Cool for about 15 minutes.

Topping for Lemon-Pineapple Cake

1 (14 ounce) can sweetened condensed milk

1 cup sour cream

¼ cup lemon juice

- In medium bowl, combine all ingredients. Stir well to blend.
- Pour over warm cake. Refrigerate.

Chocolate-Orange Cake

1 (16 ounce) loaf frozen pound cake, thawed

1 (12 ounce) jar orange marmalade

1 (16 ounce) can ready-to-spread chocolate fudge frosting

- Cut cake horizontally to make 3 layers.
- Place one layer on cake platter. Spread with ½ of the marmalade.
- Place second layer over first and spread on remaining marmalade.
- Top with third cake layer and spread frosting liberally on top and sides of cake. Refrigerate.

Easy Pineapple Cake

2 cups sugar

2 cups flour

1 (20 ounce) can crushed pineapple, undrained

1 teaspoon baking soda

- Combine all cake ingredients and mix by hand.
- Pour into a greased and floured 9 x 13-inch baking pan.
- Bake at 350° for 30 to 35 minutes.

Icing for Easy Pineapple Cake

1 (8 ounce) package cream cheese, softened

1 stick margarine, melted

1 cup powdered sugar

1 cup chopped pecans

- Combine cream cheese, margarine and powdered sugar and beat with mixer.
- Add the chopped pecans and pour over HOT cake.

Strawberry Delight

1 (6 ounce) package strawberry gelatin

2 (10 ounce) packages frozen strawberries, undrained

1 (8 ounce) carton whipped topping

1 (12 ounce) prepared angel food cake

- Dissolve strawberry gelatin in 1 cup boiling water; mixing well. Add strawberries.
- Chill in refrigerator until partially set.
- Fold in whipped topping.
- Break the angel food cake into large bite-size pieces and layer the cake and gelatin mixture ½ at a time in a 9 x 13-inch shallow dish. Refrigerate.

Cut in squares to serve.

Fruit Cocktail Crepes

4 (15 ounce) cans fruit cocktail, thoroughly drained

1 cup packed brown sugar

2 cups margarine or butter, divided

3 (8 inch) packages flour tortillas

- Preheat oven to 325°. In small saucepan over low heat, stir constantly the brown sugar and ⅓ cup margarine until sugar melts and is well-mixed.

- Use remaining margarine and brush flour tortillas on both sides. (If each tortilla is not soft enough to roll without breaking, heat 2-3 at a time wrapped in damp paper towel and covered, for 4-5 seconds in the microwave oven.) For each crepe, place 2 teaspoons of sugar mixture and 1 tablespoon of drained fruit cocktail in middle of each tortilla.

- Roll each tortilla and place, seam-side down, in an 11 x 7 x 2-inch baking pan. Spread the remaining sugar mixture on the top.

- Bake covered 10-15 minutes or until the sugar mixture is bubbling.

Angel Glaze

1 cup confectioners' powdered sugar

1 tablespoon hot water

2 tablespoons light corn syrup

¼ teaspoon vanilla

- Mix all ingredients and stir until well blended with creamy texture. Glaze should pour slowly and stay on cake long enough to soak in. If glaze runs down the side of the cake, thicken the mixture with a little more powdered sugar.

- Use on any cake that needs a light icing or a topping of something sweet.

Chocolate-Amaretto Pie

2 (7 ounce) milk chocolate almond candy bars

⅓ cup amaretto

2 (8 ounce) cartons whipping cream, whipped

1 (9-inch) shortbread pie crust

• Melt chocolate in double boiler on low heat. Remove from heat and pour in amaretto.

• Stir chocolate and amaretto for about 10 or 15 minutes until mixture is room temperature.

• Fold in whipped cream.

• Pour into pie crust. Chill several hours before serving.

Creamy Cherry-Lime Pie

2 (8 ounce) cartons lime yogurt

⅓ cup chopped maraschino cherries, divided

1 (8 ounce) carton frozen whipped topping, thawed

1 (9-inch) graham cracker pie crust

• Stir together the yogurt and ¼ cup cherries.

• Fold in the whipped topping.

• Spoon the mixture into the graham cracker crust and garnish with chopped cherries.

• Refrigerate 6-8 hours or until firm.

Frozen Lemonade Pie

½ gallon frozen yogurt, softened

1 (6 ounce) can frozen pink lemonade, undiluted

1 (9-inch) graham cracker pie crust

• In large bowl, combine frozen yogurt and frozen pink lemonade. Work quickly.

• Pile ice cream mixture in pie crust and freeze.

Five-Citrus Cream Pie

1 (6 ounce) can frozen
five-citrus concentrate,
partially thawed

1 (4 ounce) can
sweetened condensed
milk

1 (8 ounce) carton frozen
whipped topping,
thawed

1 (9 inch) graham cracker
pie crust

• Stir together the sweetened condensed milk and five-citrus concentrate until well blended.

• Fold into the whipped topping.

• Spoon the mixture into the graham cracker crust. Refrigerate 6-8 hours.

Magic Cherry Pie

2 (6 ounce) cartons
cherry yogurt

1 (3 ounce) package dry
cherry gelatin

1 (8 ounce) carton
whipped topping,
thawed

1 shortbread pie crust

• In a bowl, combine the yogurt and dry gelatin, mixing well.

• Fold in the whipped topping and spoon into pie crust.

• Freeze. Take out of freezer 20 minutes before slicing.

You could also place a dab of cherry pie filling on top of pie which will make it even better.

Limeade Pie

1 (6 ounce) can frozen limeade concentrate, thawed

2 cups lowfat frozen yogurt, softened

1 (8 ounce) carton whipped topping, thawed

1 (6-inch) graham cookie crumb pie crust

• In a large bowl, combine limeade concentrate and yogurt, mixing well.

• Fold in whipped topping.

• Pour into pie crust. Freeze at least 4 hours or overnight.

Cool Chocolate Pie

22 large marshmallows

2 (8 ounce) milk chocolate almond candy bars

1 (8 ounce) carton whipped topping

½ cup chopped pecans

• In a double boiler, melt marshmallows and chocolate bars.

• Cool partially and fold in whipped topping and pecans.

• Pour into a prepared graham cracker pie crust.

• Refrigerate several hours before serving.

Creamy Lime-Almond Pie

1¾ cup almond shortbread cookie crumbs, divided

⅓ cup melted margarine or butter

1 cup lime sherbet, softened

1 cup frozen whipped topping, thawed

• Preheat oven to 350°. Mix 1½ cups cookie crumbs with margarine and pat evenly into a 9-inch pie plate.

• Bake 10 minutes, remove and cool.

• Fold together the sherbet and whipping topping. Place in the crumb crust and sprinkle ½ cup cookie crumbs on top.

• Refrigerate 6-8 hours or until firm.

Strawberry Pie

1 (6 ounce) box
  strawberry gelatin

¾ cup boiling water

1 (8 ounce) carton
  whipped topping

2 (10 ounce) packages
  strawberries, drain one
  package drained

• In a bowl, combine gelatin and boiling water, mixing well. Let gelatin cool in the refrigerator until it begins to thicken. (Watch closely.)

• Drain one package of strawberries, fold in whipped topping and strawberries.

• Spoon into a graham cracker crust.

• Refrigerate several hours before serving.

Million Dollar Pie

24 Ritz crackers,
  crumbled

1 cup chopped pecans

4 egg whites (absolutely
  no yolks at all)

1 cup sugar

• Mix cracker crumbs with pecans.

• In a separate mixing bowl, beat egg whites until stiff; slowly add sugar while still mixing.

• Gently fold in the crumbs and pecan mixture into egg whites. Pour into a pie tin and bake at 350° for 20 minutes. Cool before serving.

Top with a dip of chocolate ice cream.

Very Berry Pie

1 (6 ounce) package
  strawberry gelatin

1 (15 ounce) can whole
  cranberry sauce

½ cup cranberry juice

2 cups whipped topping

• Dissolve gelatin in ¾ cup boiling water.

• Add cranberry sauce and juice. Place in refrigerator until it begins to thicken.

• Fold in whipped topping and pour into a 9-inch graham cracker crust.

Apricot Pie

2 (15 ounce) cans apricot
halves, drained

1¼ cups sugar

¼ cup flour

1 (8 ounce) carton
whipping cream

- Cut each apricot half in half and arrange evenly in an unbaked, 9-inch pie shell.

- Combine sugar and flour and sprinkle over apricots.

- Pour unwhipped cream over pie.

- Place 1-inch strips of foil over edge of pie crust to keep from browning too much. Bake at 325° for 1 hour 20 minutes.

  You might want to place the pie on a cookie sheet to catch any possible spillovers.

Caramel Ice Cream Pie

1 roll butterscotch
cookies

½ gallon vanilla ice cream

1 (12 ounce) jar caramel
sauce

- Bake cookies according to directions on package.

- When cookies have cooled, crumble and place in a 10-inch pie plate keeping out about ½ cup to use for topping.

- Place ice cream in a bowl to soften. Stir caramel sauce into the ice cream (do not mix completely) and spoon mixture into the pie plate.

- Sprinkle remaining crumbs over top of pie. Freeze.

Pineapple Fluff Pie

1 (20 ounce) can crushed pineapple, undrained

1 (3.4 ounce) package instant lemon pudding mix

1 (8 ounce) carton whipped topping

1 (9 inch) graham cracker crust

- In a bowl, combine the pineapple and pudding mix; beat until thickened.
- Fold in the whipped topping.
- Spoon into pie crust.
- Refrigerate several hours before serving.

Chocolate-Vanilla-Almond Parfait

1 (3 ounce) box instant chocolate pudding mix

1 (3 ounce) box instant vanilla pudding mix

4 cups milk

2 cups slivered almonds

- Using 2 mixing bowls, prepare each pudding with milk as directed. Cover tightly with plastic wrap and refrigerate.
- Place slivered almonds in a dry skillet over medium heat. Stir until almonds are evenly browned.
- In parfait glasses or stemmed glasses, first spoon small amounts of chocolate pudding, then vanilla pudding to the top of the glass. Garnish with almonds. Refrigerate until chilled.

Apricot Chiffon Pie

2 (6 ounce) cartons apricot-mango yogurt

1 (3 ounce) box apricot gelatin

1 (8 ounce) carton whipped topping

1 (6 ounce) prepared shortbread pie crust

- In a bowl, combine yogurt and gelatin, mixing well.
- Fold in whipped topping and spread in pie crust. Freeze.
- Take out of freezer 20 minutes before slicing.

Holiday Pie

1 (8 ounce) package
  cream cheese, softened

1 (14 ounce) can
  sweetened condensed
  milk

1 (3.4 ounce box) instant
  vanilla pudding mix

1½ cups whipped topping,
  thawed

- With mixer, beat cream cheese until smooth. Gradually add sweetened condensed milk and beat until smooth.
- Add ¾ cup water and the pudding mix; beat until smooth.
- Fold in whipped topping.
- Pour into a graham cracker pie crust. Top with crumbled holiday candies.

Peaches N' Cream Pie

Chocolate syrup

1 quart peach ice cream,
  softened

Fresh peach slices

¼ cup pecan halves

- Drizzle ½ cup chocolate syrup over the bottom of a prepared shortbread pie crust.
- Spoon ice cream over crust and freeze for 3 hours or until firm.
- When ready to serve, place peach slices and pecan halves over top of ice cream.
- Drizzle with additional chocolate syrup.

Sunny Lime Pie

2 (6 ounce) cartons key
  lime pie yogurt

1 (3 ounce) package dry
  lime gelatin

1 (8 ounce) carton
  whipped topping

1 (9-inch) graham cracker
  pie crust

- In a bowl, combine yogurt and lime gelatin; mixing well.
- Fold in whipped topping and spread in pie crust. Freeze.
- Take out of freezer 20 minutes before slicing.

Cheesecake Pie

1 (20 ounce) can strawberry pie filling, divided

2 cups milk

2 (3.4 serving size) packages instant cheesecake flavor pudding mix

½ (8 ounce) carton whipped topping, thawed

- Spoon ¾ cup pie filling into a graham cracker pie crust.
- In mixing bowl, combine milk and the pudding mixes. Beat for two minutes or until smooth. Mixture will be thick.
- Fold in whipped topping. Spoon over pie filling in crust.
- Refrigerate at least 3 hours. When ready to serve, top with remaining pie filling.

Banana Split Pie

3 small bananas

1 quart vanilla ice cream, softened

Fudge sauce, whipped topping

Chopped pecans, maraschino cherries

- Slice bananas and place on a graham cracker pie crust.
- Spoon softened ice cream over bananas. Freeze for 2 to 3 hours.
- Spread some fudge sauce over the ice cream and top with a layer of whipped topping.
- When ready to serve, place a maraschino cherry on top of each piece of pie.

Mint-Chocolate Pie

1 cup mint-chocolate chip ice cream, softened

1 cup frozen whipped topping, thawed

¾ cup crushed chocolate sandwich cookies with mint filling, divided

1 (9 inch) chocolate cookie pie crust

• Fold together ice cream, whipped topping and ½ cup crushed cookies.

• Place in pie crust and sprinkle remaining cookie crumbs on top.

• Refrigerate 6-8 hours or until firm.

Patrick's Pie

1 (8 ounce) package cream cheese, softened

Heaping ⅓ cup sugar

1 (8 ounce) carton whipped topping, thawed

1 cup chopped Fudge Shop grasshopper cookies

• With mixer, beat cream cheese and sugar together until well blended.

• Fold in whipped topping, mixing well.

• Add cookies and about 3 drops of green food coloring, if you like.

• Pour into a prepared chocolate pie crust. Garnish with extra crumbled cookies. Freeze.

Grasshopper Pie

22 large marshmallows

⅓ cup creme de menthe

1 (12 ounce) cartons whipping cream, whipped

1 (9-inch) prepared chocolate pie crust

• In a large saucepan, melt marshmallows with the creme de menthe over low heat. Cool.

• Fold the whipped cream into the marshmallow mixture.

• Pour filling into pie crust and freeze until ready to serve.

Peach Crunch

2 (20 ounce) cans peach
   pie filling

1 white cake mix

1 cup slivered almonds

1 stick margarine

- Add pie filling evenly in the bottom of a greased and floured 9 x 13-inch baking pan.

- Sprinkle cake mix evenly and smooth over top. Sprinkle almonds evenly over cake mix.

- Slice butter into ⅛-inch slices and place over entire surface.

- Bake at 350° for 40 to 45 minutes or until top is nicely browned.

Blueberry Cobbler

2 (20 ounce) cans
   blueberry pie filling

1 box white cake mix

1 egg

1 stick margarine,
   softened

- Spread pie filling in a greased 9 x 13-inch baking dish.

- With mixer, combine cake mix, egg and margarine. Blend well. Mixture will be stiff.

- Spoon over filling.

- Bake at 350° for 45 minutes or until golden brown.

Cherry Cobbler

2 (20 ounce) cans cherry
pie filling

1 package white cake mix

1½ sticks margarine,
melted

1 (4 ounce) package
slivered almonds

- Spread pie filling in a greased 9 x 13-inch baking pan.
- Sprinkle cake mix over the cherries.
- Drizzle melted margarine over top. Sprinkle almonds over the top.
- Bake at 350° for 45 minutes. Top with whipped topping.

Cream Cheese Crust

1 stick margarine,
softened

1 (3 ounce) package
cream cheese, softened

1 cup flour

- Combine margarine, cream cheese and flour.
- Blend with a pastry blender or with a fork until mixture can be made into a ball.
- Chill pastry for about one hour.
- Roll out on a floured surface.

  Makes one 9-inch crust.

Cherry Crisp

2 (20 ounce) cans cherry
pie filling

1 box white cake mix

1 stick margarine

2 cups chopped pecans

- Pour pie filling into a greased 9 x 13-inch baking dish.
- Sprinkle cake mix over top of filling.
- Dot with margarine and cover with pecans.
- Bake uncovered at 350° for 45 minutes.

Easy Pumpkin Pie

1 (9-inch) unbaked deep-dish pie shell

2 eggs

1 (30 ounce) can pumpkin pie mix

1 (5 ounce) can evaporated milk

• Beat eggs lightly in a large bowl. Stir in pumpkin pie mix and evaporated milk.

• Pour into pie shell.

• Cut 2-inch strips of foil and cover pie crust edges. This will keep pie crust from getting too brown.

• Bake at 400° for 15 minutes. Reduce temperature to 325° and bake for 40 more minutes or until knife inserted in center come out clean. Cool.

Easy Chocolate Pie

1 frozen pie crust, cooked

1 (16 ounce) carton whipped topping, thawed, divided

8 ounces milk chocolate candy bars

¾ cup chopped pecans

• In a saucepan, break candy into small pieces and melt over low heat.

• Remove and let set several minutes until partially cooled.

• Fold in ⅔ of the whipped topping, mixing well.

• Stir in chopped pecans and pour into pie crust.

• Spread remaining whipped topping over top of pie. Refrigerate at least 8 hours.

Butter Cookie Special

1 box butter cake mix

1 (3.4 ounce) package butterscotch instant pudding mix

1 cup oil, 1 egg, beaten

1¼ cups chopped pecans

- Mixing by hand stir together cake mix, pudding mix, oil and egg. Beat thoroughly.
- Stir in pecans. With a teaspoon place cookie dough on cookie sheet about 2 inches apart.
- Bake at 350° for about 8 minutes. Do not overcook.

Coconut Macaroons

2 (7 ounce) packages flaked coconut

1 (14 ounce) can Eagle brand condensed milk

2 teaspoons vanilla

½ teaspoon almond extract

- In a mixing bowl combine coconut, condensed milk and extracts; mix well.
- Drop by rounded teaspoons onto a foil lined cookie sheet.
- Bake at 350° for 8 to 10 minutes or until lightly browned around edges. Immediately remove from foil. (Macaroons will stick if allowed to cool). Store at room temperature.

Chocolate Crunch Cookies

1 package German chocolate cake mix with pudding

1 egg, slightly beaten

1 stick margarine, melted

1 cup crisp rice cereal

- Combine cake mix, egg and margarine. Add cereal; stir until blended.
- Shape dough into 1-inch balls. Place on lightly greased cookie sheet.
- Dip a fork in flour and flatten cookies in a crisscross pattern. Bake at 350° for 10 to 12 minutes. Cool.

Double Chocolate Cookies

6 egg whites

3 cups powdered sugar

¼ cup cocoa

3½ cups finely chopped pecans

- Beat egg whites until light and frothy. Fold sugar and cocoa into egg whites and beat lightly. Fold in pecans.
- Drop by teaspoons on a lightly greased and floured cookie sheet.
- Bake at 325° for about 20 minutes. Do not overbake and cool completely before removing from cookie sheet.

Lemon Cookies

1 stick butter, softened

1 cup sugar

2 tablespoons lemon juice

2 cups flour

- Cream butter, sugar and lemon juice slowly stirring in flour.
- Drop by teaspoons onto ungreased cookie sheet.
- Bake at 350° for 14 to 15 minutes.

Angel Macaroons

1 (16 ounce) package 1-step angel food cake mix

½ cup water

1½ teaspoons almond extract

2 cups flaked coconut

- With mixer, beat cake mix, water and extract on low speed for 30 seconds. Scrape bowl; beat on medium for 1 minute. Fold in coconut.
- Drop by rounded teaspoonfuls onto a parchment paper-lined baking sheet.
- Bake at 350° for 10 to 12 minutes or until set. Remove paper with cookies to a wire rack to cool.

Coconut Moments

2 sticks margarine, softened

½ cup powdered sugar

½ cup cornstarch, 1 ⅓ cups flour

Flaked coconut

- Beat margarine and powdered sugar until light and fluffy. Add cornstarch and flour; beat until well blended. Cover and refrigerate for one hour.
- Remove and shape into 1-inch balls. Roll in flaked coconut. Place on ungreased cookie sheet.
- Bake at 325° for 12 to 15 minutes. Watch closely and don't let the coconut burn. Cool 2 or 3 minutes before removing from pan.

Drop Cookies

2 sticks margarine, softened

¾ cup cornstarch

⅓ cup powdered sugar

1 cup flour

- Mix together the margarine, cornstarch, sugar and flour, mixing well.
- Drop on cookie sheet in small balls and flatten slightly.
- Bake at 350° for about 15 minutes; do not brown. When cool, ice.

Icing for Drop Cookies

1 (3 ounce) package cream cheese, softened

1 teaspoon vanilla

1 cup powdered sugar

- Blend all ingredients together, mixing well. Ice cookies.

Lemon-Coconut Macaroons

⅔ cup sweetened condensed milk

1 large egg white

2 teaspoons lemon juice and 1 teaspoon lemon zest

3½ cups shredded or flaked sweetened coconut

- Preheat oven to 325°. Mix condensed milk, egg white, lemon juice and lemon zest and stir in coconut.
- Drop by teaspoons, 2 inches apart, on a cookie sheet covered with parchment paper or foil.
- Bake 20 minutes or until lightly browned. Cool completely and remove carefully from the foil or parchment paper.

Cheesecake Cookies

1 cup butter, softened

2 (3 ounce) packages cream cheese, softened

2 cups sugar

2 cups flour

- Cream together the butter and cream cheese. Add sugar, beating until light and fluffy. Add flour, beating well.
- Drop by teaspoons onto cookie sheet and bake at 350° for 12 to 15 minutes or until edges are golden.

These are made even better if you add 1 cup of chopped pecans.

Gingerbread Cookies

1½ sticks margarine, softened

2 egg yolks

1 spice cake mix

1 teaspoon ginger

- In a large bowl combine margarine and egg yolks. Gradually blend in cake mix and ginger, mixing well.
- Roll out to a ⅛-inch thickness on a lightly floured surface. Using your gingerbread cookie cutter, cut out your cookies and place 2 inches apart on cookie sheet.
- Bake at 375° for about 8 minutes or until edges are slightly browned. Cool cookies before transferring cookies to a cookie bowl.

Devil's Food Cookies

1 package devil's food
   cake mix

½ cup oil

2 eggs

¾ cup chopped pecans,
   optional

- Combine the cake mix, oil and eggs in a mixer bowl; mixing well.
- Drop by teaspoons onto a non-stick cookie sheet.
- Bake at 350° for 10 to 12 minutes. Cool and remove to a wire rack.

Nutty Fudgies

1 package fudge cake mix

1 (8 ounce) carton sour
   cream

⅔ cup peanut butter
   chips

½ cup chopped peanuts

- Beat cake mix and sour cream until well blended and mixture is smooth. Stir in peanut butter chips and peanuts.
- Drop by teaspoonfuls onto a greased cookie sheet. Bake at 350° for 10 to 12 minutes. Remove from oven and cool.

Chocolate-Peanut Butter Crisps

1 (10 count) package
   8-inch flour tortillas

8 (8 ounce) squares
   semi-sweet chocolate,
   coarsely chopped or 8
   ounces semi-sweet
   chocolate morsels

⅓ cup creamy or chunky
   peanut butter

1 (14 ounce) can
   sweetened condensed
   milk

- Cut the flour tortillas into 8 wedges and place on baking sheet. Bake at 350° for 10 minutes and cool on rack.
- In a heavy saucepan, melt the chocolate over low heat, stirring constantly. Stir in the peanut butter, sweetened condensed milk and 2 tablespoons water and heat through. (If the sauce is too thick, add 1 teaspoon water at a time, until the sauce smoothly drizzles on foil.)
- Drizzle warm chocolate sauce over the wedges or serve immediately in a chafing dish or fondue pot and dip crisp tortilla wedges.

Peanut Butter Cookies

1 cup sugar

¾ cup light corn syrup

1 (16 ounce) jar crunchy peanut butter

4½ cups chow mein noodles

- In a saucepan over medium heat bring sugar and corn syrup to a boil; stir in peanut butter.
- Remove from heat. Stir in noodles.
- Drop by spoonfuls onto wax paper and allow to cool.

Butter Cookies

1 pound butter (not margarine)

¾ cup brown sugar

¾ cup granulated sugar

4½ cups flour

- Cream butter and sugars together and slowly add flour, mixing well. Batter will be very thick.
- Roll into small balls and place on an ungreased cookie sheet.
- Bake at 350° for about 15 minutes until only slightly brown. Do not overbake.

 # Butterscotch Cookies

1 (12 ounce) and 1 (6 ounce) package butterscotch chips

2¼ cups chow mein noodles

½ cup chopped walnuts

¼ cup coconut

- Melt butterscotch chips in double boiler. Add noodles, walnuts and coconut.
- Drop by tablespoonfuls onto wax paper.

Pecan Puffs

2 egg whites

¾ cup packed light brown sugar

1 teaspoon vanilla

1 cup chopped pecans

- Beat egg whites until foamy. Gradually add (¼ cup at a time) brown sugar and vanilla. Continue beating until stiff peaks are formed (about 3 or 4 minutes). Fold in pecans.
- Line a cookie sheet with freezer paper. Drop by teaspoonfuls onto paper.
- Bake at 250° for 45 minutes.

Scotch Shortbread

1 stick unsalted butter, softened

⅓ cup sugar

1¼ cups flour

Powdered sugar

- Cream butter and sugar until light and fluffy. Add flour and pinch of salt, mixing well.
- Spread dough in an 8-inch square pan. Bake at 325° for 20 minutes or until lightly brown.
- Let shortbread cool in pan and dust with powdered sugar and cut into squares.

No-Cook Lemon Balls

2 cups graham cracker crumbs, almond or pecan shortbread cookie crumbs, divided

1 (6 ounce) can frozen lemonade concentrate, thawed

½ cup margarine or butter, softened

1 (16 ounce) box powdered sugar, sifted

- Combine 1½ cups cookie crumbs, lemonade concentrate, margarine and powdered sugar. Shape into small balls.
- Roll in the reserved cookie crumbs and put on wax paper.
- Refrigerate 3-4 hours in sealed container or freeze to serve later.

Nutty Blonde Brownies

1 (1 pound) box light
  brown sugar

4 eggs

2 cups biscuit mix

2 cups chopped pecans

- In mixer, beat together the brown sugar, eggs and biscuit mix. Stir in pecans and pour into a greased 9 x 13-inch baking pan.
- Bake at 350° for 35 minutes. Cool and cut into squares.

Peanut Butter Brownies

1 (21 ounce) package
  brownie mix

1 cup peanut butter
  morsels

- Prepare brownie mix according to package directions, stirring in peanut butter morsels.
- Spoon mixture into a greased 9 x 13-inch baking pan.
- Bake at 350° for 35 minutes. Cool and cut into squares.

Peanut Butter Cups

1 (18 ounce) roll
  refrigerated peanut
  butter cookie dough

48 miniature peanut
  butter cup candy

- Slice cookie dough into ¾-inch slices. Cut each slice into quarters and place each quarter, pointed side up in a greased miniature muffin pan.
- Bake at 350° for 10 minutes.
- Remove from oven and immediately press a peanut butter cup candy gently and evenly into cookies. (Be sure you take paper wrapper off peanut butter cups). Cool and remove from pan and refrigerate until firm.

Chocolate Chip-Cheese Bars

1 (18 ounce) tube
   refrigerated chocolate
   chip cookie dough
1 (8 ounce) package
   cream cheese, softened
½ cup sugar
1 egg

• Cut cookie dough in half. For crust, press half of the dough onto the bottom of a greased 9-inch square baking pan or a 7 x 11-inch baking pan.

• In a mixing bowl, beat cream cheese, sugar and egg until smooth. Spread over crust. Crumble remaining dough over top.

• Bake at 350° for 35 to 40 minutes or until a toothpick inserted near the center comes out clean. Cool on a wire rack. Cut into bars. Refrigerate leftovers.

Snicker Brownies

1 German chocolate cake
   mix
1½ sticks margarine,
   melted
½ cup evaporated milk
4 (2.7 ounce) snicker
   candy bars, sliced in ⅛-
   inch slices

• In a large bowl combine cake mix, margarine and evaporated milk. Beat on low speed until well blended.

• Add ½ of the batter into a greased and floured 9 x 13-inch baking pan.

• Bake at 350° for 10 minutes.

• Remove from oven and place candy bar slices evenly over the brownies. Drop remaining half of batter by spoonfuls over the candy bars; spread as evenly as possible.

• Place back in the oven and bake for 20 minutes longer. When cool cut into bars.

Walnut Bars

1⅔ cups graham cracker crumbs

1½ cups coarsely chopped walnuts

1 (14 ounce) can sweetened condensed milk

¼ cup coconut (optional)

- Place the graham cracker crumbs and walnuts in a bowl. Slowly add the condensed milk, coconut and a pinch of salt. Mixture will be very thick.
- Pack into a 9-inch square greased pan. Pack mixture down with the back of a spoon.
- Bake at 350° for 35 minutes. When cool cut into squares.

Apricot Bars

1¼ cups flour

¾ cup packed brown sugar

6 tablespoons margarine

¾ cup apricot preserves

- In mixing bowl, combine flour, brown sugar, and margarine, mixing well.
- Add ½ of this mixture into a 9-inch square baking pan. Spread the apricot preserves over top of mixture. Add remaining flour mixture over top of dessert.
- Bake at 350° for 30 minutes. Cut into squares.

Chocolate Drops

12 ounce package milk chocolate chips

⅔ cup chunky peanut butter

4¼ cups Cocoa Krispie cereal

- In double boiler, melt chocolate chips and stir in peanut butter. Stir in cereal.
- Press into a 9 x 9-inch pan. Cut into bars.

Chocolate-Cherry Bars

1 devil's food cake mix

1 (20 ounce) can cherry
  pie filling

2 eggs

1 cup milk chocolate
  chips

• In a large bowl, mixing by hand combine all four ingredients, blending well.

• Pour batter into a greased and floured 9 x 13-inch baking dish.

• Bake at 350° for 25 to 30 minutes or until cake tester comes out clean. Cool and frost.

Frosting for Chocolate Cherry Bars

1 (3 ounce) square of
  semi-sweet chocolate,
  melted

1 (3 ounce) package
  cream cheese, softened

½ teaspoon vanilla

1½ cups powdered sugar

• In a medium bowl beat chocolate, cream cheese and vanilla until smooth. Gradually beat in powdered sugar.

• Pour over chocolate cherry bars.

Pecan Squares

1 (24 ounce) package
  almond bark

1 cup cinnamon chips

1 cup chopped pecans

8 cups frosted crispy rice
  cereal

• Melt almond bark and cinnamon chips in a very large saucepan or roaster on low heat, stirring constantly. When melted remove from heat and add pecans and frosted crispy rice cereal.

• Mix well and stir into a 9 x 13-inch pan. Pat down with the back of a spoon. Refrigerate just until set. Cut into squares.

Corn Flake Cookies

1 (12 ounce) package
butterscotch morsels

¾ cup peanut butter

3½ to 4 cups corn flakes,
crushed

• Melt butterscotch morsels on very low heat. Add peanut butter. When mixed thoroughly add corn flakes.

• Drop by teaspoons onto wax paper.

Butterscotch Crunchies

1 (12 ounce) package
butterscotch morsels

1¾ cups chow mein
noodles

1 cup chopped pecans

• Melt butterscotch morsels in heavy pan over a very low flame, stirring gently. Stir in noodles and pecans just until blended and coated.

• Drop mixture by teaspoonful onto wax paper. Refrigerate 30 minutes or until set.

Porcupine Clusters

¼ cup corn syrup

1 (12 ounce) package
white chocolate
morsels

2 cups chow mein
noodles

¾ cup salted peanuts

• On low heat, melt corn syrup and white chocolate chips. Pour over noodles and peanuts. Mixing well.

• Drop by teaspoon onto waxed paper.

• Refrigerate to harden. Store in airtight container.

Chocolate or butterscotch chips could be used instead of white chocolate morsels.

Hazel's Nutty Fudge

1 (12 ounce) package
  white chocolate chips

¾ cup Nutella hazelnut-
  cocoa spread

1½ cups chopped
  hazelnuts, divided

- In a medium saucepan over low heat, melt the white chocolate chips and add the hazelnut spread.

- Cook and stir until mixture is well blended.

- Remove from heat and stir in 1 cup hazelnuts.

- Drop by teaspoons on wax paper. Garnish with the reserved hazelnuts. Refrigerate until set.

  Option: Add ¼ cup shredded or flaked coconut.

Tiger Butter

1 pound white chocolate
  or almond bark

½ cup chunky peanut
  butter

1 cup semi-sweet
  chocolate morsels

- Line a 15 x 10-inch jelly-roll pan with wax paper.

- Heat white chocolate in a microwave-safe bowl on high 1 to 2 minutes or until melted. Stir until smooth. Add peanut butter and microwave on high until melted. Stir again until smooth. Spread mixture evenly into prepared pan.

- In another microwave-safe bowl melt chocolate morsels on high until melted. Pour chocolate over peanut butter mixture and swirl through with a knife until you get desired effect. Refrigerate several hours until firm. Break into pieces.

Surprise Chocolates

2 pounds white chocolate (or almond bark)

2 cups Spanish peanuts

2 cups small pretzel sticks, broken

- Melt chocolate in a double boiler. Stir in peanuts and pretzels.
- Drop by teaspoonfuls onto wax paper. Work fast because mixture hardens quickly.
- Place in freezer for 1 hour before storing at room temperature.

Butterscotch Peanuts

1 (12 ounce) package butterscotch morsels

2 cups chow mein noodles

1 cup dry roasted peanuts

- In a saucepan, heat butterscotch morsels over low heat until completely melted. Add noodles and peanuts and stir until each piece is coated.
- Drop from spoon onto wax paper. Cool. Store in airtight container.

Marshmallow Treats

½ stick margarine

4 cups miniature marshmallows

½ cup chunky peanut butter

5 cups crispy rice cereal

- In saucepan, melt margarine and add marshmallows. Stir until melted and add peanut butter. Remove from heat. Add cereal, stirring well.
- Press mixture into a 9 x 13-inch pan. Cut in squares when cool.

Honey-Nut Bars

⅓ cup margarine

¼ cup cocoa

1 (10 ounce) package miniature marshmallows

6 cups of Honey Nut Clusters cereal

- Melt margarine in a large saucepan and stir in the cocoa and marshmallows. Cook over low heat, stirring constantly until marshmallows are melted and mixture is smooth.
- Remove from heat and stir in honey nut clusters.
- Pour into a Pam sprayed 7 x 11-inch pan. With a spatula smooth mixture down in pan. Cool completely and cut into bars.

Raisin Crunch

¾ cup light corn syrup

1 cup sugar

1 cup crunchy peanut butter

1 (20 ounce) box raisin bran

- In saucepan combine corn syrup and sugar. Heat until sugar is thoroughly dissolved. Remove from heat and stir in peanut butter. Place raisin bran in a large container and pour sauce over the top. Mix in thoroughly.
- Pat mixture into a 9 x 13-inch pan and completely chill. Crunch can be cut into squares and stored in a airtight container.

Crazy Cocoa Crisps

24 ounces white almond bark

2¼ cups cocoa flavored crispy rice cereal

2 cups dry roasted peanuts

- Place almond bark in double boiler; heat and stir while bark is melting. Stir in cereal and peanuts.
- Drop by teaspoon on cookie sheet.
- Place in refrigerator for about 30 minutes to set. Store in airtight container.

Morning Meringues

2 egg whites, beaten stiff

¾ cup sugar

1 cup nuts

1 cup chocolate chips

- Add sugar to stiffly beaten egg whites. Add in nuts and chocolate chips.
- Line a cookie sheet with foil. Drop by teaspoonfuls, pressing down.
- Bake at 350° for 10 minutes. Turn oven off. Let cookies sit in oven 8 to 10 hours.

Peanut Clusters

1 (24 ounce) package almond bark

1 (12 ounce) package milk chocolate chips

5 cups salted peanuts

- In double boiler, melt the almond bark and chocolate chips.
- Stir in peanuts and drop by teaspoons onto waxed paper.
- Place in refrigerator for 30 minutes to set. Store in airtight container.

Haystacks

1 (12 ounce) package butterscotch chips

1 cup salted peanuts

1½ cups chow mein noodles

- Melt butterscotch chips in the top of double boiler. Remove from heat and stir in peanuts and noodles.
- Drop by teaspoons on waxed paper. Cool and store in airtight container.

Peanutty Cocoa Puffs

¾ cup light corn syrup

1¼ cups sugar

1¼ cups chunky peanut butter

4½ cups cocoa puff cereal

• In a large saucepan bring syrup and sugar to a rolling boil. Stir in peanut butter; mixing well. Stir in cocoa puffs.

• Drop on wax paper by teaspoonful.

Caramel-Apple Cupcakes

1 package carrot cake mix

3 cups chopped, peeled tart apples

1 (12 ounce) package butterscotch chips

1 cup finely chopped pecans

• Make cake batter according to package directions. Fold in apples. Fill 12 greased or paper lined jumbo muffin cups ¾ full.

• Bake at 350° for 20 minutes or until toothpick comes out clean.

• In a saucepan on very low heat melt the butterscotch chips. Spread over cupcakes and sprinkle with chopped pecans.

Scotch Crunchies

½ cup crunchy peanut butter

1 (6 ounce) package butterscotch bits

2½ cups frosted flakes

½ cup peanuts

• Combine peanut butter and butterscotch bits in a large saucepan; melt over low heat. Stir until butterscotch bits are melted. Stir in cereal and peanuts.

• Drop by teaspoonfuls onto wax paper. Refrigerate until firm. Store in air-tight container.

Peanut Butter Crunchies

1 cup sugar

½ cup white corn syrup

2 cups peanut butter

4 cups crispy rice cereal

- In a saucepan mix sugar and syrup and bring to a rolling boil. Remove from stove and stir in peanut butter. Add the crispy rice cereal, mixing well.
- Drop by the teaspoons onto wax paper. Place in refrigerator for a few minutes to set.

Pumpkin Cupcakes

1 (18 ounce) package spice cake mix

1 (15 ounce) can pumpkin

3 eggs

⅓ cup oil

- With mixer, blend cake mix, pumpkin, eggs, oil and ⅓ cup water. Beat for 2 minutes. Pour batter into 24 paper-lined muffin cups. Fill ¾ full.
- Bake at 350° for 18 to 20 minutes or until toothpick inserted in center comes out clean. You might want to spread with commercial icing.

Kid's Bars

1 cup each sugar and light corn syrup

1½ cups crunchy peanut butter

6 cups crispy rice cereal

1 (12 ounce) package chocolate chips

- In saucepan, combine sugar and corn syrup. Bring to a boil, stirring constantly. Remove from heat and stir in peanut butter and crispy rice cereal.
- Spread into a buttered 9 x 13-inch pan.
- In saucepan, over low heat, melt chocolate chips. Spread over cereal layer. Refrigerate until set; cut into bars. Store in refrigerator.

Tasty Treat

2 cups butterscotch
   morsels

2 cups salted peanuts

2 cups white raisins

• Mix all together and store in an airtight container.

Brown Sugar Cookies

¾ cup packed brown
   sugar

1 cup butter, softened

1 egg yolk

2 cups flour

• Cream sugar and butter until light and fluffy. Mix in egg yolk. Blend in flour. Refrigerate dough for 1 hour.

• Form dough into 1-inch balls, flatten and criss-cross with fork on lightly greased baking sheet.

• Bake at 325° for 10 to 12 minutes or until golden brown.

Macadamia Candy

2 (3 ounce) jars
Macadamia nuts

1 (20 ounce) package
white almond bark

¾ cup coconut

- Heat a dry skillet; toast nuts until slightly golden. (Some brands of Macadamias nuts are already toasted, so skip this step if they are.) Set aside.

- In a double boiler, melt the 12 squares of almond bark.

- As soon as almond bark is melted, pour the Macadamia nuts and coconut in. Stir well.

- Place a piece of waxed paper on a cookie sheet and pour the candy on the waxed paper; spread out. Refrigerate 30 minutes to set. Break into pieces.

Diamond Fudge

1 (6 ounce) package semi-sweet chocolate morsels

1 cup creamy peanut butter

1 stick margarine

1 cup powdered sugar

- Cook first 3 ingredients in a saucepan over low heat, stirring constantly, just until mixture melts and is smooth. Remove from heat.

- Add powdered sugar, stirring until smooth.

- Spoon into a buttered 8-inch square pan; chill until firm. Cut into squares.

Peanut Butter Fudge

12 ounces chunky peanut
butter

12 ounces package milk
chocolate chips

1 (14 ounce) can
sweetened condensed
milk

1 cup chopped pecans

- In saucepan, combine peanut butter,
chocolate chips and condensed milk.
Heat on low, stirring constantly until
chocolate is melted.

- Add pecans, mixing well. Pour into a 9
x 9-inch buttered dish.

Raisin Fudge

1 (12 ounce) package
semi-sweet chocolate
chips

1 cup chunky peanut
butter

3 cups miniature
marshmallows

¾ cup raisins

- In a saucepan melt the chocolate chips
and peanut butter over medium to low
heat.

- Fold in the marshmallows and raisins;
stir until marshmallows have melted.
Pour into a 7 x 11-inch pan.

- Chill until firm. Cut into squares.
Store where it is cool.

Microwave Fudge

3 cups semi-sweet
chocolate morsels

1 (14 ounce) can
sweetened condensed
milk

½ stick margarine, cut
into pieces

1 cup chopped walnuts

- Combine first 3 ingredients in a 2-quart
glass bowl.

- Microwave at MEDIUM 4 to 5 minutes,
stirring at 1½ minutes intervals.

- Stir in walnuts and pour into a buttered
8-inch square dish. Chill 2 hours. Cut
into squares.

Dream Candy

2 (8 ounce) cartons whipping cream

3 cups sugar

1 cup light corn syrup

1 cup chopped pecans

- In a saucepan combine the whipping cream, sugar and corn syrup. Cook to a soft-boil stage.
- Stir and beat until candy is cool.
- Add pecans and pour into a 9-inch buttered pan.

Chocolate Toffee

1 cup sugar

2 sticks butter

1 (6 ounce) package chocolate chips

1 cup chopped pecans

- In a heavy saucepan, combine sugar and butter. Cook until candy reaches a hard-crack stage. Pour onto a greased baking sheet.
- Melt chocolate in a double boiler and spread over toffee.
- Sprinkle with pecans; pressing pecans into the chocolate.
- Chill briefly to set chocolate. Break into pieces.

Quick Pralines

1 (3ounce) box
   butterscotch cook and
   serve pudding
1¼ cups sugar
½ cup evaporated milk
2 cups pecan pieces

- In a large saucepan, mix together butterscotch pudding, sugar and milk.
- Bring to a boil, stirring constantly for 2 minutes. Add pecans and boil another 1½ minutes, stirring constantly.
- Remove from heat. Beat until candy begins to cool; drop by tablespoonfuls on wax paper

Date Loaf Candy

3 cups sugar
1 cup milk
1 (16 ounce) box chopped
   dates
1 cup chopped pecans

- Combine sugar and milk in large saucepan.
- Cook to a soft-boil stage (234° on a candy thermometer). Stir in dates. Cook to a hard boil stage (260°), stirring constantly.
- Remove from heat; add pecans and mix well. Stir and cool until stiff. Pour mixture onto a damp tea towel.
- Roll into a log. Let stand until set. When candy is set, remove the tea towel and slice.

Pecan-Topped Toffee

2 sticks butter (the real thing)

1¼ cups packed brown sugar

6 (1.5 ounce) milk chocolate bars

⅔ cup finely chopped pecans

- In saucepan combine the butter and sugar. Cook on medium high heat, stirring constantly until mixture reaches 300° on candy thermometer. Pour immediately into a greased 9-inch baking pan.
- Lay chocolate bars evenly over hot candy. When the candy is soft, spread into a smooth layer.
- Sprinkle pecans over the chocolate and press lightly with the back of your spoon. Chill in refrigerator for about one hour.
- Invert candy onto a piece of waxed paper and break into small irregular pieces.

Yummy Pralines

1 stick butter (the real thing)

1 (16 ounce) box light brown sugar

1 (8 ounce) carton whipping cream, unwhipped

2½ cups whole pecans

- In a heavy saucepan, combine butter, brown sugar and whipping cream.
- Cook until temperature comes to a soft ball stage (about 20 minutes), stirring constantly. Remove from heat and set aside for about 5 minutes.
- Fold in the pecans, stirring until ingredients are glassy. (This will take several minutes of stirring.)
- With a large spoon, drop on waxed paper. Remove after pralines have cooled.

A

A Better Scramble 86
Adobe Chicken 213
A Wicked Meatloaf 219
Almond Asparagus 172
Amaretto 65
Amaretto Cooler 58
Amaretto Dip Spread 49
Amaretto Ice Cream 259
Amaretto Peaches 261
Amaretto Sauce for Pound Cake 261
Ambrosia Spread 85
Angel Glaze 275
Angel Macaroons 289
APPETIZERS
    Amaretto Dip Spread 49
    Artichoke Bites 36
    Artichoke Blue Cheese Dip 12
    Artichoke Spread 43
    Bacon Nibblers 33
    Bacon Oyster Bites 31
    Bacon-Wrapped Water Chestnuts 36
    Beef Roll 24
    Beefy Cheese Balls 27
    Bits of Frank 41
    Black Olive Spread 45
    Blue Cheese Ball 25
    Border Queso 37
    Broccoli-Cheese Dip 11
    Bubbly Franks 38
    California Clam Dip 22
    Cheddar Cheese Ring 31
    Cheddar Toppers 39
    Cheese in the Round 32
    Cheese It 39
    Cheese Straws 38
    Cheesy Crab Dip 20
    Chicken-Cheese Spread 28
    Chili-Cheese Balls 25
    Chili-Cheese Bites 35
    Chocolate Fruit Dip 47
    Chorizo Cheese Dip 8
    Chunky Shrimp Dip 20
    Cinnamon Pecans 50
    Classy Red Pecans 49
    Cocktail Sausages 30
    Cold Curry Dip 10
    Confetti Dip 17
    Cottage Dip 13
    Cottage Ham Dip 23
    Creamy Cucumber Spread 44
    Crispy Chestnuts 42
    Crunchy Asparagus Dip 19
    Cucumber-Garlic Dip 44
    Cucumber Squares 36
    Deviled Pecans 49
    Devil's Spread 42
    Dilly Dip 18
    Dried Beef and Chips 17
    Easy Tuna Dip 22
    English Muffin Pizza 28
    Fiesta Onion Dip 10
    Five-Minute Dip 13
    Fried Mozzarella 35
    Fruit Dip for Nectarines 48
    Fun Mustard Dip 18
    Garlic Shrimp 32
    Gitty-Up Crab Dip 21
    Great Balls of Fire 34
    Green Eyes 31
    Ham-Bone Dip 18
    Holy Guacamole 33
    Homemade Pimento Cheese 33
    Horsey Shrimp Dip 14
    Hot Artichoke Spread 43
    Hot Broccoli Dip 11
    Hot Cheese Balls 24
    Hot Cocktail Squares 41
    Hot, Rich Crab Dip 21
    Hot-to-Trot Dip 13
    Indian Corn Dip 15
    Jack Quesadillas 29
    Jiffy Tuna Spread 44
    Juicy Fruit Dip 47
    Mexican Fudge 41
    No-See-Um Chicken Livers 37
    Nutty Apple Dip 46
    Nutty Cheese Dip 9
    Olive Balls 26
    Olive-Cheese Appetizers 45
    Olive-Cheese Empanadas 26
    Onion Crisps 40
    Onion-Ham Dip 27
    Orange Dip for Apples 46
    Orange Sour Cream Dip 47
    Party on the Rye 30
    Party Shrimp Dip 19
    Peanut Butter Spread 48
    Peanut Butter Sticks 42
    Pep-Pep-Pepperoni Dip 16
    Pepper-Pot Bean Dip 18
    Picante Cream 16
    Pineapple-Island Spread 45
    Pigs in a Blanket 30
    Pineapple Roll-Up 45
    Quicky Shrimp Dunk 19
    Ranch Cheese Ball 25
    Sassy Onion Dip 12
    Sausage Balls 24
    Sausage Bites 40
    Sausage Pinwheels 40
    Sausage Rounds 29
    Shrimp Squares Deluxe 34
    Shrimp-Stuffed Eggs 34
    Smoky Gouda Spread 43

Index

Index

Master Grocery List

FRESH PRODUCE

___ Apples
___ Avocados
___ Bananas
___ Beans
___ Bell Peppers
___ Broccoli
___ Cabbage
___ Carrots
___ Cauliflower
___ Celery
___ Corn
___ Cucumbers
___ Garlic
___ Grapefruit
___ Grapes
___ Lemons
___ Lettuce
___ Lime
___ Melons
___ Mushrooms
___ Onions
___ Oranges
___ Peaches
___ Pears
___ Peppers
___ Potatoes
___ Strawberries
___ Spinach
___ Squash
___ Tomatoes
___ Zucchini
___ _____
___ _____

FRESH BAKERY

___ Bagels
___ Bread
___ Cake
___ Cookies
___ Croissants
___ Donuts
___ French Bread
___ Muffins
___ Pastries
___ Pies
___ Rolls
___ _____
___ _____

DAIRY

___ Biscuits
___ Butter
___ Cheese
___ Cottage Cheese
___ Cream Cheese
___ Cream
___ Creamer
___ Eggs
___ Juice
___ Margarine
___ Milk
___ Pudding
___ Sour Cream
___ Yogurt
___ _____
___ _____

DELI

___ Cheese
___ Chicken
___ Main Dish
___ Prepared Salad
___ Sandwich Meat
___ Side Dishes
___ _____
___ _____

FROZEN FOODS

___ Breakfast
___ Dinners
___ Ice
___ Ice Cream
___ Juice
___ Pastries
___ Pies
___ Pizza
___ Potatoes
___ Vegetables
___ Whipped Cream
___ _____
___ _____

OTHER

___ _____
___ _____
___ _____

Master Grocery List

GROCERY

___ Beans
___ Beer/Wine
___ Bread
___ Canned Vegetables
___ _____
___ _____
___ Cereal
___ Chips/Snacks
___ Coffee
___ Cookies
___ Crackers
___ Flour
___ Honey
___ Jelly
___ Juice
___ Ketchup
___ Kool-Aid
___ Mayonnaise
___ Mixes
___ _____
___ _____
___ Mustard
___ Nuts/Seeds
___ Oil
___ Pasta
___ Peanut Butter
___ Pickles/Olives
___ Popcorn
___ Rice
___ Salad Dressing
___ Salt
___ Seasonings
___ _____
___ _____

___ Sauce
___ Sodas
___ Soups
___ Spices
___ _____
___ _____
___ _____
___ Sugar
___ Syrup
___ Tea
___ Tortillas
___ Water
___ _____
___ _____
___ _____

MEAT

___ Bacon
___ Chicken
___ Ground Beef
___ Ham
___ Hot Dogs
___ Pork
___ Roast
___ Sandwich Meat
___ Sausage
___ Steak
___ Turkey
___ _____
___ _____

GENERAL MERCHANDISE

___ Automotive
___ Baby Items
___ _____
___ _____
___ _____
___ Bath Soap
___ Bath Tissue
___ Deodorant
___ Detergent
___ Dish Soap
___ Facial Tissue
___ Feminine Products
___ Aluminum Foil
___ Greeting Cards
___ Hardware
___ Insecticides
___ Light Bulbs
___ Lotion
___ Medicine
___ Napkins
___ Paper Plates
___ Paper Towels
___ Pet Supplies
___ Prescriptions
___ Shampoo
___ Toothpaste
___ Vitamins
___ _____
___ _____
___ _____

Substitutions

Food	Amount	Substitution
Breadcrumbs, dry	1 cup	¾ cup cracker crumbs
Broth, chicken or beef	1 cup	1 bouillon cube; 1 teaspoon granules in 1 cup boiling water
Butter	1 cup (4 ounces)	⅞ cup vegetable oil or shortening; 1 cup margarine
Buttermilk	1 cup	1 tablespoon lemon juice or white vinegar plus milk to equal 1 cup (must stand for 5 minutes)
Cottage cheese	1 cup	1 cup ricotta
Cornstarch	1 tablespoon	2 tablespoons flour
Cream, whipping	1 cup	4 ounces frozen whipped topping
Flour	1 cup sifted all-purpose	1 cup minus 2 tablespoons unsifted all-purpose
	1 cup sifted self-rising	1 cup sifted all-purpose flour plus 1 ½ teaspoon baking powder plus ⅛ teaspoon salt
Garlic	1 small clove	⅛ teaspoon garlic powder
Herbs	1 tablespoon fresh	1 teaspoon dried
Honey	1 cup	1 ¼ cups granulated sugar plus ⅓ cup liquid in recipe
Ketchup	½ cup	½ cup tomato sauce plus 2 tablespoons sugar plus 1 tablespoon vinegar
Lemon juice	1 teaspoon	½ teaspoon vinegar
Mushrooms	½ pound fresh	1 (6 ounce) can, drained
Mustard	1 tablespoon prepared	1 teaspoon dried
Onions	1 small	1 tablespoon instant minced; ½ tablespoon onion powder
Sour cream	1 cup	1 cup plain yogurt; ¾ cup buttermilk; 1 tablespoon lemon juice plus enough evaporated milk to equal 1 cup
Sugar	1 cup light brown	½ cup packed brown sugar plus ½ cup granulated sugar
	1 cup granulated	1 ¾ cups confectioners sugar; 1 cup packed brown sugar; 1 cup superfine sugar
Tomato juice	1 cup	½ cup tomato sauce plus ½ cup water
Tomato sauce	1 cup	½ cup tomato paste plus ½ cup water
Yogurt	1 cup	1 cup buttermilk; 1 cup milk plus 1 tablespoon lemon juice

Pan Sizes

Pan Sizes	Approximate Volume
Muffin Pans	
1 ¾ x ¾ mini	⅛ cup (2 tablespoons)
2 ¾ x 1 ⅛	¼ cup
2 ¾ x 1 ⅜	Scant ½ cup
3 x 1 ¼ jumbo	⅝ cup
Loaf Pans	
5 ½ x 3 x 2 ½	2 cups
6 x 4 ½ x 3	3 cups
8 x 4 x 2 ½	4 cups
8 ½ x 4 ¼ x 3	5 cups
9 x 5 x 3	8 cups
Pie Pans	
7 x 1 ¼	2 cups
8 x 1 ¼	3 cups
8 x 1 ½	4 cups
9 x 1 ¼	4 cups
9 x 1 ½	5 cups
10 x 2	6 cups

Pan Sizes	Approximate Volume
Cake Pans	
5 x 2 round	2 ⅔ cups
6 x 2 round	3 ¾ cups
8 x 1 ½ round	4 cups
7 x 2 round	5 ¼ cups
8 x 2 round	6 cups
9 x 1 ½ round	6 cups
9 x 2 round	8 cups
9 x 3 bundt	9 cups
10 x 3 ½ bundt	12 cups
9 ½ x 2 ½ springform	10 cups
10 x 2 ½ springform	12 cups
8 x 3 tube	9 cups
9 x 4 tube	11 cups
10 x 4 tube	16 cups
Casseroles	
8 x 8 x 12 square	8 cups
11 x 7 x 2 rectangular	8 cups
9 x 9 x 2 square	10 cups
13 x 9 x 2 rectangular	15 cups
1-quart casserole	4 cups
2-quart casserole	8 cups
2 ½-quart casserole	10 cups
3-quart casserole	12 cups

U.S. Measurements

3 teaspoons	1 tablespoon	
4 tablespoons	¼ cup	2 fluid ounces
8 tablespoons	½ cup	4 fluid ounces
12 tablespoons	¾ cup	6 fluid ounces
16 tablespoons	1 cup	8 fluid ounces
¼ cup	4 tablespoons	2 fluid ounces
⅓ cup	5 tablespoons + 1 teaspoon	
½ cup	8 tablespoons	4 fluid ounces
⅔ cup	10 tablespoons + 2 teaspoons	
¾ cup	12 tablespoons	6 fluid ounces
1 cup	16 tablespoons	8 fluid ounces
1 cup	½ pint	
2 cups	1 pint	16 fluid ounces
3 cups	1 ½ pints	24 fluid ounces
4 cups	1 quart	32 fluid ounces
8 cups	2 quarts	64 fluid ounces
1 pint	2 cups	16 fluid ounces
2 pints	1 quart	
1 quart	2 pints; 4 cups	32 fluid ounces
4 quarts	1 gallon; 8 pints; 16 cups	
8 quarts	1 peck	
4 pecks	1 bushel	

cookbook resources®

Cooking With 5 Ingredients

The Ultimate Cooking With 4 Ingredients

The Best of Cooking With 3 Ingredients

Easy Gourmet Cooking With 5 Ingredients

Healthy Cooking with 4 Ingredients

Slow Cooking with 4 Ingredients

Easy and Gourmet Desserts with 5 Ingredients

Casseroles to the Rescue

Cookie Dough Secrets

Gifts for the Cookie Jar

Quick Fixes With Mixes

Kitchen Keepsakes & More Kitchen Keepsakes

Mother's Recipes

Recipe Keepsakes

Cookbook 25 Years

Pass The Plate

Texas Longhorn Cookbook

Simply Simpatico

Mealtimes and Memories

Holiday Treats

Homecoming

Cookin' With Will Rogers

Best of Lone Star Legacy Cookbook

Little Taste of Texas

Little Taste of Texas II

Southwest Sizzler

Southwest Ole

Leaving Home

Flavors of Home™
Preserving
The Family Meal

www.cookbookresources.com

community cooks™
Celebrating The
Community Cookbook

To Order *The Ultimate Cooking With 4 Ingredients*:

Please send_____hard copies @ $19.95 (U.S.) each $_____

Please send_____paperbacks @ $16.95 (U.S.) each $_____

Plus postage/handling @ $4.00 each $_____

Texas residents add sales tax @ $1.22 each $_____

Check or Credit Card (Canada-credit card only)   Total $_____

Charge to my ❑ [MasterCard] or ❑ [VISA]

Account # _____

Expiration Date _____

Signature _____

Name_____

Address_____

City_____State_____Zip_____

Phone (day)_____(night)_____

| Mail or Call: |
| Cookbook Resources |
| 541 Doubletree Drive |
| Highland Village, Texas 75077 |
| Toll-free: 866/229-2665 |
| sheryn@cookbookresources.com |

- -

To Order *The Ultimate Cooking With 4 Ingredients*:

Please send_____hard copies @ $19.95 (U.S.) each $_____

Please send_____paperbacks @ $16.95 (U.S.) each $_____

Plus postage/handling @ $4.00 each $_____

Texas residents add sales tax @ $1.22 each $_____

Check or Credit Card (Canada-credit card only)   Total $_____

Charge to my ❑ [MasterCard] or ❑ [VISA]

Account # _____

Expiration Date _____

Signature _____

Name_____

Address_____

City_____State_____Zip_____

Phone (day)_____(night)_____

| Mail or Call: |
| Cookbook Resources |
| 541 Doubletree Drive |
| Highland Village, Texas 75077 |
| Toll-free: 866/229-2665 |
| sheryn@cookbookresources.com |

To Order *The Ultimate Cooking With 4 Ingredients*:

Please send_____hard copies @ $19.95 (U.S.) each $_____

Please send_____paperbacks @ $16.95 (U.S.) each $_____

Plus postage/handling @ $4.00 each $_____

Texas residents add sales tax @ $1.22 each $_____

Check or Credit Card (Canada-credit card only)   Total $_____

Charge to my ❑ MasterCard. or ❑ VISA

Account # _____

Expiration Date _____

Signature _____

Name_____

Address_____

City_____State_____Zip_____

Phone (day)_____(night)_____

Mail or Call:
Cookbook Resources
541 Doubletree Drive
Highland Village, Texas 75077
Toll-free: 866/229-2665
sheryn@cookbookresources.com

- -

To Order *The Ultimate Cooking With 4 Ingredients*:

Please send_____hard copies @ $19.95 (U.S.) each $_____

Please send_____paperbacks @ $16.95 (U.S.) each $_____

Plus postage/handling @ $4.00 each $_____

Texas residents add sales tax @ $1.22 each $_____

Check or Credit Card (Canada-credit card only)   Total $_____

Charge to my ❑ MasterCard. or ❑ VISA

Account # _____

Expiration Date _____

Signature _____

Name_____

Address_____

City_____State_____Zip_____

Phone (day)_____(night)_____

Mail or Call:
Cookbook Resources
541 Doubletree Drive
Highland Village, Texas 75077
Toll-free: 866/229-2665
sheryn@cookbookresources.com